From the Stage Coach

TO THE PULPIT.

H. K. Stimson

H. K. Stimson

From the Stage Coach

to

THE PULPIT,

BEING AN AUTO-BIOGRAPHICAL SKETCH, WITH INCIDENTS
AND ANECDOTES, OF

ELDER H. K. STIMSON,

THE VETERAN PIONEER OF WESTERN NEW YORK,
NOW OF KANSAS.

EDITED BY REV. T. W. GREENE,

OF KANSAS.

SAINT LOUIS:
R. A. CAMPBELL, PUBLISHER,
S. E. Cor. Fifth and Olive Sts.
1874.

ST. LOUIS, MO.,
BARNS & BEYNON,
Printers and Stereotypers,
215 Pine Street.

CONTENTS.

THE AUTHOR'S PREFACE.

In presenting this volume to the Christian Public and "the rest of mankind," I know that I am liable to severe criticism, to which I do not object if it is made in kindness. Such has always done me good.

I have had a maxim through life, I once invented in self-defense, that a man that can't spell a word but one way, is a literary fool. For the practical illustration my manuscript affords that I am not a fool in this sense, if it appears on the printed page, you can blame the editor, Rev. T. W. Greene.

I make no claim to originality, except in memory. This I have endeavored to use to the best advantage in applying other men's thoughts and principles. I believe in the largest liberty to all men in advocating their views and sentiments, if not dogmatic and superstitious. I advocate a liberal education, a liberal contribution to all benevolent institutions, and large donations to ministers.

I have no great enemies, except the devil. All others are of small calibre and not worth a notice. I love all mankind, and good horses. For the rest of the world I care but little, as I am nearly through it.

I wish you to buy the book, pay for it and read it. Then you will have a consciousness of two things: first, you own a book and are independent. Second, you are helping an old man and woman to a little support in the evening of life.

May God bless you.

H. K. S.

Burlington, Kansas, 1874.

THE EDITOR'S PREFACE.

I BELIEVE in preaching and like to preach. I also believe in writing and like to write, especially when helping to increase the acquaintance of the world with so genuine a man, and one so wide-awake for CHRIST, evenin the evening years of life, as FATHER STIMSON.

I have enjoyed the work of preparing the manuscript of this book for the press. As Dr. BUSHNELL would say, it has been play for me. It was nearly done before I knew it. Only a few weeks of an exceedingly hot season have been spent by FATHER STIMSON in preparing the pencil notes good and ample, and by myself in making them comply with the exactions of the printer, and a little more fully represent the Author; and that, too, in the midst of uninterrupted pastoral work on the part of both.

My only wish is that the book may be read by many during his life here and after he has entered on the better life, and with the same relish with which the labor of preparing it has been accomplished. Then I shall be sure it will do more good than we both could have done in the same time in any other way.

T. W. G.

JUNCTION CITY, Kansas.

INTRODUCTION.

It was in the winter of 1843, I first saw Rev. H. K. STIMSON. It was in my native town in Western New York, and at an age when my mind was very easily impressed by the presence of men of mark. The occasion was the meeting of an Ecclesiastical Council, which excited great interest in that community. Mr. STIMSON was a delegate from a neighboring church. He was then a young man, full of point, soul and magnetism, which years have not lessened. Because of his brilliancy, piquancy and quaintness, all eyes admiringly centered upon him when he spoke. To my youthful mind, he was the chief attraction of the Council. I have ever remembered him as I saw and heard him there. He then told a certain story, with such inimitable skill and dramatic power—a story having a patness and application so hitting and ludicrous—that I can never forget it or its author. Who might this curious and strangely potent man be? I wondered. It came out that he was a converted stage-driver, of Irish descent, and the wittiest minister in the Genesee country.

From that day to this I have known H. K. STIMSON, and from the time I went into the ministry he has known me, I think; and if he has not loved me, I have had the sweet retaliation of loving him. For more than thirty years in Western New York, he held a prominent place as a preacher and pastor. No man in that region stood higher as a faithful, able and useful minister of the Gospel than he. This is saying much, for he was associated with such men as Elon Galusha, Elisha Tucker, Pharcellus Church, James Reed, Ichabod Clark, William Arthur, Charles Van Loon, Daniel Eldridge, the Elliots, Harrison Daniels and Walter Brooks. In the learning of the schools, Mr. STIMSON never professed to be a proficient, but the Gospel and men he knows by heart. Wit, tact, knowledge of human nature and ready ability to use current events, superadded to a great and good heart, and to a naturally strong and withy intellect, all consecrated to God, have made him a most popular, devoted and efficient minister of Christ for forty-five years.

His auto-biography is a book over which readers will both laugh and cry. No person who has ever known this remarkable man will fail to be interested in the work, and in it thousands of others, in all Christian denominations, will find entertainment and profit. In wit and drollery, this book is keener than the works of professional humorists, in its serious portions and theological utterances, it is as sound as Jonathan Edwards; and in its touching passages and pictures, it is as tender as anything which Payson or McChene ever wrote.

As the subject of this taking volume is a welcome guest in all denominations and circles, because he is a Christian, a gentleman, a genial companion, a helpful minister and a man of the soundest common sense, so his auto-biography will be welcomed by all classes, professions and ages. The book is the man in portraiture, and this is its highest commendation. Mr. STIMSON is now well on in life, but is as vivacious, as social, as generous and as companionable as ever; and the book is just like him. When he leaves your house, wife, husband and all the children say, "come again." A book picturing such a character and life as his, so full of telling incidents, of rich personal history, of hits, of genius, of talent, of eloquence, of pathos, of piety, of good sense, must be remarkable, *a priori*. Upon examination, the work proves itself the satisfactory fulfillment of the prophecy which such a character utters.

The Editor, Rev. Mr. GREENE, his neighbor in Kansas, where Mr. STIMSON has lived for the last few years, has done his work so well, as to richly deserve the thanks of the thousands the land over who know and love the "Converted Stage-Driver," and who pray that the evening of his life may be as sunny as its noon; and that, as from the stage coach Christ transferred him to the pulpit, so from the pulpit, though not for many years, He may transfer him to Himself in glory, not only to be forever with his Lord, but with the great multitude brought to Jesus by his labors.

A. H. BURLINGHAM.

ST. LOUIS, January, 1874.

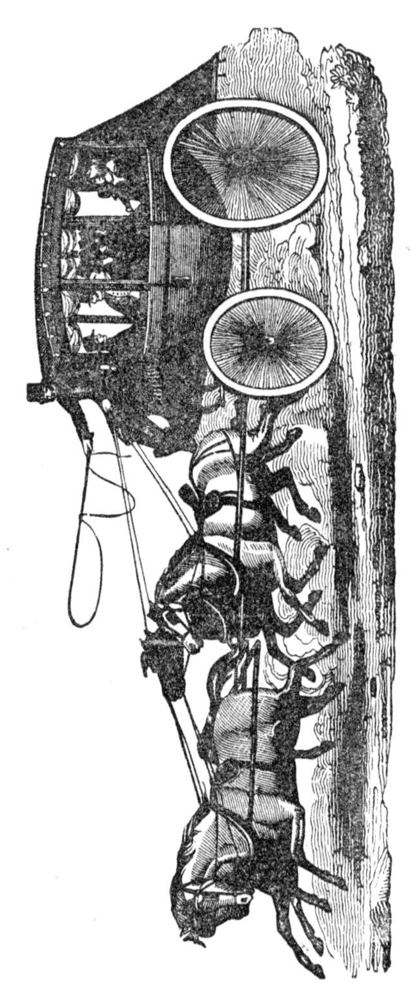

FAREWELL TO THE COACH.

Farewell to the Coach that has carried us long
  Through sunshine and storm with wheels rolling fast;
A kindly farewell in a brief, simple song,
  And a smile and a tear for its far away past.

A smile for the memories pleasant and pure,
  A tear for whatever unhallowed was there;
Let the first with all that is precious endure,
  And the last be forgotten in praise and in prayer.

How strong was your frame and capacious each seat,
  Old Coach, as you rolled on your track every day;
And how many good friends we then used to greet,
  As they climbed into you, and we sped on our way.

How waited and watched for then was our load!
  How welcome the letters we bore up and down!
How gaily our horses stepped out on the road,
  Or dashed up the street full speed into town!

Now better enjoyment we thankfully find,
  For our last whip and bottle were cracked long ago;
Though to crack a good joke we still feel inclined,
  And we bear other news as we go to and fro.

Good tidings, great blessings we gladly proclaim,
  Christ's life and His death, the epistles of Paul;
To those who will weep o'er His sorrow and shame,
  And rejoice in the news that can ransom us all.

We still hope to carry full many a soul
  From evil to good, from sin to salvation;
For the chariot wheels of the Gospel must roll
  Until the grand story is told to each nation.

CHAPTER I.

BIRTH AND BOYHOOD.

I WAS born — so I have been told — at Saratoga Springs, October 11th, 1804. My parents were of Irish extraction, having descended from an ancient stock in the North of Ireland. All I know of their religious opinions is that they were of Presbyterian proclivities, and, like most other adherents of the Scotch "Kirk," strongly prejudiced against all other denominations, especially Roman Catholics, and no less, the Baptists. This prejudice my father never overcame. My mother finally became more tolerant, but it was not until the Baptists had become quite numerous in Western New York that any of my family were immersed.

My father, who was a draper and tailor at Saratoga Springs, moved from there to what was then called the "Genesee Country," in the winter of 1811–12. Our family at this time consisted of my parents and their three children, I being seven years of age and the oldest of my mother's children. At this time nearly all west of Canandaigua was one vast wilderness, and

I well remember the contrast between our pleasant home at the Springs and the rude log hut in the dense forest in the "town" of Mendon. With the exception of an occasional visit to my uncle John Stimson, who lived four miles distant, I was constantly in the house with my mother, or with my father in the woods where he was "clearing." To one thus situated, any event which would enable him to see a company of men gathered together, was indeed hailed with joy. Such an event was the first town meeting of the "town" of Mendon, held at Deacon Eli Ewer's in the spring of 1812. During the previous winter the "town" of Bloomfield had been divided into four "towns," one of which was Mendon. It was therefore necessary to have a "town meeting" there, which was called at the house of Eli Ewer, a deacon of the Presbyterian Church. I remember feeling quite elated when I started with my father to attend the meeting. I anticipated a good time, and it seemed as though all there determined that my anticipations should be fulfilled. The deacon had the day previous obtained a license to keep a public house, and had laid in a good supply of rye whisky. He also served up to his guests a dinner consisting of baked pork and beans; a dish that may have been heard of still further east. Although a plain repast, and needing but little table furniture, his supply was found totally inadequate to the demand. His plates were of brown earthen-ware and wooden trenchers. For forks there were short sticks tipped with prongs of wire, the other part of the cutlery being supplied with pieces of scythe points and jack-knives. During the dinner hour everything was in confusion and noise, but the utmost good feeling prevailed. After dinner, games, business and drinking occupied the time till sundown, when the majority started for home, many very much intoxicated; for men got drunk even in the good old times. A few of them were beastly drunk. The beasts will please excuse me. There is one consolation, however, the whisky they drank was pure. But pure as it was, it operated badly on the deacon's windows, doors and premises generally. It had a very dilapidating effect upon them. The next day Deacon Ewer gave up his license and quit the rather expensive business of selling whisky.

In the spring of 1814, my father moved from his place in the woods to a public house on the road leading from Irondequoit Bay to Lima, where he kept tavern for the next four years. This was then the great Western thoroughfare, Buffalo being the "far West." While residing here there was no school which I could attend, and I was compelled to spend my time around the bar-room, where I was educated to all the vice and folly attendant upon such a place, but making no advancement in intellect and certainly none in moral education.

In the fall of 1818, I left home and worked at another tavern for my board, while I attended school for the first time since I was a child. In the spring of this year I had my first religious impressions, and well do I remember the occasion. A young companion of mine, Napoleon B. Stickney, and myself, attended a prayer meeting, conducted by the Rev. John Taylor, of the Congregational Church, and Deacon Eli Lyon, of the Baptist Church. Stickney and myself, both vain and wicked youths, had gone there out of mere curiosity. During the evening, Deacon Lyon gave a short but very impressive history of his experience and conversion, which, for the time, made a deep impression on my mind. Stickney was also much affected, and, on our way home, he said to me, "Hiram, I am a great sinner, and I feel as though it was my duty to quit the evil practices of Sabbath breaking, profane swearing and card playing." I at once told him of my own convictions, of my guilt as a sinner, and invited "Boney," as we called him, to stay with me at the tavern that night. He accepted my invitation, and we started for my room. The family had all retired, and the house was still when we reached it. We sat down in the bar-room where we had so often joked and made merry, but this time to talk over our deplorable condition as sinning against our God and Saviour. We had talked but a short time when "Boney" said, "Hiram, you go and get the Bible and we will read it." I stole away into the room where I knew the Bible was kept, a useless book to all the family. I brought it and gave it to "Boney." He opened at the fifty-fifth chapter of Isaiah, and commenced reading. When he closed the book he looked at me with a strange stare and said, "Hiram, pray." And there we both knelt on the floor of the dirty bar-room, filled with the fumes of whisky and the odor of burnt tobacco, and prayed in broken sentences and homely expressions, but with earnestness. What I said I know not. But after rising we mutually promised to reform and lead a better life. But how vain are most of our promises of reformation. The very next Sabbath, Stickney and

I went fishing all day. Thus may be seen how little dependence is to be placed upon resolutions of a better life when God is not really loved, and when our dependence upon Him is not realized and acknowledged with that acknowledgment that comes from renewed hearts.

From this time till I was eighteen I worked at the tavern, going to school three months each winter, pursuing only such branches as were then taught, imperfectly taught, and as imperfectly received and applied. So that when at this age the importance of an education first impressed itself upon my mind and I received my advancement, I found I could only read and write, knowing nothing or nearly nothing of arithmetic and geography. As I thought over these things, and as the value of an education arose before my mental vision, I was compelled to look about with a determination to lay hold of any possible chance that would allow me to pursue a course of study. But all was dark, dreary and discouraging. My parents were now too poor to help me. There were no good schools in that part of the country that I could attend, even by "choring" for my board. And with no means nor any way of obtaining them to pay my expenses away from home, and no kind friend to extend a benevolent hand or speak an encouraging word by way of relief, I settled down into the belief that there is such a thing as toiling for knowledge under difficulties, and that there are some lighter amusements than working one's way through school. With these facts dogging my heels, I saw that my hopes of obtaining an education at that time were vain. I soon dismissed the idea of enjoying the advantages of attending school where I was, and as to going East to attend one, that could only be done by the sons of the wealthy. This, in connection with my father's somewhat intemperate habits, led me to the conclusion that I must make the best of my poor condition in life, and so I set myself to the work of whiling away my youth in ignorance and vice.

Some time previous to this my father had given up the tavern and opened a small whisky grocery, obtaining his stock of one S——, who kept a hotel and store in the village of East Mendon. After continuing this grocery a little time, my father found himself indebted to S——, to the amount of eighty dollars, with no way to pay it. To settle the matter, S—— proposed that I should come and work it out at his hotel. A formal contract was at once drawn up, but I was to be kept in ignorance of the fact that I was working to pay for a "dead horse," or, what was in fact much worse, for whisky long since swallowed. S—— came to me and said, "Hi, I want you to work for me a year tending bar, and now and then driving those black horses of mine, which I am fitting for market. How much do you want a month?" The idea of being a kind of superintendent of a small tavern and of driving as fine a team as S——'s blacks was the height of all greatness to my mind, and we struck a bargain at eight dollars a month. Mr. S—— soon after started for New York City, leaving me to take charge of the tavern, and a young man by the name of Brace as clerk in his store.

My wardrobe at the time was somewhat scanty, and as spring came on I had need of new and more respectable clothing; that is, my position as mixer of whisky sling, gin cocktails and brandy smashes, and retailer of "penny grab" cigars required that I should appear in dignified attire. I went into the store and told Brace that I wanted cloth for a new suit of clothes, a new hat, boots, etc. What was my surprise and chagrin when hė told me I was at work to pay the old debt of my father, and he was instructed not to let me have anything out of the store during Mr. S——'s absence. At this I was indignant and not a little enraged, and I at once said, "Well, then I shall leave; you may take charge of the hotel and the horses, for I am not the boy to work for any old whisky debts, and go ragged while doing so, into the bargain." I was about to leave the store in a rage when Brace, who by the way was a good friend of mine, and in deep sympathy with me, said, "Well, Hiram, I will let you have what you want on my account. I will take the responsibility until Mr. S—— returns from New York, and then you and he can settle the matter." I at once replied, "No, I will not take a thing only on my own account and for my own labor. If I cannot have what I want on those conditions I will stay no longer, and as to working out that old whisky debt, it is something I will never do." At this decided declaration Brace replied, "Very well, Hi, it is too bad, and I will let you have what you want and you must settle it with Mr. S—— when he returns from New York City." Upon this condition cloth for a summer suit, cloth for two shirts, a pair of shoes and a hat were secured. The cloth for my suit I carried home that my father might cut them out, and my mother and sister make them. That night after going to bed my reflections were something like the following: "Now, when S—— gets home, we shall have a conflict about this matter. He and my father will lay their heads together, and compel me to work out this eighty dollar debt at eight dollars a month—ten long months. This is not right and just, I have no heart to stay and no determination to do it."

CHAPTER II.

RUNNING AWAY FROM HOME.—STAGE DRIVING AND STAGE DRIVERS.

THOUGHTS like these soon induced me to form plans for leaving my home, parents, brothers and sisters, to seek my own livelihood among strangers. The next morning I asked my mother to make my shirts as soon as possible as I was in very great need of them. She and my sister were not long in finishing them; and as soon as they were done I tied them in a bundle with the rest of my new made clothes and started apparently for the tavern, but really I knew not where. I passed out of the little village unobserved by any one. Arriving at the road leading to Bushnell's Basin on the Erie canal, I turned my steps thitherward.

I did not take the main road, fearing that I might meet some one who would detect and report me. As I wended my lonely way among the by-roads I had ample time for reflection, and my mind was filled with thoughts like these: "Now, I am taking an important step, one that will tell for good or evil on my whole after-life. I shall have no kind mother to look after me, no sweet sister to caress and respect me, no familiar friend to advise and counsel me. I am all alone, without friends or home, and now, after all, would I not gain by returning to Mendon, where I will be near my mother and sisters, and where I will see and be with those who are near and dear to me, even if I have to work almost a year to cancel that old whisky bill." Then, again, I thought: "If I do return, I must be a poor, despised lackey in a miserable rum hole; I must be an associate and companion of those belonging to the lowest grades of society; I must work and thus spend a whole year of my life for nothing that will do me any good; for something that has done no good in times past or present, and will benefit no one in time to come."

With thoughts like these I arrived at the Basin, and took my stand upon the bridge to await the arrival of the next boat. I cared not much from which way it came, whether east or west, it mattered not to me. All I cared for was to go—somewhere, anywhere, but back to Mendon. I longed to be moving. I wanted to escape from the terrible dread of working out old rum bills. I hated the very name of liquor, and despised all connected with it. I was desperate, and growing more and more so when a boat hove in sight, and I alighted upon its deck, taking passage for the East at one and a half cents a mile, board included. After a few miles' ride the captain approached me and said, "Young man, do you wish to get employment?" I said, "Yes, sir;" and we soon closed a bargain, he agreeing to pay me ten dollars a month as a hand upon the boat. As we neared Syracuse, our steward was taken ill, and had to leave the boat at that place. As we had on board a number of passengers to be cared for, a new steward must be found. After some talking and calculating, I was established in that office, or, as the phrase was, I was made "chief cook and bottle-washer." In this position I gave general satisfaction, so much so that Capt. Warren and his passengers began to praise me as a first-rate bar-tender and a number one cook.

After arriving at Albany and unloading our craft and cleaning up our cabins, I strolled up into the business part of town, and calling at a hotel, met James Herrington, an old stage driver with whom I had been acquainted at Mendon. We were both taken by surprise; and, in his rough and profane way—you don't want the profane part, and so I will leave it out—he said: "How come you here?" And then, introducing me to his companion, added: "Here is Hi Stimson, one of the smartest boys I ever knew. He can cut more tricks and make more fun than any boy I ever saw. He can sing the best songs, dance the best hornpipes, make the best flip, sling or punch any of his age: and that aint all, he is a tip-top reinsman, and can drive four or six horses to a nit's eye. Come, let's walk up and take a little; the least drop in the world won't hurt you, if you wash it down with rum." After we had drunk, James took me one side and said: "Hi, if you wish me to assist you in any way, I will do it. I think I can get you into a good berth here as a driver, for I know you are a first rate reinsman." I told him all my troubles; how I came away from Mendon, and what induced me to leave home. This so affected him that he could not restrain his tears, and, taking me by the hand, he said: "Well, Hiram, I will stand by you as long as I have a clean shirt and a shilling left." I informed him that I had all my wages due in the hands of Capt. Warren, and that I would settle with him and draw what was coming to me, if there was a prospect of employment at higher wages. He took me to the stage office, where he introduced me to the proprietors of the line, with whom I soon closed a bargain, they agreeing to pay me sixteen dollars a month, with a bonus of twenty-five dollars, provided I remained a year. I then returned to the boat, settled with the captain, and drew my balance. The captain was sorry to have me leave, but expressed himself pleased that I had found a better paying position.

I commenced work in my new vocation as stage driver the next morning. The route was the great road between Albany and Schenectady. Here my only fear was that of meeting Mr. S——, who would probably return from New York by stage. I had laid James H. under obligations to keep my whereabouts a secret, in case he should meet any one from the West that knew me.

Thus passed the summer, from May till August. Although I saw many whom I recognized, yet no one I met knew me, until one morning, about the first of September, as I drove up to the hotel in Albany. Among those who came out to take stage was one H. B., a young man of Mendon, who was well acquainted in my father's family, and whom I knew to be conversant with all the facts about my leaving home, I having met him on my way from Mendon to Bushnell's Basin. I turned my face from him, turned up my collar and drew my hat over my eyes, to elude, if possible, his recognition of me. He stood, smoking his cigar, till almost all the others were in the stage, and then, turning to me, he said: "Driver, can I ride on the box with you?" I answered, "Yes, sir; certainly." After we set out from the city, he continued to ask me questions about trifling matters, and I answered in the monosyllables "yes" and "no," until at length I turned my face toward him and he caught a glimpse of my features. With a loud expression of surprise, he exclaimed: "Oh! my ——, is this you, Hi? Your mother has cried her eyes out for you, and all Mendon is in wonder about what has become of you; but all agree that you have served Mr. S. and your father just right. But it will kill your mother, if she does not hear from you."

His conversation quite overcame me, and my hard and obdurate heart yielded to the most filial and affectionate emotions, and I found relief in tears. I then laid B. under secrecy, he promising to say nothing about our meeting to any one except my mother, and only to her after she had promised not to reveal my whereabouts to my father or to any of my family. B. was as good as his word, for on arriving at Mendon he called at my father's, and taking my mother aside, and after she had promised secrecy, told her all about our meeting and of my whereabouts and circumstances. She immediately sat down and wrote me the following kind and motherly letter:

MENDON, August 27th, 1824.

My Dear Boy: I was made to rejoice yesterday as Harry Benedict informed me that you are in Albany. This summer has indeed been a long one to me and your sisters, for we have been in constant suspense concerning you, my dear absent boy. Sally and Lucinda are not as yet in the secret of your whereabouts, as Harry has made me promise not to tell that which I have heard from you. My dear Hiram, I hope you will conduct yourself in a manner that will be creditable to yourself and your family. Remember you have now no mother near you to watch over you, no kind sisters to exert a reclaiming influence upon your wandering habits. Therefore, you must be doubly watchful over your actions and thoughts, that you bring not your family to shame and bury in grief the head of your sorrowing mother. * * * * * * *

Your father and Mr. S. have been in a rage of madness about your conduct in leaving as you did. Write me at Pittsford, and Harry Benedict will get the letter for me.

Your affectionate mother,
NANCY STIMSON.

I received this letter and read it with many conflicting emotions, and then retired to my room, there to give vent to a flood of tears, such as only an absent and erring but affectionate son who has read his first letter from a dear and loving mother can shed. As I sat there alone pondering upon my condition, thinking of my mother, sisters and home, of all the pleasant hours I had spent there, I almost wished I was in the presence of my parents even at the expense of being at work for S—— tending bar; but again the thought of that old whisky debt was too much for me, and made me resolve not to go back again; and my hatred of rum and drunkenness was stronger and tenfold deeper-seated than ever.

A call to duty in the coach-yard interrupted my reflections, but I went about my duties feeling, as I never had felt before, the influence, worth and constancy of a mother's love for an absent son. My friend James Herrington, who was at that time in the yard, observed my sad look and downcast expression, and stepped up to me and said in a bantering tone, "Well, Hi, what's the matter? Have you heard bad news from your sweetheart? Is she going to jilt you, or what is the trouble?" I begged him not to jeer me, and taking him one side showed him my mother's letter. He took it and perused its contents. As he read it I could see in his large, rough face the workings of the better man. As he finished reading, his eyes filled with tears, and in a half-choked voice he said, "God bless the old woman! Hiram, it is a fact a mother is about the only true friend that we poor devils have. Your poor old mother will stand by and comfort you when everybody else forsakes you. That is just like a mother; I know it from experience."

Feeling incompetent to write a proper reply to my mother's letter, I requested James to act as my scribe, to which request he readily consented, and in a short time he had finished the following letter, which I directed to my mother at Pittsford, care of Henry Benedict, who delivered it to its proper owner:

ALBANY, OCT. 4th, 1824.

My Dear Mother: Your kind and welcome letter came to hand last week, and I improve the present moment in writing to you a few lines. I did not leave Mendon because I did not love you and all the family, my mother and my sisters particularly. I love you as I love my own eyes and life, but to stay there and work out an old debt contracted for whisky for the purpose of keeping in operation a little seven by nine grocery, the only business of which is to finish off a few miserable old drunkards that the hotels cannot afford to do at so cheap a rate, is something I could not do. In the second place, father and Mr. S. deceived me by laying a plan to compel me to work it out and to go ragged while I was at work, thus obliging me to make a fool of myself, by being a mere lackey for a bar-room, and a buffoon for the devil.

I am now doing well and saving my wages, and will send you and the girls something nice when I get a chance. Keep it all dark about my being in Albany or anywhere else, and believe me

Your affectionate son,

HIRAM K. STIMSON.

These two letters were the only communications that passed between my mother and myself until I returned home—a space of eight months.

After this event I continued my "professional" services as stage driver and general fun-maker among the craft until about the middle of October, at which time I was taken ill with a severe fever, being obliged to give up my team and keep my bed. After two weeks' sickness the doctor informed me that I was "a very sick man," adding that if I had any friends they should be advised of my condition, for I was in some danger. Soon after he left the room, the hotel keeper came to me and inquired concerning my ability to pay for being taken care of. I sent for the agent of the line to come and see me. He and my friend James H. came in together. The agent told Munger, the hotel keeper, that he need give himself no trouble about the pay, as he would attend to all that matter. James said he would find a place where I could have better care than I was then getting at Munger's. He soon made arrangements for my removal to a private house, where I received the best attention and care that could be afforded, considering their scanty accommodations. And although it was not a sister's care or a mother's nursing, yet it was all I could expect. James, and in fact all the drivers of the "old line," as it was called, and the wives of as many as were married, were constant in their attentions to me in my sickness.

And here let me correct a false impression. It is

generally supposed that stage drivers are an unfeeling, worthless class of beings. It is true many of them are exceedingly profane, and not a few are intemperate in their habits; but, with all their rough and uncouth exterior, they are generous and frank to a fault. I have known one to pull off his overcoat in a cold winter's day and give it to a sick passenger inside, while, at the same time, a "broadcloth gentleman" of the legal profession would not even give the sick man the hind seat of the coach, thus compelling him to ride on the middle seat, rather than give up an iota of his own comfort. I have known them to contribute their last dollar to a poor, unfortunate fellow-driver. The steam engine is fast monopolizing the place of the old stage coach. The engineer is now the hero of the road, and not the old-time stage driver. The stage coach has considerable country to the west of us to subdue to the empire of the engine; but the time is coming when the last coach will make its last run, and the final stage driver will crack his whip and dismount for the last time. And having been one of the craft in the childhood of the stage coach in this country, I want to record my testimony to the noble-heartedness of the professional stage driver—a character that many young people who read this book will never meet. They have received the curses of many polite gentlemen; they deserve the blessings of thousands. The modern omnibus driver is not to be put alongside of the stage driver. He is a denizen of the city. The stage driver is a child of nature. The omnibus driver knows streets and avenues, and is often selfish and very vicious, contracting the habits of the metropolis. The stage driver has a few feelings for all men, especially his comrades and needy people, and can drive his load of precious freight from one point to another, with no human habitation to mark the road, the darkest night that ever was, with all the certainty of instinct.

Of course, the time is coming, also, when the balloon pilot will take the place of the close-mouthed, keen-eyed, steady-handed, generous-hearted engine driver. But, as that time will not fall within the evening of my day, I leave it to some abler pen to record the virtues of the noble army of engineers. But, as the stage driver, like poor "Lo"—will the former excuse the reference?—is being driven from civilized society and his services dispensed with, I want to say to the palace coach grandee that the old historical stage driver is worthy of a little corner in American biography.

CHAPTER III.

RETURNING HOME — FIRST INTERVIEW WITH MY FATHER.

BUT I must return to my narrative. After a stay of about two weeks at the house where James H. took me, the doctor informed me I had better take the canal boat for home, as I would be unable to resume my place as driver during that winter. I immediately made preparations for leaving, and bade an affectionate farewell to the family at whose hands I had received such attention and care. Accompanied as far as the boat by my friend James Herrington, I started for Mendon, over three hundred miles distant, where I arrived in the stage from Pittsford shortly after sunrise. I was hailed by my mother and sisters with joy and surprise—joy at my return, to know that I was once more among them; with surprise at my emaciated condition, reduced as I was with a long and severe sickness.

My father was not at home when I arrived, and my mother was fearful of the consequences of the meeting between us. For she knew Mr. S. had done all in his power to enrage my father against me for leaving him in the manner I did. I sent for Jeremiah S. Stone, an old friend of mine from boyhood, who kept a hotel and store just opposite the establishment of Mr. S. He advised me what to do, assuring me that I should be protected at all hazards.

While on my way home I had sewed my money, amounting to some sixty dollars, into my vest lining, to keep it away from my father and his whisky creditor. This money I now concluded to deposit with Stone for safe-keeping.

The day wore away. My father returned in the evening. I was in bed when he came in; but one of my little brothers said, "Father, Hiram's got home." He made little or no reply. I got up and came down stairs. As I entered the room he arose and gazing at me exclaimed, "What in the devil is the matter with you? You look like a ghost." I replied that I had been sick. "Sick ha! you have been to sea I suppose. What's the news in Europe?" "Nothing of importance," I replied, "except that the Dutch have taken Holland." At this he set up a hearty laugh, and thus ended the matter for the present.

In a little time I was able to walk about, and went over to Stone's hotel, being made welcome to consider it my home until I was able to go to work again, which invitation I accepted. One day shortly after this, as I was passing along in front of Mr. S.'s premises, he standing in the door hailed me in something like the following language: "That's the runaway. Walk up here and let us see how you look." As I stopped at the platform, one Hollister, an old man, took me by the hand to help me up the steps and offered me a chair; but Mr. S. exclaimed, "No"—with an oath—"he shan't sit here. I have called him up here to horsewhip him." And suiting the action to the word, reaching his hand towards the post, he took up a large black whip and came towards me in a rage. Hollister interposed, saying: Mr. S., you shan't strike a sick boy; if you do I'll make a corpse of you in two minutes; I'll make your wife a widow and your children orphans before sundown."

When my father heard of the manner in which S. had attempted to horsewhip me, he was very much enraged; so much so that he went over to see S., saying to him, among other things more forcible than elegant, "If you had struck the boy, I would have made Irish hash of you and fed you out to the devil's boarders for breakfast this morning." This caused a breach between Mr. S. and my father, which in a measure worked a reconciliation between my father and myself.

I remained with the Stone family during the balance of that winter, doing such chores about the hotel as my delicate health would permit.

My father had found out that I had on deposit with Stone the sixty dollars I had left with him the fall I came home from Albany, and was about to make a demand for it, when we compromised the matter by a contract as follows: I was to give him sixty dollars a year for my time until I was of age, paying thirty dollars in advance, and thirty dollars every six months, Mr. Stone being security for me.

Early in the spring, I engaged with Orrie Adams, of Rochester, to drive stage between that place and Avon, commencing work during the month of March. During the next July I was changed to the route from Rochester to Bergen, on the Buffalo road. I continued on this route for two years and a half, and during this time I became acquainted with a large circle of young friends who were much given to frolicking and dancing, the latter a recreation to which I was much attached from childhood.

During this time I induced my old and tried friend, James Herrington, to come on from Albany to Western New York, as an increase of the business in the West made a demand for drivers. In him I always found a true man; with all his rough exterior he was one of "nature's noblemen."

I will here introduce an incident that occurred thirteen years later. In 1837, while I was pastor at Bethany, in Genesee County, I took a journey to Michigan. On my return to Buffalo I took the stage for Batavia, the country being innocent of railroads. Coming out of the hotel, I saw upon the box of the stage, my old friend James Herrington. He had changed, but I knew him. I resolved at once to get the liberty of a seat on the box with him. So I said to him in as polite a way as I could, "Well, captain, can I ride with you on the box this fine morning?" He replied, "I am no captain, nor corporal, but you are welcome to a seat with me, as no other one has spoken for it." So up I climbed, and away we went out of the city.

I made every effort for him to recognize me, without telling him who I was. I asked him a multitude of small questions about driving, if it was not a hard life, exposed to sun and storms, what wages he got, etc., etc. To all of which he gave prompt and civil answers.

As he stopped at Williamsville, ten miles out of Buffalo, to change the mails and water the horses, I volunteered to hold the reins. "Think ye can hold 'em? You look a little too white-livered to manage these old *snorters;* but you may try yer hand at it, stranger." So I took the reins, and while he was watering he looked up and saw that I had adjusted the "ribbons" according to the rules of the "knights of the order of Jehu." As he got up on the box he remarked, "Well, I think you have handled four 'ribbons' before to-day, hain't ye?" and looked me full in the face. I smiled and returned the look. He exclaimed with solemnity, and not in a spirit of profanity, "My God! if this ain't you, Hi. Stimson." At once the tears stole down from his large eyes, over his rough, brown cheeks, as he caught me by the hand, and after a moment's convulsion said, "Well, well, if this don't beat all, that I should ride all the way from Buffalo with you and not know Hiram Stimson. How glad I am to see you! Now, tell me about yourself, and is your old mother living yet? I have heard of you a number of times in all these years, and could hardly believe the yarns told about you, that you had become a Christian and a minister and was much respected, and looked up to. Well, well, if this ain't as strange as a dream! How do ye s'pose I came to know ye? It's just this: as I stood there watering my team, and saw you holding them 'ribbons' something seemed to crawl into my head, 'I have seen him somewhere;' and then when you smiled I knew you, because you always laughed out of the corners of your eyes. Well, Hiram, we must talk fast, for its near the end of my road." I told him all: how the Lord had led me to see myself as a sinner, and to embrace Jesus as my only hope of salvation from sin, from intemperance, and a drunkard's undone eternity. And we parted with a promise and a hope to meet again.

James Herrington after this became a humble and useful Christian, the deacon of a Freewill Baptist church in the city of Buffalo, and died respected and beloved by all that knew him. The reader will forgive this episode. I must return to my narrative of thirteen years previous

At my boarding house in Bergen I became acquainted with a young friend, James Davis. He had been apprenticed to the wagon-making business in the shop of Mr. Carver. James and myself lodged together at Buel's hotel, and at night he would tell over to me all his troubles, which were simply these: His mother was a pious Baptist lady, as was also his sister Sally. His oldest brothers, Lyman and George, were also members of the Baptist Church. His family were opposed to his attending places of amusement, and dancing, and these being the order of the day in Bergen, it was almost impossible to restrain him. He soon became restive and dissatisfied with his place and occupation, and decided to leave home and seek his fortune among strangers.

I in turn gave him a history of my adventures on leaving home. And I have reason to think that it was mostly through my influence that he was induced to leave home. Hence, how true it is that "one sinner destroyeth much good." He obtained permission from Carver to spend a week at home with his mother, but instead of going home he started for Troy, in the eastern part of the State, where he had wealthy relatives, I being the only one cognizant of his real destination. Thus he had a fair start, his mother supposing him to be in the shop at Bergen Corners, and Mr. Carver supposing him to be with his mother. When they discovered that he was gone, his mother came to me and said, by way of introducing the conversation, "Young man, have you a mother?" To which I replied in the affirmative. "Well, if you had left your mother and home and gone—where she knew not—and a friend in the neighborhood did know, would it not be a mercy to your mother for that friend to inform her of your whereabouts?" This appeal to my feelings quite overpowered me, and with choked utterance and tearful eyes I answered, "I will tell you all about your son. He is in Troy and here is a letter from him," at the same time handing her one which I had just received. The good old woman took it and said, "God bless you for this relief to my afflicted heart! The death of my husband was indeed a sad bereavement, but the wandering of my dear James and the suspense I have been in to hear from him is taking my life by inches!" I then as I never had before, realized the pain and anguish I had given my own dear mother in leaving home as I did some two years before. Although I had some show of reason for doing so at the time, I now felt that I was guilty of a great outrage upon parental affection and a mother's care. As I shall have occasion to allude to this subject again, I will now dismiss it and proceed with my narrative.

I continued on in my wild and reckless career, at times keeping the whole community in a state of excitement about some practical joke. For instance, while at Rochester, on one of my trips, there came a young man into the "Eagle Hotel," of a pompous and boastful bearing, telling about his money and his ability to carry on business. He said he wanted to purchase a good mill site for manufacturing flour. I saw at once that he was a "greenhorn." So I entered into conversation with him, telling him of a grand mill privilege at Bergen, near the village, where, with a moderate dam, a twenty-foot fall could be obtained. He made inquiries about wheat, the probability of the owner selling the property, etc., to all of which I of course answered favorably. The next morning he paid his fare to Bergen, treating his new friend the "driver" at every stopping place. We arrived at Bergen about noon, and as soon as he had swallowed his dinner, off we started for the proposed mill site. Just west of Bergen is a deep gully, with banks twenty or thirty feet high. As we approached the spot, I began discussing the best place for the dam and the position for the mill. By this time we were at the top of the steep bank, when the speculator turned, and, looking me full in the face, said: "Well, but look here, driver, there is not a —— drop of water in the whole concern." To which I answered, in deep sympathy: "Well, that is a pity; but I can't help it." This dry joke cured the young fellow of Bergen and its water power. He returned forthwith to Rochester, not to hear the last of his Bergen speculation for many a day.

During all these exhibitions of youthful blood, I was not without a deep and pungent sense of my lost condition as a sinner against God, and most conscious that I was fast hastening my soul to an utter state of ruin. And at times I would go alone into the forest, and sit down and weep myself sick over my profanity and Sabbath-breaking and the premonitory symptoms of disease from my habits of intemperance, which, if continued in, would, I knew, result in my ruin for time and eternity, only to return again to the hotel, or some circle of vain and frivolous associates, and enter with more zeal and apparent thoughtlessness upon my career of sin. My pride and sense of propriety in the company of ladies exercised a restraint upon me, keeping me from appearing outlandish and vulgar in their presence. In fact, this was about my only passport to respectable society, and constituted all my capital as a decent sinner. And yet I would, when out of such restraining society, reduce myself to a common blackguard and billingsgate rough.

From early childhood I had a strong prejudice against people of color. I believe the Irish generally are not very fond of their African relatives. On one occasion, as I came up to the door of the "Eagle Hotel," to start on my drive to Bergen, the only passenger to take the stage was a large, fleshy colored woman, about forty-five years of age. Colored dames of that age have a habit of becoming fleshy very frequently. With her large bundle—they often carry large bundles also—she seated herself in the coach. As Mr. Blinn handed me the way-bill, he said, in an undertone and with a mischievous look, "I hope, Hiram, you will not get love-smitten with this fair lady and come back a married man." At which all the bystanders raised a hearty laugh, and I cracked my whip and bounded up Buffalo street at full speed. At each stopping place my passenger and I were the objects of some laughing joke. It was much funnier to laugh at colored people then than now. Why? When I got to Riga Corners, within four miles of the end of my road, while the postmaster was changing the mail, I buttoned down all the curtains of the coach and lit my lamps, though it was about noon, and drove on to the vicinity of Bergen, when I held up into a slow funeral walk, blowing my stage horn with a plaintive-toning sound, so that it attracted all the village. Taking a long circuitous turn up to the hotel door, everybody came gazing with wonder at my lighted lamps, closed curtains and slow, funeral gait. As I halted, Mr. Buell stepped up, as he was accustomed to, and opened the coach door, when out sprung her ladyship, as though she would enjoy a breath of fresh air. As she passed in with Mr. B. to the dining hall, a boisterous laugh followed. It so happened that I was acquainted with this woman, and knew her to be a pious, respectable Methodist member. As I lay down at night, this indignity to the simple-hearted, innocent old woman haunted me. All effort to sleep was vain. She was black and I was white. She was a good Christian, a child of God; I was a sinner, a child of the devil. She was despised by some low characters on account of her color, but honored of God as one redeemed by Jesus. I was despised, I thought, by all good beings, and loved by none. If ever any poor wretch was in torment, present and in anticipation, I was the most of that long night.

But how soon do all such superficial emotions evaporate in mere momentary regrets, and leave the blinded and hardened to return to their accustomed folly and vicious pursuits! On I went, involving myself in sin more and more, and as I look back upon this dreary and dark pathway of my youth, I wonder at the long-suffering of God in sparing me, a reckless sinner indeed.

CHAPTER IV.

COURTSHIP AND MARRIAGE.—EARLY MARRIED LIFE.

AMONG the many youth of Bergen who congregated for the purpose of dancing and other amusements, was Miss Almedia Gifford, with whom I had become acquainted. She was exceeding fond of dancing. She was a great singer, and seemed to be in her element when in the associations of her young companions. At all public parties she was first on the floor to lead the dance, and the last to leave the room. Between Miss G. and myself there was a growing intimacy; that is, on all or nearly all these occasions I waited on her, until the common gossip of the place among the knowing ones was, that an engagement was entered into. Some said one thing and some another. Some expressed regrets that Almedia should throw herself away on such a reckless, rattleheaded fellow as Hi Stimson. But during all this tittle-tattle of the gossip-makers, not a word or intimation had been exchanged between us about any permanent relations of after life. But the thing was a fixed fact in the judgment of these allwise persons. So much so that some of her near relatives said, "I had rather see her dressed for her grave than for the bridal chamber." All this coming to our ears had a slight tendency to irritate us, and so I left that place and went to Palmyra for a short time, our stage route now being from Rochester to Palmyra. Things passed on till all was quiet at Bergen, but not so quiet about the regions of certain hearts.

On the 11th of October, 1825, my twenty-first birth-day, I sat down in a by-place and soon found myself in a reflecting mood. My thoughts took a direction something like this: "I am now twenty-one years of age. If I am ever to reform in my habits, now is my time. The past has only revealed the fact that I am growing worse and worse. I am profane; habits of intemperance are getting a fast hold upon me; a large share of my companions are not the most desirable in their conduct and character. What the friends say in Bergen is too true. I am confident though, that I possess the ability to be a man and a gentleman." And I then and there resolved to go back to Bergen and conduct myself with a little more reserve and propriety. So when I got into Rochester, I effected an exchange with a young brother of mine who had now become the driver to Bergen. The same day that I returned to Bergen was Thanksgiving day, and the youth of the place were celebrating it with a ball. Strange as it may appear, this was our understanding of gratitude to the Giver of all good, and our expression of it was by dancing.

Here I met again Miss Gifford, and soon improved an opportunity to have a little close conversation with her about the matter of our previous intimacy, and the common talk that had been going the rounds. She frankly informed me that much had been said to her about me, and her friends had prohibited her associating with me. I then suggested an interview to which she consented, and a time was appointed, at which time we negotiated the matter, and on the 11th of January, 1827, we were united in marriage at Bergen.

In the autumn and winter previous to our marriage, there was in the Presbyterian Church at Bergen, a considerable religious awakening. I believe not many conversions were the result, but the church was much improved in its religious condition, and among those who were affected by Divine influence, was a young man by the name of Harry Everett. One evening I attended their social meeting; and this young man arose, and in a very feeling manner addressed himself to the youth present. I returned from that meeting to my boarding place with deep and pungent convictions. I realized myself a sinner against God; and now believe if some Christian friend had just commenced a course of conversation and instruction and prayer with me, it would have saved me at least a long and severe career of open rebellion against God's truth. I was made sensible of the depravity of my nature, and how utterly vain it was for me to hope for reform while I was without a good hope in Christ, and my heart unrenewed by the Spirit of God. So I again procrastinated the all-important matter of my soul, to what I considered a convenient season, which never came. I still persisted in my course of sin, with but little restraint, all the while growing harder in heart, and more confirmed in my bad habits.

In my connection for life with the woman of my choice, I had a most congenial spirit as a lover of mirth and amusement, but differing from me in this particular: She detested anything like vulgarity and profanity, and utterly detested all habits of intemperance. Poor girl! she little knew then that the very man she had forsaken all for was hastening, with rapid strides, to a full and complete inebriate, and in a few years, if left to go on, would fill a drunkard's grave and a drunkard's undone eternity. The fact is, I was already a confirmed drunkard, in all the essential particulars. True, I did not get so intoxicated as to stagger on the streets, or to fall into the gutter. But I was under the power of a confirmed and unrelenting habit of the constant use of strong drink, though often disguised. During the first two years of our marriage, she had the worst evidence that her fate was that of a drunkard's wife.

She possessed two important elements of character, viz: kindness of heart and resolution of purpose. When she saw the sad evidences of her husband's ruin, she manifested the spirit of an angel in manner and in conversation. Yes, I have still in vivid remembrance her benignant look, as she spoke to me about my wayward course. Her resolution to endure all the privation and grief, growing out of her connection with the fallen and prospectively ruined companion of her youth, who, day by day, was perfecting himself for unutterable shame and sorrow, was worthy of a saint.

As an illustration of the desperation and rapidity

of my ruin, I will sketch to the reader the following: Soon after the birth of our first child, I removed to Mendon, the place of my early childhood and where I had experienced, only a few years previous, such a conflict with my father and Mr. S——, as to induce me to leave my home and the care and counsel of my mother. I came back to Mendon with the ostensible purpose of carrying on the cabinet business. Here I found a large group of young men who had been raised up with me in childhood, now matured into vigorous manhood; and many of them had made fearful advance in habits and practices of vice, especially intemperance. As a matter of course, we were congenial spirits; and "birds of a feather" will "flock together." Every leisure hour was spent in some place of amusement, at card playing or dancing, or, what was still more degrading, drinking and carousing.

It so happened during this summer, 1828, that the scarlet fever prevailed in the community to an alarming and fatal extent in many families. A large share of my time was occupied in my shop, making coffins for the dead; and soon my own family was visited with this terrible scourge. Our little boy, then eight or ten months old, was stricken. My wife was assisted by my kind-hearted mother and sister in caring for the sick infant, while I was occupied in my shop as stated, preparing those last conveniences for the dead. I came in one evening from my workshop and found my child in no better condition, and with the sad evidence that but little hope could be relied on of its recovery. My wife had so long applied her energies by night and day in a mother's care and love for her suffering babe, that I saw she was unwell and nearly exhausted. I said, "Almedia, I will step over to the hotel a few minutes, and then I will sit up a part of the night, while you get rest." So out I went, and soon fell into the company of my companions, who suggested a drink and short hand at "Loo." I consented, and down we sat at the gambler's table. The excitement of the game and the fumes of the liquor soon effaced from my mind my obligation to my weary wife and sick and suffering child. And so the whole night I remained away, or until one of the comrades said: "Boys, it's time to quit; it's plump three." I started from the place with amazement, and, with a hurried pace, arrived at my house, where a dim light was burning. And then fell upon my mind, like a thunder-burst, my neglect of wife, of my sick child, and my own debased condition. As I looked through the window, and there saw my pale and weary Almedia swinging the fan over her babe, that was scorched and writhing with a burning fever, oh! what a mountain-load of guilt and self-reproach crushed my conscience! I was half inclined to go and conceal myself in some unknown place; but I advanced to the door and silently turned the latch; but it was fast. I then went to the back door, but that was fast also. I then knocked for admittance. She came softly and opened the door. As I came into the room, I said: "How is the child?" She replied, with a stifled voice, "No better." There was a solemn pause. I said, "Almedia, come, you go and lie down, and I will take care of him until daylight." To which she replied, "Hiram, you are in no condition to take care of this dying child. You are not able to take care of yourself. You are under the influence of liquor. It does seem to me, if you loved your wife and child as a husband and father should, you would not have remained away 'till this late hour. Come, go and lie down, and when you are yourself I will talk with you about it." Oh! if a thousand thunders had uttered their voices of condemnation and death, they would not have struck greater consternation to my withering soul! I felt my way up stairs and there lay me down, but not to sleep, not to rest. And as the dawn of day and a bright August sun came into the east window, as I was recovering from the effect of my intoxication, all seemed to join with the admonition of Almedia and the groans of my suffering babe, to say: "Wretch! wretch! wretch! You are, indeed. You are now only fitted for ruin. How can you ever look your kind-hearted wife in the face again? Is this fulfilling the solemn vow you made to her when, against the advice of friends, she gave you her hand and heart, and who has done all in her power to make you and your home happy? Is this the example you are setting before your child, if God should spare its life?" It was a number of days before I fully recovered from the dreadful sense of my outrage upon the relationships of our home life.

In my temptation to engage in drinking and card playing, while my child was so near death and my dear wife so nearly exhausted, I now recognize most clearly the influence of a personal devil. My utter neglect and forgetfulness cannot be accounted for even by drinking and the excitements of gaming alone.

I believe the devil had possession of me, and obliterated for the time, home and wife and child. Young man, you had better keep clear of the devil's church, the drinking and gaming room. He always is on hand where his disciples congregate. To keep out of his clutches you'd better keep out of his places of meeting with the children of men. If Satan comes also when the sons of God meet together, you may be sure be does so when the sons of Belial come together.

One of the principal means that facilitated my degradation on this occasion, was a barrel of cider brandy that my partner in business and myself had bought, and kept on tap in the shop. You may be sure we had plenty of company while the brandy lasted, and we were expected to drink with each one who called for the brandy's sake. This wholesale provision for drinking, in connection with the horrible night's debauch and gambling, led to a little sober reflection, which resulted in a secret resolution to stop drinking for the short period of four days. I made the resolution during the night, went into the shop in the morning, and worked until breakfast was ready, and drank nothing. Then felt a strange want of something, but could eat no breakfast. So by the time the fourth day came, I was all lassitude, and generally wanting in energy. I had kept my secret pledge *all of four days*, and then returned again to old habits, but with a deep, penetrating conviction: "This you ought to have continued. It is your only hope of salvation from all the dreadful consequences of intemperance."

CHAPTER V.

A TURNING POINT—VICTORY OVER WHISKY—A SHOOTING MATCH—ETC.

MATTERS thus passed on until Christmas; 1828. There was to be a shooting match in the village that day. As I awoke in the morning these thoughts were suggested to my mind: "Now it's Christmas, and I shall go out with my associates to-day, to join in the sports and dissipations of the holiday. The result will be, I shall add another pang to my distracted and aching heart. I made one half-hearted effort to abstain from drink; it failed for the want of *determined, uncompromising resolution, a will to conquer or die.* I have fallen into the same sin and shame that I have abhorred in others. Here I have a beautiful and kind-hearted wife; I have a child that Heaven has spared to us, while others have been taken all around us. My dear mother and sisters are yet spared to me, but I fear only to be brought to anguish and shame by my reckless conduct. And now before I get up, I must decide this all-important question. And I

WILL. I WILL NOT DRINK NOR TASTE OF IT. I WILL NOT GIVE IT TO OTHERS, OR PROCURE IT FOR THEM." This was at four o'clock on the morning of Christmas. *It was an awful moment.* I arose and went about my morning duties, and at the time of the gathering at the shooting-match grounds, I put in my appearance.

My first shot drew a turkey. And as the custom was on such occasions, the successful one was expected to bring out his bottle; and so a number cried out, "Come, Hiram, bring on your 'clearance,'" as was the phrase. But I said, "No. If you don't get anything to drink until you get it from me, you will never drink." Then I made my second shot, and drew another turkey. At this they were more clamorous than before, and one cried out, "There are cobwebs in our throats!" I replied, "If they are not washed out except by liquor that I buy, young spiders will hatch out by hundreds."

It was enough. My companions knew by the look of my eye and tone of my voice, that I was not to be trifled with.

EDITOR'S REMARKS.

[When a man steps out of his former self, and turns the scale in which his past life is in one balance and his future life in the other, there is something about him that forbids vulgar familiarity. Such a passage in life is of too supreme importance to leave its hero at the sport of common-going souls. They at once shrink back. They do not comprehend the solemnity of the situation, nor the new—new to them—manifestation of human nature. For it is within the compass of our strange organism to change the whole bent and issue of our lives in a moment. Those who think that moral changes in man must be wrought slowly like the changes in man's physical nature, have never thoroughly comprehended the problem of human life. All souls are not capable of the sudden transition from a state of aimlessness to one of unswerving purpose; from a state of servitude to any vice, or habit not commonly called vicious but destructive of true development, to a condition of victorious self-reliance, and of course they are incapable of comprehending the idea. But a live man, whose instincts are keen, whose glance can comprehend a complicated situation, and whose resolution shrinks from no hazard and no mountain weight of effort, can in a moment's time become a totally different man from what he was, even mentally. It is not one in a thousand who has the courage to grasp this reversing lever and pull it down at a stroke, even with the bright prospect of a total change for the better immediately before him. The latent ability is lodged in many, perhaps all men, but practically it is used by the very few. But this does not invalidate the truth that men—some men—can in a pulse-beat, forever bid adieu to the character they have been years in slowly building up, and as suddenly begin a career on a different plan and according to different principles, resulting in the growth of a character as different from the former one as Jacob was different from Esau, as Abel was from Cain. Here is a man of passionate nature, cultivated by years of indulgence, and worse, inherited. His speech continually betrays him. He has the most intense loves and hatreds, the latter not entirely free from prejudice. And yet he has no patience with prejudice. His soul abhors mush and milk men. He has no patience with living antediluvians. He thinks the only place they are entitled to is in the ground. Contact with them, or more properly, against them, stirs his whole vehement nature, his tongue included. He has no thoughts, feelings or words of excuse for their last century modes. If it wasn't wrong, he would banish the whole tribe to some island, or perpetual "sleepy hollow," or more likely to the ground. This man stops. Some one in whom he has unbounded confidence may stop him. He says, "I see this fiery temper and tongue are the bane of my life. I could augment my influence five-fold were I to part company with them for good." The resolution is formed. The will has reversed the whole mechanism of the man. Henceforth he is patient. He can think out an apology for old fogyism, if need be, or for sly, plausible devils, under some circumstances. He can associate with those whose ideas in many respects are antagonistic to his own, and yet not chafe himself. He can speak peaceably to and of those who stand on the other side of a great dividing line. He is as impetuous against wrong as ever, but he is tolerant of slowness and feebleness. He burns against intelligent, deliberate wrong-doing as hotly as ever. But towards those who are to be pitied rather than blamed, even if their presence is oppressive, he has forgiveness and tolerance of heart and tongue. He is a self-controlled, care-taking man. He is a new man. His life is keyed on a different note. The course and issue of his existence are totally different. What is true in this respect holds good when it comes to the conquering of a dominant habit that has gathered to itself all the power of the will. The "awful moment," as Father Stimson calls it, comes when the man may liberate himself. The will summons its energies and offers itself as champion of the enfeebled nature, before making a final surrender of itself. The issue is met and passed in a moment. The die is cast, and the man goes forth, forever confirmed in his slavery to the habit, or forever free from it. In such a struggle, brief as it is fierce, one wants no aid from friends. He must be alone. It is purely a self-conquest. It is an "awful moment."

And why is it that men will admit this marvelous capability of human nature over itself, and yet stagger at the truth of Revelation, that the eternal God can suddenly change the currents of a man's moral nature; can in a moment conquer the opposition of his selfish will? If we admit the miracle as within the scope of man's own power, why deny a similar though greater miracle, perhaps, as within the compass of Divine power? And as to its fact, there are personal, experimental proofs of it in every community.—Ed.

On the evening of the day of the shooting-match, we all repaired to the hotel to raffle for the turkeys and other prizes, among which was a fat beef, just slaughtered. As the evening passed, strong efforts were made to induce me to drink or treat, as I was considered a lucky man in shooting and raffling, and I now had, in addition to turkeys, etc., a hind quarter of the beef. But I refused as persistently as I had in the day time. Then a friend, who had observed the conversation and who was acquainted with me from a child, knowing all my reckless habits, spoke up: "Boys, Hi is right; I have a mind to see how many will join in 'kegging' up for a month? All that will, step this way, and I will take your names; and a month from to-night all meet at my house, to talk over the matter and see how we can stand it." Twelve put their names to a simple pledge not to drink for thirty days, at the end of which time we were to meet at the residence of Gen. Cady, a man of wealth and highly respected, though he had long carried on the distilling business in that town. This was the first temperance effort in East Mendon.

At the expiration of the thirty days we met at the General's house. The community had in the meantime become not a little excited on what they called the "cold water question." That unhistorical, but not altogether uninteresting group, is worthy of a moment's scrutiny. There were old men who had "followed strong drink" from childhood—blear-eyed and red-nosed. There was the temperate drinker, expressing his opinion that "a little was for health." There were the young men and youth of the place, looking on curiously to see what would be the upshot of the "cold water movement." One man said he put his name down on Christmas and had kept his pledge until that last day, but would not suffer again as he had during the month for the best farm in Mendon; and he had stopped on his way there and improved his liberty by taking a drink. He felt better. This man died a drunkard in Mendon. I was called upon to express my views. I said I had been in a commingled state of mind and feeling during the last thirty days. The first ten days, everything went like dragging a cat by the tail, hard pulling, with much squalling. But for the last twenty days everything was changed for the better. Wife was better; little boy was better; neighbors were all changed for the better; and the world seemed to be made on purpose to make me and everybody else happy. I knew of but one thing as a drawback to keep us from all being happy—the devil in the shape of whisky. Forty more added their names that evening, some for a month, others for a year. Ethan Allen, a young man about my own age, joined for "ninety-nine years." I was not to be outdone by him, and put my name down for *one hundred*.

This move was the foundation of subsequent events not looked for by me, or remotely anticipated by others. My attention was soon arrested by an uncommon concern of spirit about myself as a sinner in the sight of God. My mind was never before so directed to the great fact. It followed me by day and night. I resorted to every expedient to dissipate these unwelcome and melancholy impressions. I had no inclination to attend the meetings in the community, and still I felt a kind of compelling power to attend, that I could not resist. I assumed the office of critic, making remarks about Christians and their manner of praying, speaking and singing. Sometimes I would attend the Baptist meeting, and then pretend that I was disgusted with their order of conducting worship; and especially disgusted with Rev. E. Weaver, the pastor of that church.

I would mimic him, by getting a crowd together and haranguing them in a mocking manner, and by paraphrasing the hymns sung at the Baptist meeting. Thus I went on from bad to worse, until one Sunday I went to hear Mr. Weaver, when his text was "Who for a morsel of meat, sold his birthright." (Heb., xii. 16.) The very announcement of the text meant me; all the illustrations meant me; and when he made the application, I was quite positive that he meant to insult me, and that some one had told him all about me, and my conduct was all known to him. I went out of the house quite in a rage, and expressed to one of the members my hatred of the man that would single me out before a large congregation, in the way he had that morning. The friend replied that he presumed that Mr. Weaver knew nothing about me and that no one had told him a lisp about me. The same friend came to me in a few days and said: "I spoke to the Elder about that sermon, and he says he did not know you were in the congregation, and had no knowledge of you, only that you were like other young men in the village, 'a common sinner on the devil's common.'"

All this while my distress of mind continued, and every shift I made for relief only increased my horror of soul, until at last this thought impressed me, that I had committed the unpardonable sin, and I had now better give myself up to sin and the enjoyment of life the best I could; I had gone beyond all reasonable expectation of deliverance from sin. The Spirit's influences had left me forever, and I was just as much damned as if I was already in hell; and if I would only go back to my cups and old associates again, I might enjoy life for a while at least. But damned I must be, damned in the end to all eternity.

The effect of this temptation was, that instead of being led back to my old companions, their company and presence were made all the more disgusting to me; so that I resolved to keep out of their way, and seek seclusion from all society. I had made two or three efforts to pray, but it seemed like solemn mockery, and only aggravated my distress.

One evening as I came from my work, my wife said we needed something from the store, and I at once started to obtain it. As I came near the store, the thought of my resolve not to put myself in the way of my old associates, came to me, and so I passed by the store to see if any of them were in. If so, I would return without the article. I saw the store was empty, and went in. But no sooner had I got into the room than in came Mr. U. T. James, the hotel keeper. I at once turned my face from him, determined I would not sin any more by joining with him in ridicule of sacred things. I had no sooner thought it than he came up to me, saying in a bantering, sneering, devilish tone, "Well, Hiram, I understand you are crying 'Abba Father.'" My first impression was to deny it by cursing and swearing. The next impression, as quick as thought, was, "Confess it and confess Christ." I replied, "Mr. James, it is time I cried for mercy and relief from sin. You and all of us as sinners need to cry to God to be merciful to us." He at once turned as pale as ashes and trembled in every muscle, while George Allen, the clerk in the store, looked at me with blank astonishment.

Then something seemed to say in a superhuman whisper, "*Now go and pray*, and you shall be heard in heaven, and Jesus will relieve you of all your burden and apply His blood to cleanse your pollution and make you whole." Away I went to my home, only stopping long enough to leave the article on the table, and hurried to the barn, behind which I kneeled and opened my mouth in confession and prayer to God. And O, such relief! O, such joy!

O, such views of Christ and of the plan of salvation! And what a debasing sense of myself, of my misspent life, of my awful sins against God and His holy law!

I at once went into the house and exclaimed, "Almedia, God for Christ's sake has had mercy upon your poor, miserable husband." And to my mother I said, "Your son that was dead, is alive; was lost, is found." Soon the Christian neighbors came rushing into my humble cottage, and expressed their gratitude to God in hymns of praise, and the prayer of thanksgiving to Jesus the Savior of sinners. At midnight, we closed the delightful exercise by singing that old hymn, now found only in books that are out of print:—

"Away my unbelieving fears;
Fear shall no more in me have place.
My Savior doth not yet appear;
He hides the brightness of His face.
And shall I therefore let him go,
And basely to the tempter yield?
No! in the strength of Jesus, No!
I never will give up my shield."

That was my birth night. The Kingdom of God had come down to me. I was a new man in Christ.

After this first morning, I had an opportunity to

receive the congratulations and advice of not a few veteran Christians of the different denominations in the place,—among them, Dea. Barrett and DeWolf, of the Baptist, and Hon. Timothy Barnard and Deacon Ezra Sheldon, of the Presbyterian Church, and a large company of young converts, who had, within a year or two, been brought to a knowledge of the truth. I commenced attending the social gatherings of the new company, who assembled for the purpose of mutual conference and prayer—that is, the company was new to me, and I found myself astonished at the perfect contrast between what I heard, what I saw, and, more than all, what I felt now and only a few days before in the society of my old cronies. Only a short time before, I hated these men, now I loved them; once I could not endure to listen to their addresses in such meetings, but now I was interested like a charm in all they said, in every hymn sung. And, although I felt weak and insufficient, yet I desired to bear some part, though humble, in the worship of God. I felt it was a special obligation resting on me to confess Christ in public and in private. Wherever I went, whoever I saw, Christian or not, I either expressed my new love for Christ, or rather His old for me, or I invited some poor fellow-sinner to go with me to "Mount Zion."

Although I expected to join the Presbyterian Church, yet I knew no difference in my love between that and the Baptist Church. Christian men and women were now the excellent ones of the earth to me; and I was just as much at home in one meeting as the other. I soon discovered, however, that Almedia had no relish for the Baptists; and, joined as she was by my relatives in this opposition to them, it became a source of great irritation to her and my sisters whenever I attended one of the Baptist meetings. And they commenced paying me off in the same coin, with compound interest, for my ridicule of the Baptists. They would put themselves energetically at work to invent some caustic joke at my expense: calling me, for instance, "the Weaver sprout of the last growth;" "the second edition of Elder Weaver, abridged and bound in calf;" "my dear Elder Hiram ·" "Brother Stimson;" "Our Elder," etc.

But they soon found that this was all useless, for the same grace manifested to turn the current of my affections from error to truth, from hatred to love, from sin to holiness, could not be moved by any mere scoffing and silly laughing ridicule. I had been too well schooled in that kind of appliance, and too perfectly understood its powerless effect against the spirit of Jesus and the love of God filling my heart. I had tested it in the times of ignorance and opposition to Christ, "whereof I was now ashamed."

This was soon changed for more stern opposition against not only the Baptists, but against all vital godliness and zealous Christians of every name. But in the midst of it all I came to the conclusion: "This is all right in the Divine economy of salvation. The Master means to show me how cruel I have been in pouring contempt on Christians, in ridiculing them to their faces, and how wicked I have been in my profane conduct and open opposition to Him and His anointed ones."

After a few weeks had passed, my attention was called to the duty of connecting myself with some church. I need church-fellowship for my own welfare, and in order to increase my influence over my fellow men. But above all, I saw it was a positive command of the great Head of the Church.

CHAPTER VI.

A SEARCH FOR A CHURCH.

NO one had said a word to me, however, concerning the matter, but I knew that I needed the advice of intelligent Christians. So when on the Sabbath, the pastor of the Presbyterian church gave notice of the preparatory lecture on the following Friday, and also stated the session would meet immediately after the lecture, to receive applications for membership, and also stated that on the next Sabbath the ordinance of baptism would be administered to infants and adults, I immediately said to myself: "I will improve this opportunity and offer myself as a candidate for membership;" not for baptism, for I supposed that I had been baptized. "I will also bring my children—we now had two—forward for baptism." This I expected to do, as much as I expected to live till the next Friday and Sabbath. On Monday morning the pastor of the Presbyterian church called upon me at my shop, and after making a few inquiries about my hope in Christ, he asked if my children had ever been baptized and if I intended to present them at the administration of the ordinance? I replied that they had never been baptized, and said I would present them, if I could get the consent of my wife. After a few more remarks upon the subject, the minister went out.

There was at work in the same shop, John Woodbury, before named in this narrative, a staunch Baptist. He heard my conversation with Mr. Anderson, the minister; so, when he had gone, Mr. Woodbury came to me and said: "Brother Hiram, did I hear you say that you intended to have your children baptized next Sunday?" I replied that such was my intention. He continued: "Do you think it to be your duty?" "Certainly, I do." "Well, Brother Stimson, if it is your duty, it must also be my duty, must it not?" I replied: "Of course it is; and here is where I think you Baptists are in error, in not having your children consecrated to God in baptism." He said: "If this is commanded in the Bible, we are in error, indeed." I at once replied: "Well, it is commanded in the Bible; I can show it to you in ten minutes, or could if I had the Bible here. I will look it up when I go home to dinner, and show it to you this afternoon." "Very well, when you do so I will have all my children baptized." "But," said I, "Elder Weaver will not baptize them." He replied: "Well, then, I will join the Presbyterian Church, and have Mr. Anderson do it." I now thought, "I have caught him;" for I supposed that I could find it, or rather that my mother could, and I knew that the Presbyterian Church would be glad to receive so good and worthy a man as John Woodbury. When I went home to dinner, I took up the Bible, at the same time relating to mother, who was then present at my house, the conversation with Brother Woodbury and the proposition he had made, adding, "and now, mother, let us find it and see if he will stand to his proposal." Upon which, she adjusted her glasses to her eyes, saying at the same time: "Well, the Bible is all full of it." So we sat down together to find this very easy and common command upon all parents. I of course depended on her, as I was ignorant of the Bible on all questions. She looked here and then there—first in the Old, then in the New Testament. Soon dinner was ready. "Come," said I, "let us sit down to the table, and after dinner we will find it." She replied, "No, you sit down and eat your dinner, and I will find it, so that you can carry it back to Mr. Woodbury." But at the conclusion of our meal, the said precept or example either was not forthcoming; and still the dear old lady was confident the good Book was full of it, and she could find it by the time I came back to my tea.

I went to the shop feeling a little puzzled what to say to my dear friend Woodbury, if he should ask for it; but not a word was said by him, and I was sure I should not say anything if he did not, and so the afternoon passed away. At the tea hour, I hastened home to get the required evidence on infant baptism. As I came in, I saw the Bible was put away, and mother was employed knitting as usual. "Well, mother," said I, "have you found the passage on infant baptism, yet?" She replied, "No; I can't find it. I thought it was in Ezekiel or Jeremiah. I have forgotten just where it is, but I know well enough it is in the Bible. But, Hiram, let me say to you, you had better keep away from those Baptists; they are always dogging converts about baptism." The manner and spirit in which it was said at once indicated to me a little distrust about the existence, in fact, of the thing I was in pursuit of. But I replied, "Mother, John Woodbury is a candid and pious Christian man, and the request he has made of me is a reasonable one; he has used no influence to proselyte me, nor has any other Baptist, to anything but the truth and the salvation of my poor soul to Christ. And now, mother, I am not going blindfold one single step. I have been a miserable, deluded sinner all my life, and my eyes begin to be opened, and my prayer is for more light. I shall search the Bible for myself, and what that requires of me I shall do with Divine assistance. Without it I shall fail and stumble; with it I am confident of ultimate success and correct direction." She said I'd better go and see Mr. Anderson; he would tell me all about it and find the passage for me. I replied, "It will be a pleasure for me to do so, and I will this evening." So off I started to converse with the Pastor of the Presbyterian church. He received me very kindly, and made many valuable suggestions about my future prospects, and the delight it gave him to know that I had seen my folly and turned to God, exhorting me to fidelity in my Christian course. I then said to him that I was in perplexity about infant baptism, and informed him what had taken place that day, since I saw him in the morning at the shop. After a minute's pause, he said, and with some hesitation, "Mr. Stimson, that is a subject you had better leave to take care of itself. You come right along and put yourself within the church, and this whole subject will adjust itself to your mind without any perplexity, in a little time." So back I trudged through the dark, made doubly so to me since I had not got the passages on infant baptism, with which to meet Brother Woodbury. When I arrived at home, I told mother of my ill success with the pastor in my search after light, and sat down with my Testament to see what I could gain from that to help me out of my trouble. In the morning, as I resumed my employment in the shop, Brother Woodbury came along to my bench and said, "Well, Hiram, I have waited twenty-four hours for that Scripture on infant baptism; have you found it yet?" My reply was in the negative, of course, but qualified by the remark that "mother had been looking in the Old Testament for it, and that I was looking in the New, and if it was there, we should find it." I saw a slight smile irradiate from his face as he said, "Well, you have got the best part of it. Your mother will look in vain in the Old Testament for baptism, but you will find it is a very plain subject in the New Testament. There's not a word of it in the Old."

Here the conversation ceased, and during the day I resolved on two things; first, I will not join any church until I see my duty made plain from the Bible on the subject of baptism. Second, I will take the New Testament as my only guide and counsel in all religious faith and practices. When I had made these two resolves, I felt such a confidence in Christ and His blessed Spirit as I had never experienced before, and from that day I commenced the study of the Bible, with an intensity and determination to know all the truth, but without the least expectation of ever being a Baptist, or thinking them correct in faith or practice; no more than I had of supposing Mahommed was right. I really expected to find sprinkling and pouring as the common, if not the only act for the ordinance. But three short weeks revealed to me, and to my utter surprise, that I was mistaken. My investigation was carried on in this manner without any assistance from Baptists or Pedobaptists: I commenced at Matthew, first chapter, and first verse, and continued through by course, to the last chapter and verse of Revelation, marking every passage on baptism, pouring and sprinkling. When I had finished I reviewed the whole, to find the results. I found the words baptism, baptizing and baptized eighty-one times; pour, pouring and poured, seventeen times; sprinkle, sprinkling and sprinkled, seven times. Where the subject of baptism was alluded to, if qualified at all, it was by "going into the water," "coming up out of the water," "being buried with Christ in baptism," "baptized into Christ," etc., etc. The word *pour* was qualified, but had no connection with baptism whatever; and the same held true in regard to the word *sprinkling*.

Just as I had closed this investigation in my own simple and private way, the Rev. Mr. Anderson preached a sermon on baptism, taking for his text, Acts viii. 38: "And they went down both into the water, both Phillip and the eunuch, and he baptized him." The first sentence of the sermon was: "This refers to the apostolic mode of baptism by immersion," and he went on to say, "No reasonable doubt can be entertained but that Jesus of Nazareth was thus baptized in the river Jordan;" but he undertook, with a great show of words, to prove that other modes were equally as well. It was indeed a Godsend to me. My duty was now becoming plain. This first remark of the preacher, and my own silent investigations, left but little doubt as to what was the true course for me to pursue. All this while nothing had been said to me on the subject by any one. So the Monday evening following this discourse of Mr. Anderson, I walked over to see him unbeknown to any one.

I have so far neglected to state one important fact in my early history, which is this: While my parents resided at Saratoga Springs, and while I was an infant, I was taken seriously ill, and my parents, fearing I was about to die, called in a Presbyterian minister, who sprinkled me for baptism. I had always depended on this as sufficient until within the past three weeks, but now all my dependence on my infant sprinkling was gone. I found Mr. Anderson in his study, and he gave me a hearty welcome and at once inquired: "Well, Brother Stimson, did you get any new light on the subject of baptism?" I readily answered, "Yes; I am glad to know that your sermon and my investigations of the New Testament convince me that the apostles immersed, and that the Savior was baptized by immersion in the river Jordan; and my business here to-night is to see if you will immerse me." "I will do so," he replied, "if you cannot be satisfied with anything but immersion and you have never been baptized by any other mode." I replied, "I must confess to you the truth;" and I proceeded to give him the history of my being sprinkled when an infant. He then said to me, "Such being the facts, I cannot immerse you, as I would consider it sacrilege so to do." "What can I do then?" I inquired. "You can join the Baptists; they will immerse you on profession of your faith, notwithstanding your previous baptism." To this I objected: "I cannot do that; they are close-communion." "Close-communion! Pooh! They are no more close-communion than we are. We take no one into the Church until he has been baptized, neither do the Baptists; the only difference being in what we consider baptism." This opened the matter in an entirely new light to my mind and completely changed my views upon the question, and I said to him: "I'll go home and think upon this matter." As I walked along, I could but admire the man for his magnanimity and generosity. The next morning, I called upon Deacon Woodbury, a brother to John, and asked him a few questions about the Baptist Church policy, of their faith and practice; and after getting a candid exposition of the matter, I informed him of what I had been doing the past three weeks, to which he made a remark of commendation and said: "Move on, Brother Stimson, with caution; you are taking the right direction, and if you keep near the Cross, all will result for your advancement in the Divine life."

But now the most trying point in all this conflict was yet to come. The opposition of my wife, connected as it was with that of my other relatives and friends, against the Baptist denomination, would be no surface agitation, I was satisfied; and how to broach the matter in such a way as to evince a Christian spirit and not excite a disposition to contend, was a question of the first moment to me. I had ample time for reflection. From Tuesday morning to Friday evening, this subject was constantly on my mind. After supper on Friday evening, I said to Almedia, my wife, "Come, go along with me to the Baptist covenant meeting to-morrow afternoon." "Not I!" was her prompt reply. "Why not?" I inquired. "What do you desire to go there for?" she asked. "I am going to join the Baptist Church, if they will accept me," was my quiet answer. "*You* join the Baptists! Well, you will go alone, then." At this moment my mother came in, and Almedia saved me the trouble of informing her. My mother commenced weeping and talking at the same time. "Well, Hiram, you are the only child of mine that has experienced religion, and I was in hopes you would feel it your duty to join the Presbyterian Church, and I think you are hasty in the matter, and have been influenced by Elder Weaver and the Woodburys." "Not so," said I; "I have not exchanged a word with Elder Weaver on the subject of baptism; and as to the Woodburys, all that has been communicated to me is this: John Woodbury asked me to find infant baptism in the Bible, and you and I have made an effort and could not produce it. You then sent me to Mr. Anderson, and he could not produce it; and last Monday evening, I told him my convictions, and he says I am a Baptist, and as an honest Christian minister has advised me to join them, and the Lord Jesus helping me, I shall do it. I want to do right, and I am confident the Bible directs in this way." This last remark put an end to the conversation for the present.

CHAPTER VII.

THE CHURCH FOUND.

THE next day, in the afternoon, the covenant meeting convened, and a large concourse of people assembled. Among the number, were Heber C. Kimball and Brigham Young. Brigham spoke. At that time he had left the Methodists, and belonged to what were called the Giffordites. He was quite fervent, and spoke with much feeling and effect. He was regarded as stronger in heart than in head. His faith and piety were counted of more force than his intellect. Heber C. Kimball, on the other hand, was respected as a man of much more mental power, but not of great devotion in comparison with his associate, Young.

[A recent interview with Brigham Young, on the part of the editor, in company with Rev. E. P. Hammond, letters of introduction being given us by Father Stimson, satisfied him that this estimate of him by Father Stimson at the time of his conversion would require modification, and much of it, to be applicable to him now. His piety can hardly be spoken of as dominant. His will can. His ambition can. His selfism can. His power over men can. His early simplicity of heart and devotion have certainly deserted him. A more Jesuitical, autocratic ruler of men, cannot be found on the globe. Men change. Brigham is a puzzle; and Mormonism is puzzling. The latter because of the former. Men who have known him longest, acknowledge that they know the least about him. He is fearfully and wonderfully made; especially the former. And yet he will talk to you with the greatest apparent relish, of pure and undefiled religion. Abandonment of principle is followed by either open wickedness, or habitual hypocrisy. Brigham is an exception: in his case it has been followed by both.—Ed.]

At the meeting referred to, thirty-one converts related their experience to the church, and the next day (the Sabbath) they were immersed in the likeness of Christ's death and resurrection, and among them was myself. A day never to be forgotten by me. The Baptist church in Mendon then numbered about four hundred, a united and happy people. Their zeal and devotion were known in all the land. God was with them in the power of the Spirit. My new relation to the Baptist church I found a very pleasant one. A large number of ardent Christians and warm-hearted friends, both old and young, stood ready to counsel and encourage in every good word and work, and the summer and autumn of eighteen hundred and twenty-nine was enjoyed by me as no former season of my life had been. In fact, this was the only drawback to the gliding days and months: my dear companion had no good hope in Christ, and no sympathy with the people with whom I was identified, and in whose society I found such delight and Christian fellowship. I could, however, see most plainly that she at times made great efforts to render herself agreeable to those with whom I came in contact, but it was also as plain that their society was not agreeable to her. She was unwilling to attend the Baptist meeting, and would refuse to interchange visits with persons of that society, only in such cases as would be a breach of good manners, and sometimes she was not so careful even about that. All this grew out of one fact, a want of a change of heart and love to Jesus, as the sequel will show by her own confession in a subsequent work of grace, and as was manifested in a life altogether short of consistent devotion and application to the duties of a wife and mother in the Christian sense.

It gives me pain to refer again to the opposition evinced by her during eighteen long months after I had hoped in the pardoning mercy of the great Redeemer; and I have only consented to do it since her conversion to Christ magnifies the grace of God. "Where sin abounded, grace did much more abound." As I have before stated, she was possessed of a nature of kindness and a very benevolent disposition. Nothing was wanting to make home all that could be desired, except the one thing needful on her part. She opposed prayer in the family, and would absent herself from it, if possible, and often would resort to extra efforts to disconcert its order. She was unwilling that the pastor, or any of the Baptist society, should interchange visits with the family.

All this rendered necessary, at the commencement of my discipleship, the very important grace of patience. In all that I have named, I saw in miniature what I was when in a state of alienation, fighting against God and resisting the truth of the Holy One of Israel.

My own soul was in deep agony for sinners. I constantly felt a weeping solicitude that they might be brought to the Saviour, and I envied the talent and ability of any one that was qualified to expostulate with and win souls to Jesus. But what could

I do? All my childhood and youth had been spent in sin and folly, and now I had come to the years of mature manhood, involved in the darkness of ignorance. Religion don't educate a man, though it often makes him feel his need of education and gives him fixedness of purpose in acquiring it. No education! no character! and in no condition to obtain the one or strengthen the other, and with no hope of either, at least without the interposition of God's sovereign grace.

To say a word to any living creature about my feelings and anxieties, I could not. If I should, I would be laughed at as visionary, or rebuked as ostentatious. In this state of mind, I resolved to make such improvement as I could under the circumstances. So I obtained a dictionary, and stented myself to study six columns a day, by spelling the words and committing the definitions.

A dictionary is the first thing instinctively sought by every ignorant person who is bent on educating himself. Without knowing why, they all feel that a knowledge of words lies at the foundation of all that needs to be known, or can be known. Here is a good point for philologists.

My wife heard my lessons at night. This she did

with cheerfulness, little knowing what use I intended to make of my knowledge. During the day I would fix the dictionary before me on the bench, and would repeat the spelling and definition of the words to myself while I was busy at work with my hands. Every evening found me a little further on, till in this way I went through the entire book. I have found this systematic study of the dictionary of invaluable benefit to me during all my public life. Having had so few school privileges in early life, and having spent so large a portion of my time in the society of those whose language was as imperfect as it was impure, my knowledge of the spelling and meaning of words was very limited. I was at this time furnished with a few religious books and the *New York Baptist Register*. The books were, Baxter's "Call to the Unconverted," his "Saints' Rest," "The Evidences of Christianity," and "Butterworth's Concordance." These, with the Bible, constituted my library. But I made good use of them.

CHAPTER VIII.

A YEAR OF JUBILEE.

ABOUT the first of June, 1830, a powerful revival of religion began in the Baptist church of Mendon, but extending to adjacent towns, and continuing into the autumn of the year; and then increased in power as the winter set in. A year, blessed be God! never to be forgotten by me, nor by a multitude of others, redeemed as the purchase of Christ's precious blood. Among the number was my dear companion. This fact makes it the year of jubilee to me. She had not been to the Baptist church for months previous to the evening of her surrender to Jesus. She was induced to go by some means, I knew not what; and although we had had no preaching for weeks on account of the illness of the pastor, the meetings were continued from day to day and from evening to evening by the members of the Church, in a manner to interest and profit all. This evening the pastor thought it his duty to preach, as a large congregation had come out, and though quite feeble, he held the audience spell-bound, from the text, "It is a fearful thing to fall into the hands of the living God." During the whole delivery of the sermon my soul was weighed down with such a spirit of prayer for my wife as I had never before experienced, for her salvation. It seemed to me that all I had ever felt for her before was merely the result of sheer selfishness, a desire to make me and my home, in a domestic point of view, more comfortable. God never answers selfish prayers. He cannot consistently. But now I saw, independent of my interest in her as a companion, or as the mother of our children, that she had a soul to save, for which Christ died, and which, if saved, would be a star in His crown of rejoicing; but if lost, would be lost in unutterable despair for eternity. And oh! what a sense was impressed on me of that word, eternity! "Oh! will she submit to-night to the Spirit's blessed influence?" As the preacher closed his discourse, he said, "If any poor sinners will now yield to the Lord Jesus, let them manifest it." And while he was yet speaking, before any one had moved, she left her seat and came down the aisle, and as she came, said, "O, my dear Christian friends! will you pray for me a sinner? O, my husband!

can you forgive and pray for me?" And then bowed herself, burying her face in the lap of the pastor's wife. Others came forward for prayer, and found peace in believing, almost immediately. But Almedia remained in her kneeling posture for a long time, under great agony of spirit, but at length arose with a countenance beaming with a heavenly smile, and broke the silence of the moment by saying, "Can such a sinner as I am hope for mercy at the hands of an insulted Savior? Yet I have insulted His Spirit, I have insulted His children, and," turning to me, "I have been angry at God for converting my dear husband. But with all this aggravated sin, my heart says I will believe in Jesus and I will follow Him by His assisting grace."

Perhaps it will not interest others to relate all that transpired for the next two years after her conversion to Christ. I will simply state the fact, that at the first covenant meeting she offered herself to the Baptist Church for membership. And although the day of her baptism was one of intense cold, she, with others, followed the Savior with a joyful heart into the liquid tomb; and from that day, was a practical illustration of the Scripture: "Even so we also should walk in newness of life."

The next spring, we found it for our interest to move to a place called Sibleyville, near West Mendon, and so changed our church membership to Rush. In Sibleyville was a large business carried on in the manufacture of carding and agricultural implements.

The factory was under the proprietorship of Hiram Sibley & Watson. The former of these gentlemen has since become wealthy, and, with a wise generosity, has given a large sum of money to the Rochester University, with which "Sibley Hall" has been erected, one of the first educational buildings in the land. Though not a member of the Baptist Church, his sagacious eye has seen the immense advantage to a city and commonwealth, for all time to come, of the establishment of such an institution of liberal learning on the most permanent basis, and his hand has given accordingly.

In my new employment, I was connected with a class of hands numbering some eighty in all, and not one of them a Christian, except an old man by the name of Kimble, a Methodist, pious and godly. The whole company, with this single exception, was given to drinking, profanity and Sabbath desecration. I proposed to Kimble to start a meeting in the place; but he thought it useless, as our associates were so irreligious, the most of them being drunkards and scoffers at sacred things. "Well, then," said I, "let us get up a temperance meeting, and see if some of them can't be reformed." But he said, "No; we can't do anything for them." "Well, I shall make an appointment, and you must come out and act as chairman of the meeting." He finally consented, if I would take the responsibility of the result. "I will assume that," I replied. So I made an appointment at the school house, giving a written notice. It so happened, without any design on my part, that it would occur on "town meeting" day. I went to East Rush and selected a young medical student to come up and be secretary. His name was Howard. The evening of the meeting came, and the whole crew in and about the shops had been to the "town meeting," and were well liquored up. Kimble saw the cases we had to deal with, and regretted that we had hit upon that evening. But in we went, and found the school-house jammed with all classes. Many were respectable young men and women, while a host were hard cases, highly fired up with "town meeting" whisky. As we came in with our associates, all manner of remarks were made: "There come the cold water devils;" "hold your breath, Jake—you will take fire from that candle," etc. Then followed a loud laugh. Kimble looked as pale as ashes. I arose and said: "It is time to organize the meeting, and I will nominate Mr. Kimble as chairman and Dr. Howard as secretary." The Doctor seconded the motion. "All in favor of the motion, will say, aye." "I;" "I;" "I will;" "I won't;" "I shan't;" "I can't," went up on all sides. "Contrary-minded, say no." "No—no—no—no, not I;" "No, not you, old 'Kib." The whole scene was not the most orderly imaginable, nor calculated to quiet delicate nerves. Kimble took the chair, with about as much grace as a dog gets over the fence after he has been caught stealing sheep. He called on me to pray, which I did as well as I knew how under the undevotional circumstances, when they began hooting and jeering again. But I at once arose and commenced addressing the meeting something as follows:

"My dear neighbors of Sibleyville, I rejoice to see so many of the respectable inhabitants of this place out to this meeting to-night. It argues well for your respect to the cause of sobriety and the cause of humanity. The occasion is most auspicious, for more than one reason: It is town-meeting day, or the evening of our town election, in which a few have not only exercised their right to the elective franchise, but to improve the right of drinking egg-nog well seasoned with bad whisky, and such other drinks as men indulge in to make fools of themselves, and to disgust all good and honest-thinking people; and as we have a few specimens of that disgusting and degrading class present this evening, I propose to talk to you about *Temperance*."

As soon as I had pronounced the word "*temperance*," a pettifogging lawyer of the town rose in his place and interrupted me by asking: "What is the definition of the word 'temperance'?"

I saw at once that it was all done to disturb the meeting and get up a row, and, if possible, break up the meeting by disorder and drunken slang. I knew him to be a man of some education,—in fact he had been a school-teacher in the town, and was in repute as a man of intelligence. So I replied, "I presume every person in the congregation is quite familiar with the definition of the term, except Mr. *Townsand*; and as he has been so long accustomed to the other side of this important word, and has now nearly finished his course of intemperate education, I propose, now, that we buy him a Webster's spelling-book and send him to a good school, to some woman teacher for three months; and at the end of his time, if he has not learned the signification of the term *temperance*, that we then put him on a course of simple diet of buckwheat cakes and cold water for three months more. And if that don't effect his knowledge of the *word*, at the next town-meeting we will turn him over to old '*Aunt* Cloe,' the goddess of his passions."

At the conclusion of this reply, the entire congregation were in a perfect storm of laughter at poor Townsand's expense.

I then made an appeal to the young men, sighting them to the class present who had given us, there and then, such a demonstration of the effect of a drunkard's life and character, and asked them to decide that night which side they would take; and every man and woman present, who was not identified with that company of the baser sort, came up and signed the pledge—among the number, Hon. Hiram Sibley and his partner in business, Mr. Watson. After this, temperance was the order of the community.

Poor Mr. Townsand never heard the last of the proposition to send him to a woman's school.

CHAPTER IX.

SHALL I PREACH?—FIRST PASTORATE.

IN my new relation with the church at Rush, I found a more ample field in which to develop the ardent desire of my heart. The church was small in comparison with the one at Mendon, which at the time numbered some four hundred. At Rush the numerical strength was one hundred all told, mostly poor and not well-trained in Christian work. In fact, many of them did not believe in the benevolent efforts made for the extension of the Messiah's kingdom, while a few believed in every good word and work. The pastor was a young man from the Mendon church. Partly owing to this, I was at once put forward by the working members of the little church, and encouraged by the young pastor to enter every open door of usefulness—the Sunday school, prayer meeting, the conference meeting. In a short time we established a number of out-stations, some in considerable-sized towns near by.

My effort at the temperance meeting had created quite a stir among the better class of the community, and not a little rage among the baser sort. Thus I was called upon to address gatherings at Sunday school meetings and temperance societies. I was at home with all classes of working Christians: Methodist, Presbyterian and Baptist.

Long before I left Mendon, I was impressed with the duty of preaching Christ to all my fellow-sinners, but was always met with the depressing fact of my unfitness for a work of such magnitude and responsibility. No expectation of even a common education, I yet had an insatiable thirst for knowledge, that I might tell the story of Christ's love to a world of lost sinners, what He had done and was doing for their salvation.

Many dear friends said and did much to encourage me to enter just as I was upon the work, while others suggested that I might perhaps go to Hamilton and take what was called the "short course." But this looked well-nigh impossible, for two reasons: *First.* In that case, my wife and children would be without any visible means of support, while I was twenty-six years of age and not instructed in even the common branches. What little knowledge I did possess, was in a crude and disconnected state. *Second.* The church in Rush was quite divided on the question of licensing me to improve my gifts in preaching. Something was the matter, first of all, with my doctrinal views. A part thought I was not exactly sound on the election phase of the Gospel, whatever that is; while others thought that if this was true, it might not work great mischief to let me try and do all the good I could in the name of my newly-adopted Master, Christ the Lord. As to my own views, I did not know which I was, or on which side of these questions I properly belonged. But this one thing I did know, that Jesus Christ came into the world to save sinners, and the Gospel was the power of God unto salvation to every one that believeth.

I continued to hold meetings in such communities as opened a door to my poor efforts, so that all my Sabbaths were occupied. At length the pastor pressed the church to give me a regular license to preach wherever God should cast my lot. The "hypers" opposed and the "lowpers" pressed it to decision. The vote was finally decided with six majority in my favor, out of about fifty votes. The clerk refused to make a record of the action, because the sisters voted. The pastor and friends asked him to give a certificate of the vote, which he also declined to do. The devil shows his ingenuity in inventing such men and getting them into the Church. He generally only loans them to the Church, for in nine cases out of ten, he receives them back again. This man was not an exception. He continued to show his pious zeal for having all things work according to "Gunther" in the church. When I received a call to the little church in the "town" of Alabama, Genesee County, and decided to accept it, the question of my receiving the license came up again; but he, with the same holy love of meanness as ever, stoutly refused it. He was shortly deposed from the clerkship, excluded from the church, and imprisoned on being found guilty of theft. His name was Murray.

During the pendency of this certificate business, I kept still, having very little confidence in paper credentials, paper creeds, paper religion or paper sermons. (Skip the last word, or read it in a whisper.)

I soon moved to my new field, where I found my hands and heart full. I was shortly ordained by a council of churches, represented by the following pastors: Elijah Weaver, G. B. Davis, Roswell Kimble, Martin Coleman, Samuel Gilbert, Horace Griswell, Stephen A. Weaver, and Wm. Barrett. I think all these have passed away to their rewards, except the last named, who left the Baptist Church and joined himself with the Methodists.

The church in Alabama was organized in 1831, with twenty-one members. The following year they reported to the Association one hundred and ninety-two. I remained with them until 1835, when I accepted a call from the church in Parma.

This was a very trying year to me. During it my dear Almedia sickened and died, leaving me with four small children, and myself with impaired health.

I have had misgivings about the right of leaving Alabama at the time I did; yet I then thought it duty. Certain after developments have led me to question the correctness of the step. The whole time of my connection with the Alabama church was one of uninterrupted prosperity.

Many incidents occurred in this country church, which are worth remembering. In one portion of the "town" was a community of Universalists, who controlled the school house in that district. There was then but one pious family in the neighborhood, the man a deacon in my church. He was quite desirous that an effort should be made for the reformation of his neighbors. But many of the church thought it impossible (at least inexpedient,) for so young and inexperienced a person as myself to be brought into contact with these semi-skeptics with any advantage to the cause. But I told the deacon that if he would get the right of the house, and he and his wife and little Adney would stand by the cross and pray for salvation, I would come over and in the name of Jesus I would "strike for liberty and salvation."

He and "Aunt Eliza" gave the best of assurance of fidelity to the work at whatever cost. So we gave out the appointment for Wednesday evening, and the meetings to be continued day and night, for time indefinite. It was early in March, and farmers had not much to do. Wednesday evening came, and with it, a crowd that filled the house in every part. A murmur was heard in a certain corner, with such remarks as: "I smell brimstone;" "the devil will get you;" "look out for the bottomless pit;" "hell will be your portion;" "now for a gospel storm of hail and hot damnation, mixed."

While this was going on, I called on the deacon,

his wife and little boy to pray. Such pleading with God it seemed to me I had never listened to before; and soon all was still as the hour of death. At this moment came in Mr. McC. and wife, carrying a light stand and two candles, also a chair apiece. As the Squire, for such he was, took his seat in front of the desk and fixed his writing apparatus, an audible smile arose from all over the room. I arose, called on all to sing the fifty-fifth Psalm, in Watts' old book,

"Let sinners take their choice, and choose the road to death,"

and announced as my text, when they had finished singing; "I am not ashamed of the Gospel of Christ, for it is the power of God unto salvation to every one that believeth."

As I was about to proceed with my sermon, Squire McC. interrupted me by saying, "Will you repeat your text again?" I did so, calmly, and then went on. In a short time, "Will you wait a minute till I take that down?" I waited. And so he continued to interrupt me at almost every step for about twenty minutes, all this time the congregation evincing more or less merriment at the sharpness of Squire McC.

All this time, the Deacon and "Aunt Eliza" were

groaning in spirit for Divine help for the stripling of a minister. When it came in point, I quoted from Mark iii. 28–29:

"Verily I say unto you, All sins shall be forgiven unto the sons of men, and blasphemies wherewith soever they shall blaspheme:

"But he that shall blaspheme against the Holy Ghost hath never forgiveness, but is in danger of eternal damnation."

"Put that down, Squire McC.," said I; "and don't forget the chapter and verse." I went on: "Our Universalist friends say that there is no eternal damnation. Jesus says there is. Whom shall we believe?" The Squire pushed back his chair and paper, and that was the last of his note-taking that evening. He sat the rest of the time with bowed head and downcast looks. The next morning, he and his wife called at the Deacon's and requested prayer, and confessed their skepticism and sin. They were both converted.

Major Richards lived in this community, and a day or two before the meeting, he thought to nullify all the effect of the meeting by alluding to it in something like the following: "Stimson is to hold a protracted meeting in our school-house next week." "So I hear," would be the response. "Well, I will tell you what I have been thinking about," he would continue; "and it is this: you, Mr. A., (or B., as the case was,) will be among the converts." "Not I—not I," would be the natural reply. "Well, I will bet two shillings on it, anyhow." And, "I will take that bet," his friend would say. Then the Major would go to the next, and make the same wager. In his round he came upon Capt. H., who refused to bet money, but would bet a bushel of potatoes against twenty-five cents.

The meeting continued a number of days, when one evening a lady came and invited me to go and stay with her family that night. I consented. She had come to the meeting on horseback, and her husband left the house first to go on and start the fires at home. On the way she told me that her husband was under deep conviction, but he had made a bet with the Major of a bushel of potatoes against twenty-five cents. He did not know what to do. Not that he cared for the potatoes, but the bet was a sin in his view now.

When we arrived at their log house, we found the captain quite depressed in spirit. I at once commenced conversation with him about his state of mind as a sinner, and put to him this question, "Capt., are you willing to do any and everything you can for salvation in Christ?" "Yes; all I can do." "Will you pray in your family and begin here now, to-night?" He hesitated. "Well, now Capt.," I continued, "this is the turning point." He still hesitated. "Come, Capt., now resolve to pray, and ask God to forgive your sin of trifling with sacred things; and to-morrow morning go to the Major and pay the potatoes, and tell him you have lost the bet, fair play." And I quoted Ecclesiastes v. 4–5: "When thou vowest a vow unto God, defer not to pay it; for he hath no pleasure in fools; pay that which thou hast vowed. Better is it that thou shouldest not vow, than that thou shouldest vow and not pay." He hesitated no longer, but cried out, "O, Elder, do pray for me!" We all bowed, and God delivered his poor soul that night from con demnation. The next morning he went, paid the potatoes like a man, and confessed to the Major, and warned him to flee from the coming wrath.

Thus the work went on against the deep laid plans and open opposition of the enemy. The third Lord's day after the meeting began, twenty-three were baptized; Capt. H. and wife, C. McC., Esq., and wife, among the number. In all, eighteen heads of families and five youths. And we continued to sing,

"O, careless sinner, come,
Pray now attend;
This world is not your home,
It soon will end.
Jehovah calls aloud,
Forsake the thoughtless crowd,
Pursue the road to God,
And happy be.

During this year a squad of blacklegs came to town, and as usual, made an onset upon the morality of the community. They secured a large field adjoining the house in which we worshiped, and fitted it up for the races. I trembled for our youth in view of this moral pest. Horse-racing, like circuses, may be all right *per se*, only they are never found *per se; per contra* is the attitude in which they stand to all morality.

The Sabbath before this devil's protracted meeting began, we held forth the word of life from the text in Psalms xvi. 9: "Gather not my soul with sinners nor my life with bloody men." It had the desired effect. Not a Christian of any denomination attended, with a single exception; and he was disciplined, and confessed his wrong doing. The Lord's day following the races, we preached from the text, John viii. 44: "Ye are of your father the devil, and the lusts of your father ye will do; he was a murderer from the beginning, and abode not in the truth, because there is no truth in him. When he speaketh a lie, he speaketh of his own; for he is a liar, and the father of it." The chief man among the gamblers was present, and listened with marked attention to all the scathing utterances of the young preacher, with all the decorum of a saint. He had won a thousand dollars at the races the week previous. As the congregation was dismissed he took his position near the door, and as I came out, he reached me his hand, and with a smile, said, "I am happy to hear you to-day, and should be pleased to make your acquaintance, Mr. Stimson. Good day, sir," and he passed off among the crowd. In shaking hands he had left a five dollar note in my hand.

On my way home I commenced the following close conversation between myself and this son of Belial, now absent in body but present in spirit; "Well, Mr. Devil Jr., you think you have caught me in a trap, but I will let you know that I don't bite at any such poison-bait. If you have paid this to buy your conscience ease, it will only increase your pains fourfold." I thus went to my home and told my wife what had occurred, and showed her the note. She smiled, and remarked, "Quite a nice donation." I replied, "Not so nice for me. This is hush money. And I will make the devil's children wish they had kept it out of my hands."

The next morning I went to the hotel, and asked the clerk for Mr. R. He directed me to his room, where he greeted me with all the suavity of Lord Chesterfield. Mr. R. with his companions, were surrounding a table loaded with liquors of different brands in fine cut glasses. I walked up to the table and laid down the bill, saying: "Here, Mr. R., is the bill you left in my hand yesterday. I now return it to you as "base gain," illy gotten by you, and probably given to a poor minister to ease your guilty spirit, or as a pretext for scandalizing the servants of God, by saying 'they will preach against our profession, but are as eager as other men to get the avails.' Gentlemen, I cannot take a bribe. You are young men that appear well in exterior, but inwardly are corrupt. You have brought to our town, and have caused to congregate here during these days of races, the vilest prostitutes, to poison and pollute our young men. The worst forms of intemperance follow in your wake, as a besom of death and destruction to all that come within your power. May the Spirit of God follow you, and hedge up your way to despair. Good morning, gentlemen."

During this little speech each man sat as still as if made of marble. In a few days it was ascertained from the landlady, that it was a plot designed to bring scandal on the minister; that he would as soon take money from gamblers as from any other source. But it failed this time. I was gratified in after years to learn from J. H. Green, the reformed gambler, that this same Mr. R. became a reformed man and a Christian, and related to Mr. Green the circumstances of the foregoing plot, and requested him if he ever came North, to find me out, and if living to extend to me his grateful emotions for kind and plain dealing.

The following winter was a time of general refreshing in all the churches in Western New York. Our dear church in Alabama had a divine portion meted out to them, but not as extensive as that of a year or two previous. The church was well united, and quite happy in their covenant relation with each other. There remained, however, not a few in the community who had not been personally brought to accept Jesus. Among others there were three young men, whose names we shall not mention, whose enmity to the truth had increased in the same proportion as they had resisted Christ and grieved the Spirit.

Among others that they didn't like, was the pastor of the Baptist church. I had a young and spirited horse which needed a vigilant eye, and careful handling. My carriage was a rude sort of concern, mostly manufactured by my own hands, but answering all the purposes of a poor minister in a new country. It was early in March, when I had an appointment at an out-station where these young men resided. My appointment was on the evening of Sabbath. I arrived at the usual time, and as a light snow was falling, I covered my animal up snugly with the blanket, and went into the school-house. All were waiting for the minister. In the course of the evening, in came these three young men, and quietly waited till the meeting closed. I got into my buggy, if it could be dignified by such a name, and drove carefully home as usual, not mistrusting the least harm to myself or property. There had been a

February thaw, and as the ground froze up again it left deep ruts, which I let the buggy follow; got home between ten and eleven o'clock, put up the horse and went to bed, unconscious of any danger to which I had been exposed. As I went to the barn in the morning, in passing the vehicle I noticed a linch-pin was missing, and on examination found that all were gone. On going into the barn, I found that the harness was cut in a number of places, and only held together by mere strings; if any part had given way, or a wheel had run off, a shipwreck would have taken place, and life or limb would have been in jeopardy in the darkness of the night.

I went into the house with a deep sense of God's preserving care impressed on my heart, and with a strange wonder as to who could be our enemy. At family devotions I rendered thanksgiving to God for protection, and then prayed for those who had sought our hurt, but failed in their malice. After prayer, wife said: "Why, husband, what has happened that you should be so exercised at prayer this morning?" I tried to evade her inquiry, as I was unwilling she should know what peril I had been in, or that she should think I had an enemy so malicious. But all my attempts at concealment only made her the more inquisitive—for some women, even, are inquisitive—and earnest to know the facts. I told her, and showed her the buggy and harness; and we mutually agreed to keep it a secret and let time develop the mystery, as I had all the time an impression that it would.

This occurred the first of March. Things moved on for a month or more, not a word coming to our ears from any source by way of explanation of the affair. As we were going to the same school house one Sabbath morning to fill an appointment, I saw in the distance a young man, sitting on a log by the roadside, and at once recognized him. What can it mean, I thought, that he should be out here Sabbath morning, a mile and a half from home? As I neared the spot, he arose and came directly to the carriage—by using different words to designate what I rode in, I may hit it—and after saying "Good morning," asked if he could ride with me to the meeting. I stopped, and as he got in he looked over the dash board of the ark at the harness, first one side and then the other. The place where the tugs were mended was visible to the naked eye. He then hung his head, as if in a deep study, and with a woebegone countenance. There was perfect silence for a few moments. At length he said: "Mr. Stimson, I have come out to meet you this morning to confess an awful crime of which I am guilty." At this he choked up, and became convulsed beyond utterance. After a moment's pause, he said: "Will you stop here in the woods?" It was a dense forest. By this time he had so far got the control of his emotions as to speak distinctly. He proceeded, "I am one of the men who cut your harness and took out the linch-pins of your buggy. I do not want you to ask me who were with me and are equally guilty as myself. I told them last evening that I was going to confess to you the whole matter, so far as I am concerned. Now, Elder, can you and will you forgive me, and pray God to pardon me for this awful, malicious sin?" He went on to say: "The night we committed the act I did not close my eyes, and all the next day I dreaded to hear from the Lewiston road lest the news should be, Elder Stimson's horse ran away with him and killed or hurt him; and when I understood you were about as common, I went into the stable and wept like a child. The entire six or eight weeks since has been a constant hell of torment to me, day and night. Now, Elder, tell me what I must do to satisfy you, and then what I must do to find peace with God and my almost distracted mind." "Well, my friend, you have nothing to do to satisfy me. As far as I am concerned, it's all cancelled. As to your relations to your Maker and Savior, all I have to say is, in the words of Paul to the jailer, 'Believe on the Lord Jesus Christ, and thou shalt be saved.' Go into the meeting this morning and confess yourself a sinner, and ask Christians to pray for you. Now, will you do it?" To which he replied, in a subdued tone: "I will, God helping me." And we drove on to the meeting. The young man was as good as his word. At the close of the meeting, he got up and confessed his sins and asked Christians to pray for him. His sister, who was a godly woman, shouted out, "Praise God!" While this young man was speaking, the whole church was in tears, and two other young men were noticed to be quite restive in the back part of the room. I at once called on others who felt the need of prayer and salvation to express it by rising and speaking, and seven or eight at once improved the moment; but the two restive young men did not leave their seats. We closed with a solemn season of prayer. and two found peace in believing. But the young man was left in a state almost bordering on despair. The next day he called at my house to pay the damage to buggy and harness, but I declined to receive anything whatever.

This was the opening of a new refreshing for the church. In the course of one or two weeks, two other young men called at my residence, and wished a private interview. We went into an adjoining room, and as soon as seated, one of them commenced by asking me if a Mr—— had in any way implicated them in a certain transaction quite disreputable? I answered, "No." "Did he implicate himself in the matter?" "What matter?" I inquired. "Any matter of injury to yourself or property?" I answered, "Gentlemen, any matter confided to me of a personal nature, not affecting the public interest, I am bound by the laws of Christian honesty to keep; and as a minister of Christ, I am protected by the law of the land from divulging it even in a court of justice. (The only good law for which we are indebted to the Catholics.) So I hope you will not press me to answer any questions in regard to Mr——." "Well, Mr. Stimson, we are involved in all the guilt of that malicious act in exposing your life on that night you came from the —— school-house, and have come here to-night to settle the matter, if we can."

"So far as I am concerned in this affair, I have no price to set, no sum to ask. Have you arranged the matter with your God and King? Your sin against Him is vastly of more importance to you than all my interest. Do you feel that your acts in this case are a great sin against God? and that unrepented of and unforgiven, they will peril your interests in eternity? I hope, young gentlemen, you will consider this matter in its true light, and bestow on it the thought its importance demands."

"We called, Mr. Stimson, to adjust the damages to your property, and we are willing to satisfy you for all the inconvenience and loss you may have sustained. If —— had kept still and not acted the fool by exposing the matter, nothing would have come of it. It will teach us after this to know what company we keep. Will you tell us how much we must pay you for your damages? We are willing, Elder, to give you a good round price to settle it." I said *sternly*, "Why, dear young men, no money consideration could tempt me to expose my life as it was exposed on that night. Sitting in a conveyance behind such a spirited horse as that of mine, if one of the reins or tugs had given way, or a wheel had run off, the human probability is, I should have been severely injured, if not killed outright. I appeal to you, as common-sense men, what is the price?" "Oh, well, we only meant the damage to the carriage and harness. We are willing to pay a good round price for our folly. Now, tell us how much and we will pay it if we can." "I shall take nothing. The mere expense of repairing buggy and harness is trifling. I shall take nothing from you. I would like to see you in the same deep exercise of mind about your sins and lost condition, as your friend was a week ago last Sunday. It would be worth more to me than money counted by hundreds." "Oh, well, Elder, he believes in a judgment day, and in hell, and eternal punishment, and all that kind of thing. We do not. We believe God loves and will be merciful to His erring creatures, and will not be as exacting as men are to their fellow-men. It's getting late, and we have a long way to go, and if you won't take anything for your expenses and trouble, we will be going home." "Be pleased to wait a moment. I will call Mrs. Stimson in, and we will have a season of prayer before we separate." To which they reluctantly consented. After worship they departed, saying at the door, "We hope, Elder, you won't make this matter public." I replied, "It will be public enough at the judgment day, and I fear, to your everlasting regret."

The next Saturday, at our covenant meeting, the first-named of the three young men applied for membership, relating his experience to the church, and the day following, "obeyed from the heart the form of doctrine he had received." On the Sabbath, I preached from these words—Luke xvii. 17 : "And Jesus answering said, Were there not ten cleansed? but where *are* the nine?" The effect upon the congregation was subduing. Many wept aloud and others shouted for joy. It was a good day to the people of God. The two young men were not present, but had gone to hear the Rev. Mr. Hiscox, who preached in another part of the "town," where they heard hell spoken of as an "old heathen fable."

The end of the two young men—they both became confirmed Universalists. One descended to a country tavern-keeper of the lowest grade, and died a drunkard in Michigan. The other became a poor, wandering vagabond, and died a few years since near Battle Creek, in the same State. The first of the trio sustained a good character from the time of his uniting with the Church, respected and loved by all who knew him. He often expressed his joy and wonder at the amazing grace of God in his salvation, and would sing:

> "Why was I made to hear thy voice,
> And enter while there's room?
> When thousands make a wretched choice,
> And rather starve than come.
>
> "'Twas the same love that spread the feast
> That sweetly drew us in;
> Else we had still refused to taste,
> And perished in our sin."

During this summer I had more appointments up in the town of Royalton, then quite destitute of religious privileges, given to Sabbath desecration and trifling amusements. The place of holding meeting was a new log school-house, surrounded with a settlement composed mainly of Mohawk Dutch. They thought they were Christians by birth-right. They had the vaguest idea of what the latter term means. Of course, there is no such thing now; so that for being ignorant of an obsolete idea, we could hardly blame them. But, to think and call themselves Christians, when they were destitute of the first principles of practical Christianity, was hardly as excusable. Still, they had all been sprinkled in infancy—so they learned from their parents or near friends, if they ever took the trouble to inquire—and of course this made them Christians. If such a method of entrance in the Kingdom of Heaven involved any conflict—and the Bible speaks about a conflict—it must be the physical conflict of the infant in resisting the performance of the rite.

After the second or third meeting, I was informed, as I came into the place, that I could not have the school-house any more, as I had offended one of the trustees by what I had said about whisky-drinking, Sabbath-breaking, dancing, etc. I was further told that the said "Christian" trustee had locked the school-house, and had the key in his pocket. But, if I said so, the house should be opened, if they had to have a fight for it. "O, no! O, no!" said I; "we can have meeting as well out-doors as in a log school-house. God is not confined to temples made with hands." So I drove up to the place, and there sat the trustee on the door-sill, with eight or ten of his friends surrounding him as a kind of body-guard, for they evidently expected a conflict of "Yankee snap with Dutch muscle." All about the house were men, women and children in waiting for meeting to open, or the battle to begin, as the case might turn. The old two-hundred-and-twenty-five-pound avoirdupois trustee looked daggers at me, and knit his brow in true Mohawk style. He evidently was carrying a heavy cargo of whisky.

I at once said, "Brethren and friends, make some seats out of rails and billets of wood, and back up your wagons, and we will extemporize a meeting-house." And I struck up singing:

> "Religion is a glorious treasure;
> It fills our hearts with joy and love."

Soon all were in a comfortable situation to hear the Gospel of Jesus.

I announced as my subject, "Love;" text, Romans xiii. 10: "Love worketh no ill to his neighbor; therefore, love *is* the fulfilling of the law." I arranged it thus: 1. What is "Love?" 2. Who is in possession of it? 3. Its effects. As I proceeded, the audience increased till there was no more sitting room—rails and wagons all full. I stood in my carryall for a pulpit. When the noise of carriages and wagons coming up interrupted, I would sing a moment, and then go on again.

At length my big Dutch trustee friend arose from the door-sill and cried out: "Holdt on, Domina. I'll unshet de schule-house, un de vimmin and little schildren may go in, and de mans and pigger poys may stay as dey am." I said, "Thank you, Mr. B. I knew you were a good neighbor, if we could only get it out of you, and here it comes." So we sang:

> "From whence does this union arise,
> That hatred is conquered by love!"

In closing up my sermon I did not fail to "improve" the circumstance in hand, making a strong point of my stout Dutchman. This was the last of any trouble in that place as long as we held meetings there.

CHAPTER X.

LEAVING ALABAMA—PARMA.

THE Church in Parma extended me a call to become their pastor, in the fall of 1835. The first thought of such a move did not impress me favorably. It was here in Alabama I commenced my ministry, and was ordained to the sacred work of preaching Christ. I had enjoyed the confidence of a noble young church. Many of its members I had baptized and introduced into the body. I then thought there was not another such church on the face of the earth.

On the other hand, the church in Parma was smaller and more compact. As a consequence, they would not require as much pastoral work and out-station preaching, giving me more time for study; which I much needed and could not easily get in Alabama, with a field twelve miles square and six out-stations. Parma had a good meeting-house, and was considered a strong church. They would give me a better support. I accepted the invitation, and moved into the field in December.

But it took only a few weeks to prove to me that I had not found the paradise I had anticipated. I hope I shall not be misunderstood, or seem to complain. By no means. There were excellent men and women, not a few whose memory is blessed. Refreshing is it to call them up as they appeared to us then, and if it were not that it might appear invidious, we would give their names. A number of things made the contrast between the two churches plainly visible, especially to a pastor: first, the church at Parma was slow to move out of the deep-worn ruts of bad habits—one was to have but one meeting on the Sabbath. A previous pastor had produced this custom, by preaching one *good*, *long*, *doctrinal*, *sound*, *orthodox*, *Calvinistic*, *Baptistic* sermon. The adjective "long" meant, when practically translated, two hours. Two hours of monotonous voice are equal to a dose of opium.

My first effort was to break in upon this custom, by having a second service in the school-house in a central place. This would be Sabbath evening. But as soon as I suggested it, I met opposition. The main reason was, "We once tried it, and a class of roughs came in, and so disturbed the meeting that we had to give it up." "Well, will you come and sustain the pastor by your presence and prayers? I think I can manage any rude and disorderly persons." They finally consented that I should make the appointment. I did so, and the next Sabbath had the meeting at the L—— school-house.

Just as I had announced my subject, the door opened, and in came about a dozen men and large boys, with fantastic dress and most indescribable faces and general appearance, for a civilized community. Every seat being taken, they stood up around the stove. Of course a general snicker, and then a burst of laughter, arose through all the house. I stopped and stood silent and still for a minute or more, looking at these sons of the lost tribe of the devil, for I could think of nothing else but some infernal prison-house, and these as the product of its general jail delivery. Some of the men were dressed in women's clothing; others had broad shirts over their outer garments. Others still had small baskets on their heads instead of caps. Some had leather and some rude tin spectacles. One had a kitten for a handkerchief. He would take it from his pocket and wipe his nose on it; then pass it to the next. One had a large sheepskin with the wool on, through which he had a hole cut in the middle. Thrusting his head through the hole, it came over the upper part of his person like a shirt.

I said to some small boys in front, "Will you please to give these friends your seats?" They at once complied and the group started forward and occupied them. When quiet was restored, I attempted to proceed with my discourse, but had gone on only a very short time when one took the basket from his head, put a few biscuits into it from his pocket, then taking out a bottle, began passing it around to his crew. I stopped and looked at them with a steady gaze for a moment, and then addressed the audience as follows: "Well, friends, I have seen something of the world in its worst forms, and humanity in its most forlorn and depraved condition. I have been among stage drivers and sailors, among lumbermen and raftsmen; I have been among Indians and plantation negroes, among drunkards and desperadoes. But what I have seen to-night caps the climax. Here in Parma can be seen babboons and monkeys, jackalls and ourang-outangs, and all walk upright, just as the individuals of the human species walk, and come to a Christian meeting to show that they are not far removed from some idea of human intelligence. It may be they have come here to-night for the noble purpose of seeking an interest in the salvation of sinners. If so, let us pray that God will enlighten them."

By this time deep silence pervaded the congregation. All was as still as a grave-yard. Each rowdy looked at his fellow rowdy with blank astonishment, when the leader got up and began saying, "I am ashamed of myself and of my conduct, and now, boys, let's behave like human beings, and I promise this community and this minister that I will never do the like again. And if you will not believe it and take my word for it, I will give good security for my behavior hereafter." This man J. H. was outwardly a moral fellow, and his wife was a member of the church; yet he had let himself down to the idea that it was smart to act like a fool. And the boys thought it a privilege to act the fool under such a leader. But this was the last disturbance at the L. school house.

During this winter and spring I enjoyed a precious revival, and was assisted for a number of days by that able preacher, the Rev. Ichabod Clark, D. D., of sweet memory, and Rev. Zenas Case, of Ogden, whose praise was in all the churches as a man of God.

In the spring, I organized our Sunday School under a new management, and made a change also in the order of our worship, having two sermons at the meeting-house instead of one. But the old settled habit of the church was a wet blanket on the enterprise. They would have opposed a second service of any kind, a prayer and praise meeting much more than a preaching service. As soon as the sermon was well under way, the next thing in order was sleep. This was bad habit number two. As soon as the morning service was over, there was a general start for home, parents taking the children. So the Sabbath School service was small comparatively, and the afternoon was sparsely attended, plenty of empty slips at a discount.

But I prayed for patience to endure all things for the elect's sake. And we had many sympathizing friends in the church who stayed up our hands in the day of battle. Among the number was the widow of the late pastor, Rev. Stephen H. Weaver.

Here let it be remarked, that if a church is so fortunate as to have such a widow of a pastor as a member, every effort ought to be made to render her stay in the church and her widowhood as protracted as possible. For, of all helpers to a pastor, *if he is married*, the widow of a former pastor *may be* the most helpful. There is a difference in widows; I wish to have it understood. A widow of a pastor, she being a widow indeed, and moreover, an unselfish Christian, is a bright jewel in any church. Such know more than any one else about the real character of the different members, and they get at the very gist of the difficulties in the way of the cause. They have gone through the whole round of the life of the church, and are now living in an exalted sort of existence, where their vision is unclouded with personal feeling. Such widows of former pastors are a sort of presiding angel band to the churches. Very occasionally there is a slight deviation from this angelic rule. Once in a great while there is a great deviation.

But Mrs. Weaver was one of the desirable kind. She said: "Brother Stimson, don't let these things trouble you so. It will injure your health and unfit you for labor in the future. I think it affected Mr. Weaver so, and was one of the causes of his early death." This was a sort of "bitter sweet" consolation to my restive spirit, and I tried to make the application as best I could. That word was a godsend to me.

As I remarked, the unholy custom of sleeping in church had been brought on imperceptibly, by long, monotonous sermons of a previous age, and had been imbibed by the younger people by force of example. One sinner destroyeth much good, was illustrated in this case. I resolved on a reform by mild means, such as short sermons, brief reading, singing two to four stanzas—some of the hymns had twenty—short prayers, and then a sudden start right off with the discourse—no apologies. Apologies are bad, especially in the pulpit. But all this strategy failed, and I was irritated like a hornet in a spider's web: plenty of fluttering and buzzing and trying to sting, but nothing accomplished. "Caught," I thought, "and how to get away is the question."

At length we hit upon a new expedient. The chorister of the church, a brother S., was a grand singer; his two daughters sang like nightingales, and his son was capital on the bass viol. I called on him one Saturday, and made this request: that the next day at the morning service, he and his daughters should arise at any time during the sermon that I should think best, and sing the hymn:

"Awake, my soul, in joyful lays,"

There must be no pitching of the key, no bass viol, but a prompt start, right off, like a steamboat. He consented, and I retired to the study, to arrange for the new tack on the sleepers. I arranged two sermons. One from Isaiah lii. 1, "Awake, awake, put on thy strength, O Zion." The second was from Matt. xxvi. 45, "Sleep on now, and take your rest." So after the preliminary exercises of the morning, I started out on the former text, "Awake, awake," etc., quite moderately, in a measured tone, making a statement of the importance of the church being awake, in an active state of spiritual enjoyment, etc. I had proceeded only about ten minutes, when in all parts of the house, in the galleries and below, could be seen heads thrown back and eyes closed, others nodding, and still others with heads too devoutly bowed on the railing in front of them. I stopped *short*: "Will brother S. sing two or three verses of a hymn while we look up another text, as we see the one we have is not appropriate this morning?" And off the singing went: "Awake, my soul," in a good, lively manner.

The whole congregation was like a miniature resurrection; men snatching up their hats, women adjusting their shawls, others rubbing their eyes as if to discover the situation, and some taking out their watches to see what time it was. And still the singing went on to the fourth stanza:

> "Soon shall I pass the gloomy vale,
> Soon all my mortal powers shall fail."

When the singing ceased, I called their attention to the other text: "Sleep on now, and take your rest." The most of them had thought meeting was out, and were very reluctant about sitting down again, and still were unwilling to leave without the benediction; and so, quietly and deliberately took their seats, while I explained the reason for the second subject, and announced the following order:

1. Why this liberty? 2. The bad influence of sleepy Christians. 3. The application of the subject to our present condition.

I have always felt somewhat gratified with the reflection that at least one discourse of mine in Parma was listened to without a sleepy Christian in the house. Twenty years after, I went back to assist their pastor in a meeting, and many referred to that sermon as the cause of their resolving never to sleep again in the house of worship

It is now a sweet reflection, after nearly forty years

are passed, that many of them have "fallen asleep in Jesus," waiting for that delightful morning of the resurrection of the just, which God will hasten in His time. Then, blessed thought, there will be no more slumbering.

The following tenth day of November, I buried the wife of my youth.

OBITUARY.

DIED at Parma, New York, on the tenth day of November, eighteen hundred and thirty-six, Mrs. Almedia Stimson, wife of Rev. H. K. Stimson, aged twenty-eight years.

Mrs. Stimson first embraced religion and united with the Baptist church at East Mendon, Morris Co., N. Y., in the fall of eighteen hundred and thirty. During her short and unostentatious career, she honored her Christian profession by a consistent walk, a cheerful consecration of herself to the service of the saints and a ready co-operation in the various measures connected with the advancement of the Kingdom of Christ.

During a protracted illness she bore her sufferings with Christian meekness and patience, and the latter part of her time, with confidence of hope, often observing that death would be a welcome messenger. When the period of her dissolution approached, and her exhausted frame sunk under the chilling dews of death, she requested her husband to bid her friends farewell for her, and as if longing to depart, exclaimed: "Come, Lord Jesus; come quickly!" and with these words fell asleep.

Thus another servant is dismissed from the field of toil, and gone to rest. A husband with four small children survives to mourn his early loss. May he have the sympathies of his brethren, and what is infinitely more, the favor of Him whose grace can irradiate the darkest scenes, and make us joyful even in tribulation.

WILLARD JUDD.

The same month, I received a call to become pastor of the church in Bethany, Genesee County, New York. The Baptist church in Bethany was then one of the strong churches in the Genesee Association, with one of the best church edifices in Western New York. Its membership was composed of the best and the most respected portion of the community. Its congregation was large, and made up mostly of the young people of the town, with a complete choir of singers led by James Prescott, for years a man of blessed memory.

After an acquaintance of a few weeks, I accepted their call, and at once felt at home among them. There was but one drawback to produce discontentment. My family was broken up, my dear children were scattered in three different families, all in Parma. I was fortunate in getting them good places, where I was confident they would receive all the care dear friends could render. Still they were motherless and homeless, and absent from father; and I felt my separation from them. Still, everything was done by the congregation to make my situation pleasant and my ministry effective, as results will show.

There were evidences at once of a Divine work

all over the town. The three congregations of the place joined in a series of meetings, commencing with the Baptist church, and holding there twenty-eight days; and then at the Presbyterian as long. All winter there was a continued refreshing of the Spirit, in which large numbers of the youth, and many of the aged, were hopefully led to embrace Jesus as their Prophet, Priest and King. Just a little unpleasantness was felt because so many of the converts joined the Baptist church. Out of one hundred, about eighty were baptized in the likeness of Christ's death and resurrection, and joined our church.

For all this I was not to blame. I never proselyted. Only I could not turn those away who voluntarily offered themselves. This was a prosperous year to the church, in more than one sense. It was a year of numerical growth among the members, and it paved the way for subsequent advancement upon the powers of darkness, and made the people ready in every way for greater things to come.

Late in the fall, I began to be depressed in spirit about the condition of sinners who were without hope and out of Christ. So deep and constant was the distress, that I could not sleep or enjoy my daily food. And, what added to the acuteness of this state of mind, was the fact that the church did not seem to realize its responsibility. After receiving the tokens of God's matchless goodness during the year now passed, there was a singular lack of deep anxiety for sinners. There were no divisions among us; no heart-burnings between brethren; congregations large and attentive to the Word and Ordinances of God; still, sinners, unmoved by the truth, perished.

Thus things went on until the last of November or first of December, when my depression in spirit became almost intolerable, and it was with great effort that I could get my consent to preach; and when I did, it seemed like speaking against a strong wind, only to be blown back upon me. I thought the time had come to close my connection with the church at Bethany, if not to close my ministry altogether. While in this state of mind, I had an appointment at an out-station called "White's school-house" for Sabbath evening. The night was dark, and a drizzling rain set in just as I started from home. This, added to my already darkened and dampened spirits, made everything appear beyond endurance, and I was wholly unhappy and unfit to preach.

As I had gone along, I concluded that, as it was rainy and dark, there would be few or none at meeting, and I should be relieved of the duty of trying to address the people. But as I got within hearing distance, the voice of singing greeted my ears, and as I neared the house, I saw that it was jammed full. I exclaimed, in the bitterness of my soul, "My God, my God, why hast thou forsaken me?" As quick as thought, "There, that is a good text to preach from; try it, try it to-night." I thought to myself, "Where is it? No matter where it is, try it. They are the dying words of Jesus on the cross." I hitched my horse and went in, to find the large congregation composed mostly of youth. I called on Brother Russell Morley, who was a man of power with God, to pray. But I got no light or relief, only a constant ringing in my ears, "My God, my God, why hast thou forsaken me?"

I asked them to sing the hymn beginning:

"'Tis a point I long to know,
Oft it causes anxious thought;
Do I love the Lord, or no?
Am I his, or am I not?

(There *may* be special occasions when the singing of these lines is of some benefit to some one.) They sang it through, many with subdued voices. I could not sing at all. All was dark as midnight with me. An awful dread weighed upon me as the time drew near. As I arose and repeated the words of the dying Son of God, I made these impromptu divisions: 1st. Why God forsook His beloved Son. 2d. Why He will forsake impenitent sinners. And on I went in the dark. Oh, that darkness I shall never forget! Perhaps I talked thirty minutes or more, and closed the meeting as though it had been a funeral, and went home, all but determined not to preach any more.

The next Thursday was the dedication of the Presbyterian meeting-house, in which services I was invited to take a part. If I could have declined I would; but could not without giving offense. So I went as the ox is led to the slaughter, and remained in great distress of mind. As the meeting closed, I hastened out to go to my home, but while on the steps of the house, a young lady touched my elbow in the crowd, and as I turned about to see just who it was, I discovered a Miss Evaline T., who said: "I would like to talk with you a few minutes, Elder, if it would be convenient." I replied, "Certainly." She then went on to say: "Your sermon last Sunday night has brought me to see myself as a lost sinner, and this morning I found peace in believing in Jesus; and I wished to see and tell you and everybody that God, for Christ's sake, has forgiven my sins." I at once felt light breaking in upon my mind like a sunburst in a dark day. I said, "Well, Miss T., I rejoice with you; come, go to my house, and tell Mrs. Stimson of it. She will be glad to hear of your joy and conversion to Jesus." As we came into the parlor, I said: "Wife, here is Miss T., who has good tidings of great joy to tell you;" and she went on and repeated the simple story of her conviction and conversion. "Now," I said, "I have one request to make of you. Next Lord's day, at the close of my discourse in the morning, I want you to tell the congregation what Christ the Lord has done for you." She replied, "O, I shall be most happy to do so."

I well knew the effect it would have, for she was a proud and giddy girl. All her family were of a like stripe. Her father prided himself on their pleasure-seeking habits. The father and daughters, being good singers, generally sat in the gallery. Sabbath came, and a large congregation filled the house. As I entered, I thought it was like Israel's Bethel, "None other than the house of God and gate of Heaven." "*God is here.*" The text was Isaiah li. 3: "And he will make her wilderness like Eden, and her desert like the garden of the Lord; joy and gladness shall be found therein, thanksgiving and the voice of melody."

I felt like another man, and all the church seemed transformed into a better state of religious life. As soon as I closed my talk, Miss T. rose up in her place in the gallery, and poured out a full soul of joy, and then of invitation to her young associates in sin to come to Jesus and be saved. It was like a shock of electricity on saints and sinners. In a few days I baptized the father, mother, Evaline, Emily, Roscoe, Clarence and Dell.

Now, our work had assumed such proportions that I felt the need of aid. So I resolved to get an early start for LeRoy, nine miles off, and get Brother Ichabod Clark to come over and help us. I arrived before any of the family was up. As he opened the door, he exclaimed: "Why, Brother Stimson, what brought you here so early in the morning?"

"The Lord," I replied. "Well, then, I am glad to have you come. Take a seat, and I will stir up a fire." "I have come after you, Brother Clark, and you must go with me to Bethany, 'for the Lord hath need of thee.'" I went on to tell him what the Master was doing among us, and he replied, "We will see after breakfast."

So, after the meal and devotions, we went to his study. He began by saying: "Now, Brother H. K., I could go to Bethany if it was duty to do so. But God has manifested himself to your people by his Spirit in a most wonderful way, and you and your church, under His guiding hand and Spirit's influence, are all the help you need. Now, go home and hold on to Jesus by prayer, and do not go after any minister or man. I will pray for you, but can't go." Anybody that ever knew Ichabod Clark can imagine with what decision he said this.

I thought it a "bitter pill," and went home to my work with less confidence in self or any man, but with stronger confidence in God and the Spirit's power to carry on the revival.

During the progress of the gracious work, there was not a little agitation in some quarters on the subject of baptism. A Dr. J. K. B. was quite zealous in opposing the ordinance as we administer it, and, as they admit, is Scriptural. Whenever a chance occurred, he would improve it. He had been a "head-center" in one of the churches in town for a number of years, and was chagrined to see the Baptists prospering, while his own denomination had run down to such an extent that the meeting-house was sold for a school-house. He was one day called on to attend a family professionally, for he was an M. D. There were a number of ladies from the neighborhood present, but none of them Baptists, except one old lady from New England, a Mrs. P. She was seated quietly in the corner. Some of the women asked the Doctor how the revival was progressing in the "Center." He replied, "Oh, they are going on as watery as ever. I expect we shall have a great time of sickness this spring, as that pale-faced Stimson is dipping them every Sunday in the creek, cutting the ice and wading through the deep snow, enough to kill an Indian. Half of them will have the consumption in less than a year. As for Stimson, he won't live till April, the way he is going on. I wish there was some law to stop this foolish waste of human life."

Mother P., who had heard it all, conceived that he had spoken disrespectfully of her pastor, and interrupted him in his tirade by saying: "Doctor, I don't like to hear you talk so about our dear minister. We all think he is a good man, and the Lord is manifestly blessing his labors here in Bethany and all around us." The Doctor interrupted her with: "Oh, Mrs. P., I did not think you were a Baptist when I spoke. Beg your pardon, madam. I have not a word to say against Elder Stimson. He is a good neighbor, and as social, friendly a man as we have at the 'Center.' I was only saying, Mother P., that I thought it imprudent for him to be going into the water this cold weather in the winter, exposing himself and others." She replied: "Well, Doctor, we Baptists believe this to be the right way, as Jesus went into the water and the eunuch went into the water to be 'baptized;' and then young converts are always so happy when they come up out of the water. I know I was when I was 'baptized,' and it was a cold day too, and it never hurt me a bit." "Oh, nonsense," says the Doctor; "I was happy when I was baptized, and I was not immersed, either."

"Well, doctor, *du* tell me your experience about

that, for in Connecticut I have seen a great many sprinkled, grown-up people and babies too, and I never heard any express a bit of joy—no more than they would at a funeral. Come, now, *du* jest tell us all about it." "Well, mother P., it was on this wise: My parents had neglected to have me baptized when a child. I was a young man when I thought I'd better join the church. So we all went down to the little brook, one bright June morning, and *I went down into the water*, mother P., and kneeled down, and the minister dipped up some water in his hand and poured it on my head, saying, 'Jonathan K. B., I baptize you in the name of the Father,' and my heart dilated with joy; and then he dipped his hand in again and poured the water on my head, and said, 'and in the name of the Son,' and I was so happy I thought the very heavens would open; and then the minister dipped his hand the third time in the water, and poured it on my head, and said, 'in the name of the Holy Ghost;' and I was so filled with joy that I felt that I should go up through the clouds." "Why, *du* tell, doctor,"—the old lady was looking him full in the face—"*du* tell, doctor; if you had gone in all over as we Baptists do, what would have become of you?"

All joined in a hearty laugh at the doctor's expense. The old lady's logical conclusion was more than equal to his trumped up wit. As soon as I heard of it, I called on the doctor to know about how much he had made off mother. His reply was: "Not much."

The revival went on in grand majesty, clear into August of that year. The church was edified, and much people was added to the Lord.

The Genesee Baptist Association was then among the largest in Western New York, and had as efficient a class of ministers as could be found in any part of the land. But few of them had what is called a liberal education, but they were men of great common sense, and of deep piety. And those among them that had enjoyed the advantages of a classical and theological training, did not assume that they knew *all;* that their brethren of less advantages knew little or nothing. But there was a mutual disposition to help, among the two classes of the precious brotherhood. The learned always gladly and fraternally instructed and advised the younger and less learned. Criticism was not given in an officious, offensive way, but always with a kindliness that evinced the spirit of love and good will. It was also received in the same spirit of fraternal affection.

So in their labors. If the interests in one part of the Association demanded help from outside, the field brethren would go and stay one, two and four weeks at a time. Thus a familiar and happy state of feeling was kept up. Our associational conferences were great sources of instruction and help to the youthful ministers. As for myself, they were a real theological school in which I received lessons of great usefulness in our practical pastoral work, and in preaching the Gospel to my people.

In many cases they were also sources of spiritual profit to the churches where they were held. The members would come out and fill the house day and night. They were not cold, formal convocations, presided over by the spirit of ministerial etiquette and dead formality. We had no "D. D." among us then as we knew of. And yet we had, if it means *teacher of Divine Truth*. If it ever had any meaning, that's it. We were not slaves of technical, parliamentary rules. We were constrained chiefly by the loyal law of love. The motto of all seemed to be, "Work much; love much."

The decay of the old fashioned Associational

meeting is certainly to be regretted. Whatever may have led to this decay, I do not pretend to say; but of its fact and calamity, there can be no question. Even young men can remember the time when the "Association" meant much more than it does to-day, and they deplore it—at least some of them—as well as we whose steps are nearing our resting place. I am told by some apologists of the change, that this is an age of steam and electricity, and that everything is changed in consequence. That may be the cause; if it is, the fact is just as much to be regretted. For we cannot love each other by steam and electricity. They may be good in their places, but they can never take the place of fraternity. As a substitute for the old methods of conveyance, and intelligence even, they do not work to the increase of our religious gatherings. When the travel was by wagon and horseback, the brethren would come together from a wider circle of country than now, and the place would be filled with the people and with the presence of the Master. It may be we have outgrown the necessity for such religious gatherings. It may be that they belong to a past age, and cannot be revived in their primitive power. If so, I am glad that I, too, belong to a former generation. All these inventions having in view quicker transit and more general intelligence, are good and to be sought for, *provided they are used for God and His Truth*. But if they are not used by us for this noble end, their materialistic influence will creep into our spirits and deaden them to higher spiritual things. "The earth" must be made to help "the woman."

Perhaps I should give a list of these ministers then in the Genesee Association. Many of them have passed away. I will mark such with a *:

Joseph Elliott,* of Wyoming; Ichabod Clark,* of LeRoy; W. W. Smith, of Batavia; William Arthur, of Perry; Abraham Annis,* of Warsaw; Jesse Elliott, of LaGrange; James Read,* of Castile; O. D. Taylor, of Attica; Leonard Anson,* of Pine Hill; Martain Coleman,* of Byron; Elon Galusha,* of Perry; B. N. Leach,* of Middlebury; Harrison Daniels, of LeRoy; H. B. Ewell, of Pavillion; R. C. Palmer, of Wyoming; Bela Wilcox,* of Darien; I. H. Roscoe, of Pembrok; David Taylor, of York; C. M. Fuller,* of Pike; John Trowbridge, of Wethersfield Springs; S. M. Stimson, of Batavia; Augustus Warren, of Alabama; W. I. Crane, of Middlebury; Emery Curtis, of

Morganville; S. A. Esty,* of Batavia, and James Mallory.

There may be others whom I have failed to recollect. Here are twenty-six, and just one-half have gone to the better land. Thirteen, besides myself, remain. The most of them are younger than myself, three or four are older. Those of the above number, who enjoyed a partial or a full course of study, also number thirteen. Only three, I believe, had received a full course at college.

At our ministerial conferences, we had the custom of giving out subjects for essays, exegeses and sketches of sermons, purely for the sake of mutual improvement—a good plan, wherever it is practiced. The young ministers were recommended to write sermons and deliver them to their congregations, and then bring them to the conference for criticism. Among other young men to whom was assigned this part was myself. I begged to be excused, as I was not in the habit of writing sermons. But no excuse was allowed, and it was urged it would improve me in composition and the arrangement of sermons. And, then, I would have three long months in which to prepare. So I reluctantly accepted the situation, and as soon as I got home I set myself about my task.

First, I got me a quantity of sermon paper. *Second*, I had to find a text. I chose Jonah iii. 2: "Arise, go unto Nineveh, that great city, and preach unto it the preaching that I bid thee." *Third*, I commenced writing. I went on awhile, and then tore it up and put it in the fire; began again, and then quit; and after a month's work on it, had got a short introduction that I was not willing even my wife should read, and did not like to look at it myself a great while at a time. Went on again at odd spells, and the second month was nearly out and I had not finished up "*firstly*." I tried to hurry up, and the more I hurried the slower the thing went. I began to be worried. Time was short, and I was a slow writer, that was evident. I now resolved to double my diligence and put the thing through by daylight and lamplight. The Saturday night before the conference, about midnight, I wrote that expressive word, "*Amen*." As the rule was to read it, or preach it, to my own congregation before I presented it to the body for whom it was principally prepared, I hid the *precious thing* in my overcoat and started for the meeting-house. While the choir was singing the first hymn, I removed the document from my coat pocket to the Bible. I got a deacon to pray, for I dare not. The choir sang the hymn:

> "Oh, for a thousand tongues to sing
> My dear Redeemer's praise."

I read my text, and just at that moment a tall brother up in the gallery stretched up his long neck to see what I was about, and I lost my place by turning over two leaves at once. By that time fifty eyes were gazing from each side of the gallery, with a silent wonder, "what is the matter with the minister?" I then re-read the text; but, "no go." I got out of my fix by saying: "If the Lord had called me to preach, He never had intimated in the call that I should read my sermons." On which I laid the precious effusion one side, went about preaching as usual, from the same text, and had a good time. I related the facts to the Association, and the brethren very kindly excused us, and never appointed us to read a sermon again. We make no war on written sermons, but, as they say out West, they are not our "best holt."

CHAPTER XI.

A TRIAL OF OPEN COMMUNION.

IN the town of Bethany was a "Free Will Baptist church," of quite a large membership. This same great revival had extended into their families extensively. Their children had a strong preference for our services. Already a few adults had joined with us recently from the F. W. church, as our chorister and his family, and one of our deacons, had joined us from them some years before. But still the objection existed in the minds of many of these youth to that great bug-bear, close communion. For some cause, they had become alienated from the "Free Church," as it was called, and did not want to join there. So here they stood. The subject was discussed in private circulars, and ministers were imported into town who encompassed (if not sea and land) every school district at least, and the "war-whoop" was heard on every hand, "close communion."

I kept about the Master's work, taking no conspicuous part in this side issue, as we were quite confident the Baptist church in Bethany could live with Divine help, if these persons did not unite with us. Still, the door was open—the doors of a true church are always open. No minister has the power to open them. Jesus Christ openeth, and no man shutteth; and shutteh, and no man openeth. And they could come in if they would.

At a covenant meeting with a full attendance, and when many were presenting themselves as candidates for baptism, and all were in a high state of religious enjoyment, a prominent member of the church arose and moved "that the pastor be instructed to invite to the Lord's table, all such Christians as had been immersed on a profession of their faith, and were in good standing in evangelical churches." His motion was at once seconded. All was as still as a dark cellar. The old men and women of the church appeared to be "dumfounded." The brother who made the motion was a man of large influence in the community and in the church, as was the brother who sustained the motion. I suggested, "Brethren, this is an important step. Let us move cautiously in the matter. If any brother or sister has any remarks to make, use your liberty and speak freely. Due deference will be paid to your views and feelings." Not a word was spoken. All silent. "Brethren, what will you do?" "Question," "Question," from a number. "Are you ready for the motion?" "The question is called for." And the vote was carried without a single negative. Eighty voted for it.

The result was, these "Free Will" friends came into the church like a flock of sheep over a stone wall, scared by wolves on the other side. "The after clap": The church was like the boy who drew the elephant: no hay to feed him on—no stable to put him in. Decidedly a big thing on our hands. The next day we baptized thirty-three, and at the communion, followed the instructions given by the church in Bethany (not so strictly those in our commission from the Lord).

Eighty-four came to the Supper from the Presbyterian, Methodist, and Free Will Baptist congregations, and two from the Universalists. They said "they had been dipped; and thought the Universalists were evangelical." (Our elephant began to bellow for food, and not a lock of hay to give him.) The next month at the Lord's Supper, there came thirty-one. At the third, thirteen of the invited guests. At the fourth, five. (Our big animal gave signs of falling into a decline.) At the end of eight months, none of our invited guests cared to take the trouble to commune with us. (He had died a natural death.)

The church soon rescinded the motion by an overwhelming majority, and voted to give letters to all discontents. Five took letters. Three of them went to the "Free Wills," and two to the devil. (The elephant was buried.)

[A few Pedobaptists, like Dr. John Hall of New York, have the magnanimity to accept the statement of the communion question as we Baptists put it. Which is the more bigoted? The "bigotry" to hold conscientiously to a valid principle, if it is unpopular, or the practice of ignoring the issue we make, and raising an issue wholly foreign to the question, that we do not make? If it isn't bigotry or dishonesty to talk as many Pedobaptists talk on this communion question, as related to the Baptist practice, it is great ignorance and stupidity. ("We use great plainness of speech.") In no sense is the communion a test of Christianity. To say that by our practice we "unchristianize" other denominations, is most absurd. It is too puerile to deserve refutation, especially as it has been refuted from time immemorial. But Pedobaptists, we are inclined to believe, feel the real point of our protest against their practice much oftener than they are ready to admit. The issue is the baptismal question, and they must know it, if they stop to think a moment. They are not *confident* generally, in their practice of sprinkling and pouring for baptism. Our protest against this disturbs them. If we admitted their practice as Scriptural on the question of baptism, they wouldn't care enough about our communion to say a word on the subject.—ED.]

Dr. Hall says in his recent book, entitled, *Questions of the Day:*"

'Close communion,' that is, the restriction of the Lord's table to those who have been baptized in the way held by the denomination, is being assailed by many in the interests of catholicity. Whether the assailants act wisely or kindly in that matter, or not, is an open question. It is a course of doubtful catholicity to raise a popular cry against a most valuable body of people, who honestly defend and consistently go through with, what they deem an important principle; and more particularly when they have some little internal embarrassment on the subject. Our love for the brethren should include, surely, the Baptist brethren.

'Charity suffereth long and is kind.' And it is doubtful if, considering the lengths to which liberal ideas have been carried in the country, there be not some gain to the community as a whole from a large denomination making a stand at a particular point, and reminding their brethren that there are church matters which we are not bound, are not even at liberty to settle according to the popular demand, as we should settle the route of a railroad.

Equally candid and unusual are the remarks of the *Interior*, of Chicago, one of the ablest Presbyterian papers of the country:

We ask at the hands of our sister denominations the liberty to execute our own laws, to know our own theology, and to manage our affairs, without being made the subjects of ungenerous criticism. And this which we ask for ourselves, we very freely accord to others. The difference between our Baptist brethren and ourselves is an important difference. We agree with them, however, in saying that unbaptized persons should not partake of the Lord's Supper. Their views compel them to believe that we are not baptized, and shut them up to close communion. Close communion, in our judgment, is a more defensible position than open communion, which is justified on the ground that baptism is not pre-requisite to the partaking of the Lord's Supper.

To chide Baptists with bigotry because they abide by the logical consequences of their system is absurd. We think that they are wrong in reference to the mode and subjects of baptism, and should not hesitate to take ground against their interpretation, but we would not be silent about the interpretation, and then charge them with bigotry for a consistent adherence to their interpretation.

CHAPTER XII.

AN OLD SORE—SECOND WIDOWHOOD.

ON opposite sides of a narrow street in Bethany, lived two neighbors, who were also brethren in the Baptist church. They were also wealthy, one of them the richest man in the church. They had never lived in peace with each other. Their chief quarrel, which became chronic, was about "line fences," and where the water should flow, that the Lord sent in showers on their large landed estates. And then, on all the matters of common dealing, and they are numerous in a rural neighborhood as was ours, there was no real agreement. But the influence of the almost continued revival for four years, had kept the thing in check, so that no serious eruption was visible until 1839–40, when the thing assumed such an aggravated form that "catnip tea" or "poppy-blow leaves made into a poultice," would not cure or even ease the pain. (Both the patients suffered terribly. So did the patience of those who had anything to do with them.) The whole community was cognizant of the unhappy state of affairs in the Baptist church: so much so that it was talked of in all circles. Men of the world would throw it in our teeth on the street and in public places. The church had made a number of efforts to conciliate them, and in some way settle their difficulty permanently. But all in vain.

A medical council was held. Dr. Discipline and Dr. Chairman of the Committee reported the case incurable, and the moral constitution so impaired that amputation had become necessary, to arrest the spread of gangrene through the whole body. Mr. Outside said, if we did cut off these excrescences, we should be prosecuted for malpractice. Mr. World said, we cannot take them into our infirmary without bonds well-secured for good behavior. That of course we could not give, knowing the cases in hand.

Thus the thing stood for months, and we were afraid the disease would become a contagion; and so we proposed to leave the situation to other parties, if something was not done speedily, to save the body by prompt surgical operation. So a day was appointed, and the doctors and the nurses, with their bandages and lint and bottles of lotions and all-healing ointments, came together. The patients came, and the operating table was brought out. As *Man-order-of-the-day*, I tried to magnify my office and not give offense to either the body in health or the affected members. The doctors had decided to operate on one at a time, meantime giving the other an opium pill. After cutting awhile and bandaging—the *dullness of the instruments* having much to do with his flouncing—the amputation was safely effected; and the night coming on, the other case was postponed indefinitely.

A singular sort of delirium set in, during which the patient made me the sole object of his spleen, turning away altogether from the one with whom he had had such frequent and unholy conflicts. The church had peace as a consequence of this necessary action; but I had none. Wealth and family relations did all that could be done to make my situation uncomfortable, and to hinder my usefulness.

Here it might be remarked, that the devil is more devilish in a Baptist church than anywhere else. The freedom given the individual in this Church fosters both the growth of the graces in true Christians, and develops the satanic traits in the human devils who creep into the fold. The most execrable specimens, most filled with unadulterated, cunning devilishness, of the *genus Christian* that we ever met with or heard of in an evangelical church, we have "seen and handled" in a Baptist church.

The only principle on which you can account for the continued presence of such satanic hirelings in an otherwise good and peaceful and devoted church, even against repeated protests, sometimes formally made, is this from Holy Writ, that "whom the Lord loveth He chasteneth."

[No Roman Inquisition is equal in diabolical ingenuity of torture to these "sons of Belial" in some of their practices, especially invented for the destruction of the peace and usefulness of pastor and church. Get rid of such characters, if they own half the kingdom; and when out once, keep them out.—Ed.]

It is said that trouble never comes single-handed. Just at this juncture, when this man was trying me with all the arts of wicked cunning, my dear wife sickened and died of consumption, leaving me the second time in sad widowhood. We had been married less than three years. My children were yet small, and, in addition to the four left by my first wife, my second wife left a daughter eleven months old.

In 1837, I was married to Miss Loretta M., daughter of Dr. Isaac Olney.* She was at this time a teacher in a select school at Sodus, Wayne county, New York.

The following obituary was written on her death:

DIED—On the 22d day of May, 1840, at Bethany, Genesee county, New York, Sister LORETTA M. STIMSON, wife of Elder H. K. Stimson, in the 28th year of her age.

In her death, Zion has lost one of her warmest friends, her husband an affectionate wife, and her children a careful and tender mother. In her case, there was a most striking exemplification of the power and efficacy of Divine grace, in causing the soul to triumph in the prospect and pangs of death. It may truly be said of her, that in health she was amiable and devout, in sickness patient and submissive, and in death peaceful and triumphant. The funeral was attended by a numerous concourse of people, all of whom seemed to feel that in the departure of the deceased they had sustained a great loss.

The occasion was improved by Elder I. Clark, D. D., of LeRoy, in an appropriate and impressive discourse from Phil. i. 21: "For to me to live is Christ, but to die is gain."

This is the second time that Brother Stimson has been thus bereaved, and he is now left with five small children and other dear relatives to mourn the loss.

While thus sorely and repeatedly afflicted, we would bespeak the prayers and sympathy of the Christian community in his behalf.

---

* Dr. Olney was a graduate of the medical college at Fairfield, New York. In the war of 1812 he was a surgeon in the United States army, under the command of Gen. Brown, and stationed at Sackett's Harbor. Soon after the close of the war, he moved to Parma, New York, and commenced the practice of his profession, which he followed until his death, which occurred in 1832, leaving his family of six children, five daughters and one son, to the care of his widow. Dr. Olney was a Christian gentleman and highly respected by all who knew him, and esteemed as a physician and surgeon of great skill. All his children became teachers.

Ah! dear LORETTA, whither art thou gone?
  And what thy state, and who thy partner now?
Ah! tell me, dost thou dwell alone?
  Or with the heavenly myriads bow?

My dearest husband, Heaven's now my resting place;
  Joy is my state and Christ my partner here;
He takes me in His near embrace,
  And makes me His peculiar care.

O. D. TAYLOR.

The following lines were composed by Mrs. LORETTA STIMSON, May 13th, 1840:

How glorious is our God,
  Who sent His Son to die,
That we, His creatures, full of sin,
  Might reign above the sky.

He sends His love to me,
  In times of sorest need
He will His good bestow on thee,
  If it of Him thou plead.

In the autumn of 1840, by the advice of the ministers and others of our Association, I devoted the winter to labor among the churches in holding meetings with the pastors, and supplying destitute churches for a longer or shorter time. There were great revivals at Batavia, Attica and West Middlebury.

CHAPTER XIII.

EVANGELIZING.—PASTORATE AT WARSAW.

HAVING resigned my pastorate at Bethany, I accepted a call from the church at Warsaw, Wyoming County, New York, and in April, 1841, began my pastoral work under the most forbidding circumstances I had ever experienced in eleven years as a pastor. They had been a large and efficient body, but divisions and bad management had reduced them in numbers and spirituality. The singular, unpardonable whim of having their house of worship a full half mile from where it ought to be, for the mere sake of having it on a hill, also operated most injuriously, as might be known on general principles. What with distance and bad sidewalks, the congregations were of course small. Talmage or Spurgeon couldn't have made them very large. The house, after you had reached it, was as uninviting as the walk was unwelcome, even in hot or cold weather. Though it had been built fourteen or fifteen years, the interior of it had never been painted. When will the children of light be as wise in their generation as the children of this world?

The church had enjoyed the ministrations of some of the best talent in the denomination: Peter Freeman*, Walling, Joseph Elliott, Daniel Barnard*, B. Wilcox, and Abraham Annis, all good men and true. Two or three of my predecessors had made efforts to move the meeting-house into the village. But they always ended in bad feelings, and were the cause of separation between pastors and people; the south portion of the church contending for the old situation "on the hill where it could be seen."

With this state of things existing, I entered the field. It had but one redeeming feature, so far as external appearances were concerned, viz: the town had become the county seat of the new county of Wyoming. In my engagement with the church, I suggested a new house of worship, or one *in* the village. "I am not going to talk about it, but when the time comes, I want you all to lift until you can see stars, and no flinching."

Things soon changed "on the hill," and in the village. We had secured a good choir. In the village we had organized a first-class Sabbath school, and secured a good room in which to hold it and evening prayer meetings. And things went on that summer with a good degree of zeal and harmony. The next winter we had a pleasant revival, in which the church was strengthened in spirit, and an addition of twenty-eight new converts made to the membership; and all with the disadvantage of "the old house on the hill where it could be seen."

In the course of this year we had learned that one man stood in the way of moving the house, he claiming a moneyed interest in it to the amount of five hundred dollars. In a pleasant conversation I had with him, I got his consent to a removal of the house, but when the time came for him to sign the contract for the removal, he declined, saying that: "there was no need of a Baptist church in town." He had once been a member, but was excluded for immoral conduct. In the majority of cases, it is a safe rule to have but little to do with excluded members of Baptist churches. They are not to be trusted. They are fit for "stratagems and spoils."

A subscription was started the very hour he declined, nine o'clock A. M., and at ten o'clock P. M. we had on it two thousand eight hundred and twenty-five dollars for a new church edifice in the village, and in less than one year the house was dedicated; the best then in the town. And the crowning glory of all was, the church was permitted to enter it in a full blaze of revival work. On the first Lord's day after we entered our new house, six were baptized; the next, fifteen, and so on for eleven Sabbaths in succession.

But no sooner than it became quite certain that the Baptists were going to have a house in the village, than a different manner was evinced towards the church and pastor. We were all right when up on the hill, but now things were changed. The sweet treatment of the pastor by the other ministers had changed to "cold shoulder," and that without "bread or mustard." Our sentiments were not orthodox, as we did not believe in the good old New England practice of infant church membership, and sprinkling for baptism. *That was a change.* When we were up "on the hill" where we could be "seen" we exchanged pulpits with those in the village, but now it was not desirable to exchange with us. The Baptists had but a small congregation when they were worshiping on the lofty "hill." Now they had a large congregation, and as large a Sabbath school as any in the place, and composed of a class of people as "good as the best of mankind." *All that was a change.*

Then there were many who had met with a change of heart, and not a few had changed their views in regard to baptism and had been immersed, in obedience to the command of Jesus. This last change was the provocation of a wordy war. The pulpits in town were like so many batteries turned upon the Baptist church, for changing their location and coming into the village. As though they had a religious pre-emption right to the territory of the town! "Up on the hill where they could be seen" they were permitted to enjoy uninterrupted peace. Some of our brethren thought we ought to respond to these broadside attacks of the big guns, lest it should be implied that we were a little cowardly. But we replied, "No, by no means; God has more important work for us, and we ought to be contented as long as souls are being converted to Christ every day, and every Lord's day we are going to the stream to baptize. God is blessing us in a wonderful manner, and we will not be guilty of stopping the work by engaging in controversy. If it shall ever seem necessary to expose their false and unscriptural attacks, and I am not equal to the emergency, the church will be at liberty to dismiss me, and get a man who is equal to the task."

This quieted the disposition to reply to the attacks made upon us, and the work continued under the reigning power of the Spirit until about June. But the war against baptism did not abate, for a lawyer* in the place, a man of influence, who had been educated for the Episcopal ministry, had the independence to ignore his infant sprinkling and former connection with that church, and had requested baptism as a believer in Christ and salvation by faith. The church had received him as a candidate for baptism, and had requested him to give his reasons for this change in his views. He consented, and the next Sunday was appointed for his doctrinal experience, and baptism. In the morning, he occupied the pulpit an hour and a half with a clear and searching history of sprinkling as a substitute for the ordinance of immersion, and his reasons for change of belief and church membership. It was a complete vindication of the Baptist practice.

Soon after this, I was informed that one of the ministers of the place had an appointment on a

* Hon. J. R. Doolittle, now President of Chicago University.

week day to preach at East Orangeville on the subject of baptism; and a convert invited me to attend and listen to an *expose* of the Baptist fallacy of immersion. He had been induced to join the Methodist class, and had been sprinkled by this Rev. Mr. Judd, with the assurance that it was Scriptural baptism, and he would prove it to him at this Thursday's meeting at East Orangeville. I consented to attend.

It so happened that I went into the house in time of prayer and was unobserved, taking a seat in the back part of the room, and the reverend gentleman being near-sighted, did not discover that I was among his hearers. So he commenced his tirade of misrepresentation of the Baptists, with a plentiful quantity of abuse heaped on Elder H. K. Stimson. He tried to be sarcastic, but his points were too clumsily made and too stale to have any power. I sat quiet and took notes. (I have them yet.) He held the congregation an hour-and-a-half (not spell-bound, but by the "button"). At the close of this "sermon," he called upon a brother H. M. to pray. Now, this brother was a Methodist exhorter and a warm friend of mine. He knew I was present, and made special mention of me in a prayer, saying he "blessed God that Brother Stimson had been sent into that valley, and had been so successful in winning souls to Christ."

All this time, Rev. Mr. Judd was peeking about the house to see where I was. He then called upon the congregation to sing:

"A charge to keep I have."

At the conclusion of the song, I arose from my corner and said to Mr. Judd, "Can I give out an appointment?" To which he replied, "Certainly." I then gave notice that the next Lord's day, at one o'clock P. M., I would discuss the following propositions:

1st. That infant church membership, with sprinkling for the ordinance of baptism, was a tradition of man and without Scripture proof.

2d. That the "Methodist Episcopal Church" was a human institution and without Divine authority.

3d. That believers are the only proper subjects of baptism, and immersion the only valid *act*.

4th. That Mr. Judd had told six lies.

If you have ever seen a hornet's nest disturbed by throwing stones at it, you can have some correct idea of the situation within those four walls. One good large sister approached me, saying: "Well, I think you are a pretty man to come here and charge our minister with lying." To which I calmly replied: "Then, my good sister, you should have a minister that won't lie about his neighbors and brethren." I also invited all to attend and bring their Bibles with them. I returned home and set to work preparing for our next Sunday's meeting.

The excitement all over the country spread like the fire in the Philistines' corn, with Samson's foxes on the full run. I had made such preparation as the short time would afford. At one o'clock in the afternoon of the Sabbath, not only the house, but the streets and vacant places about the house, were alive with human beings. As I went in, I found in the doorway five clergymen: three Methodists, one Presbyterian and one Congregationalist. I found that they had no seats, so I arranged to accommodate them with comfortable places. I also took in, with help, a two-bushel basket full of books, many of them I had sent miles to obtain for this occasion. The ministers looked a little wild at the books.

After the opening song, I called on one of them (not Judd) to pray. I then made the following statement: "If in this discussion to-day I make any misrepresentation, or false quotation of the Pedobaptist authors, or misstatements of any minister's words, I shall be obliged to any clergyman or other gentleman to call my attention to my mistake, and I will stand corrected, if found in an error." I stated the *why* of my appearing in a discussion. I had called upon a friend to read from the authors the quotations that I might make.

We will not detain the reader to rehearse the arguments by which we sustained our first three propositions. Suffice it to say, we were not called to order by any one present, and so we concluded we did not misrepresent their position or misquote their authors. We came to the fourth proposition, and sustained it to the satisfaction of every candid hearer; and "Brother" Judd, then and there, "swallowed" three out of the six falsehoods he had told in the pulpit. The only apology he offered was, he "was told so."

We occupied three hours and fifteen minutes in this talk, without intermission. And thus ended this "bloodless, wordy and watery war." About the only reference, to the subject afterwards, was made the next year by Mr. Judd's successor, and by the way, a very clever Christian gentleman, and on this wise: My garden lay beside the walk on the main street. This brother and his wife came walking along one evening, just as I was watering my cabbages with a common watering pot. "Ah!" says he, "then you do believe in sprinkling, I see, Brother Stimson?" "Oh, yes," I replied; "for cabbage-heads—it may do them good." He and his good wife laughed and walked on.

During the following winter, the community was a good deal exercised upon the subject of "Millerism," or the speedy coming of Christ (time set to a minute), and the destruction of the world and the wicked. Two prominent lecturers came into the place, Rev. Mr. Beach and Rev. Elon Galusha. The public attention was taxed with this exciting subject, until nothing else could gain the popular mind. So, I only sat as a looker-on, occasionally witnessing a demonstration of the subject on charts. We thought then, and think now, that we had no objections to the Lord's coming; but we did not see that their figuring was exact authority, according to "Dayball's." We had always heard that "figures would not lie," and our confidence in their veracity, up to that time, was unbounded; but we thought then we saw them lying—at least, the only excuse we can discover for the behavior of the figures in this particular case is, that they were very unfortunate in being thrown together with such guess-work, by which even a cypher would change the whole tenor of Revelation on the subject. To say the least, the "exact mathematics," as applied to the doctrine of the "second advent," after a continuous effort for a generation, and the most repeated and signal failures, better withdraw from the field. Before the time for the event is fixed again, we suggest to those having the matter in charge to fix upon a "standard of time;" and then apply their mathematics to the calculation of the variation for different localities, owing to the difference of latitude and longitude. The devil must fear this doctrine, or he wouldn't have set such "minute-men" to preaching it, and so brought it into such deserved contempt. The Bible just as plainly teaches that Christ is coming the second time, bodily and personally and visibly, as that He came and was crucified, "dead and buried," and rose again and ascended up on high. If He ever came once, He is coming again. But He as expressly says that no man knoweth when, "no, not the angels of Heaven, but my Father only." To what order of beings do these mathematical, "second-advents" belong?

But no harm came of it to our church. Not a single member went off with it, and not a soul was converted to Christ in all these efforts. As soon as the excitement had subsided, I called the attention of my people to the fact that sinners were dying all around us, and that whether Christ came at once, or a great while in the future, they must be saved by Him, or lost forever. God revived us again, and that spring I baptized a goodly number of youth—some of them exceedingly interesting cases—and the church was replenished with the Spirit's influence "to the edification of itself in love."

The year 1844 witnessed the great Presidential campaign contest between Clay and Polk, and little could be done for religion, except simply to maintain the ground. The church and congregation had become deeply imbedded in my heart. Many of the church had been received by myself through the significant ordinance of initiation into the household of God, instituted and submitted to by Christ. But "God's ways are not as our ways, nor His thoughts as our thoughts."

At the close of my vacation, which I had employed in traveling through the country in that part of the State, on returning home, the brother who had "supplied" for me intimated that he would like my position, saying that "a number of the brethren had suggested that a change of pastor was desirable; that I had been there quite a while, and might be more useful somewhere else."

I said, "Very well, I will accommodate them." The next week was Covenant meeting. I wrote out my resignation, and at the meeting handed it to the clerk, with the request for him to read it at the close, for special action of the church at that meeting. He complied. There was some agitation in consequence. "Why, what can it mean?" One of the deacons moved to lay it on the table, to which, of course, I objected; but all in vain. On to the table it went without a negative. The truth is, one man was a little excited on account of my "abolition" proclivities. For I was what they called a "hair-brained, fanatical, one-idea abolitionist."

He had fooled the poor, dear, little minister into the belief that he could get the place, if I was only out of it. I was willing, if the church so wished. But they were so incensed they would not hear him again. Six weeks after, at a special meeting, my resignation was accepted, and I out on the open road to seek a new field.

CHAPTER XIV.

WHEATLAND.

THE church in Wheatland, hearing that I had resigned at Warsaw, invited me to visit them at my earliest convenience. This invitation I accepted, and was settled as their pastor in January, 1845. In leaving Warsaw as I did, I was liable to the charge of undue haste—a charge that might frequently be set to my account. I have been addicted to hasty action, more or less, all through my life. In some instances, doubtless, great harm came to churches in consequence of my haste in leaving them. If I had not stayed with them any longer to speak of, but had given them a little more warning in case of my leaving, some injury, doubtless, might have been prevented.

But, on the other hand, some of the best moves I ever made, I think, were impromptu—and this move to Wheatland was certainly one of them. I never had any regrets in the case, as I had in leaving Alabama. As soon as my family were comfortably settled, I began exploring my field. The church then covered a large extent of country, parts of four "towns," besides all of Wheatland, with small villages, Scottsville, Mumford, Churchville and Clifton. In each of these, I had an appointment regularly. The church was mostly composed of farmers, men of integrity, intelligence and wealth, and a large circle of youth who had been brought up to revere religion and attend the services of the church. A number of them were already members, and examples of Christian deportment.

All these facts impressed me with the belief that, with God's blessing on the joint labors of pastor and people, a work could be accomplished to the honor of the Gospel and the enlargement of Zion. There was one thing only that acted as a hindrance to immediate advancement. The church edifice was one of the first built west of the Genesee river, and time had made its marks upon it; and its architectural construction was not in keeping with modern ideas. To many of the members, as well as to the society, it was distasteful—high, deep galleries; seats with high, straight backs, with a sharp rib called a railing, and a lofty pulpit, with a long stairway coming up both sides into a little box with a board seat, the whole as large as a common bureau when the doors were shut. Two common-sized ministers would fill it full.

The church was organized in 1811, and had been under the pastoral instruction of some of the ablest men in the denomination. Elder Solomon Brown, the first pastor, died in 1813. E. Stone was with them four years. Aristarchus Willey, Horace Griswell, John Middleton, Daniel Elbridge, Gibbon Williams, who was my immediate predecessor, completed the list of their pastors—choice men and gifted, and some of them highly educated.

One fact is worthy of notice. This church had a practical system of management by which they conducted all their finances. They were never perplexed with any old, long arrearage. Their church book was as complete as any business man's ledger. At the end of each year they knew to a cent what they had paid out, not only for home expenses, but to the different benevolent objects of the day. It was under the supervision of the deacons of the church. All moneys passed through their hands. I was surprised, at the close of my first year, when the deacons called to settle with me, to find that every cent paid to me was on their book, and the exact amount due, which was two hundred and sixty-three dollars and twenty-seven cents, was on hand with which to pay me. A thing that had never happened to me before in fifteen years of ministerial life.

Everything was done by equality. One was not eased and another burdened, as in too many of our churches. The two acting deacons worked together in perfect harmony. Deacon Jirah Blackmer was church clerk, and had been from the beginning, more than thirty-five years. Deacon Charles Tenney was collector, always heading the list in every good work. The senior deacon, Rawsom Harmon, had become aged and had retired from active responsibilities. He was a man of great natural force of character. His bugle-voice was yet heard in prayer and exhortation. A few, that spring, were converted and added to the church.

In June, after a long consultation and mutual agreement, we entered into a remodeling of the church-house, at an expense of seventeen hundred dollars. The contract was let. The work was nearly completed, and we were in anticipation of entering the house in a few days, when, one morning about three o'clock, while all in the neighborhood were sleeping, the cry of "Fire! fire!" was heard; and lo! our new place or worship was all in flames, and before daylight, all in ashes. The evening of that day had been appointed for a donation visit at the parsonage. It was a sad gathering of all the church and society. In spite of the depressing circumstance, they brought generous offerings to their pastor, amounting in all to one hundred and ninety dollars.

At this donation visit, a society and church meeting was arranged for the next evening, to take measures for rebuilding. There was perfect unity. Their motto was, "The God of Heaven, He will help us; therefore, we His servants will arise and build." The next Lord's day, I preached from Isaiah lxiv. 11: "Our holy and our beautiful house, where our fathers praised Thee, is burned up with fire, and all our pleasant things are laid waste." The money was soon raised to construct and complete a new house.

This year we were quite disconcerted in our Sunday school and congregational meetings, for a convenient place in which to meet. But God was in it all, disciplining the church for greater work yet to come. The eighteenth of the next November the new house was entered, the Rev. Whitman Metcalf, of Brockport, preaching the sermon. In the evening, the Rev. N. Murdock, D. D., of Albion, preached. There were already manifestations of the Divine presence, as the church held days of fasting and prayer prior to the opening of the new edifice ; and yet there were no conversions.

That winter, I was engaged, with others, in the Monroe Association, to raise a large amount to help meet the deficit of forty-three thousand dollars in the treasury of the A. B. M. Union. We had three meetings—one in Rochester, one in Wheatland and one in Mendon. Rev. Alfred Bennett was invited to be present and preach at the meeting in our church. After the sermon a collection was taken up, amounting to five hundred and sixty-six dollars. I felt relieved; and I believe the work of replenishing the treasury that year was finally accomplished.

The tenth day of March following, light from above broke in upon us. Sinners became alarmed, and the cry was heard, "What must we do?" Men and women of age and standing, youth and children, were seen flocking to Zion's gates, "as clouds and doves to windows." Our meetings continued day and evening from the tenth of March to July. For thirteen Sabbaths we visited the pools of Zion to baptize rejoicing converts to Jesus, their new-found King. The Spirit of reclamation went over the land like sunlight and shower in May. Old hopes were renewed in the Spirit, and persons who had grown gray in neglect of God and salvation had now a family altar. Young men would call me up at midnight, to pray for them and direct them what to do. There was not a dog to move his tongue, except one. The Rev. Mr. Ashman, of Riga, pastor of the Congregational church, became quite incensed because a number of his people had called for letters, in order to be baptized and join our church. He said, on one occasion, that "Nobody but the *rabble* would go to see these Sabbath-breaking immersions; and I feel it to be a grievous wrong to grant letters to any member of our church to join a church that will not admit us to the Lord's table." This so offended the better portion of his church that he was summarily dismissed. He went back to New England to get refreshed. In the course of the work we received fifteen from the Pedobaptists; and I could not feel myself to blame.

Thus the year 1847 closed, with the church greatly enlarged in spirit and in numbers, having doubled its membership and also its ability. It was their custom to increase in ability in proportion to numerical increase; if not in giving ability, in doing ability. A donation visit was made to the parsonage every winter by members of the church and congregation. The time for it had come and the day was set. The invitations had been sent out. The usual order was for the older folks to come in the afternoon, and the younger to come in the evening. But, on this occasion, it seems it was a concerted plan among the younger people to come in the day also, and then make the older people stay in the evening; and it worked like a charm. Each district in the parish tried to outdo the others. On one four-horse load of hay that drove up, were, besides ten or twelve men and women, the following articles, good to read over: four barrels of apples, two barrels of flour, ten bushels of oats, fifty pounds of dried meat and butter, in addition to turkeys, chickens, cakes and pies by the dozen. It is needless to mention that it took four horses to draw this load. It came from "Palmer street." One woman threw up her hands as it approached, saying: "There comes all Palmer street, and it has outdone us all." Our donation receipts footed up on this occasion to the considerable sum of two hundred and sixty-five dollars. Donation visits are not very bad things to receive occasionally.

The next spring I held a meeting of days in an out-station called "Harman's Burgh," now Clifton. The Rev. J. B. Olcott and the Rev. H. Daniels came to our assistance, and rendered most valuable service. In that neighborhood, twenty-eight were added to the company of the disciples in that village.

This year I attended commencement at Hamilton. I had attended before when it was a simple seminary; but now it had become a "University." This was the first occasion on which they had ever conferred honorary degrees, a ceremony I had never witnessed. The first man to receive this was our warm friend, Rev. Pharcellus Church, then pastor of the First church in Rochester. The duties of conferring the weighty affair devolved upon Dr. A. C. Kendrick, then one of the Hamilton faculty. I supposed he would converse about the matter in English; but when he began, I soon saw it was all "ash dod" to me. (I was told that he chose to converse in Latin.) As soon as all was over, I started off in the stage for home. Arriving in Rochester before daylight, I proceeded at once to Church's residence, and rung the bell. He came to the door in his night dress, and asked, "Who's there?" "It's me," I replied. He opened the door, and I caught him by the hand, muttering, "Juck, dio postate pulanto dignite, fortunate vis to dogme ito Pharcellum Churchum." "Why, Stimson, what is the matter with you? Are you crazy, or are you dr——?" a condition I had not been in for twenty years and more. I replied, "I have made you a *doctor of divinity*." The daily paper was just ready to go to press, and I slipped down to the *Democrat* office and had the fact inserted in the news column. When he saw it in print, he regarded it as *official*.

The Monroe Association was one of the most efficient religious bodies in the western part of New York. It was composed of a class of ministers godly and efficient—Rev. P. Church, of the First church, Rochester; Rev. H. Davis, Second church, Rochester; Rev. Z. Case, Ogden; Rev. Jonas Woodward, Webster; Rev. A. C. Kingsley, Parma; Rev. Martain Coleman, Bergen; Rev. Whitman Medcalf, Brockport; Rev. J. B. Olcott, Grece; Rev. A. Annis, East Mendon; Rev. H. Stanwood, Rush. A number of the above are still living, some at an advanced age, while others still have "gone up higher."

About this time some dissatisfaction began to be manifest about the management of our educational matters at Hamilton. Friends in the East and West were beginning to make an effort for its removal to Rochester. In all good faith I joined in the general movement, and spent much of my time and exerted all my influence to secure that end. Bad blood was stirred up on both sides, and many things said and done that we have repented of. I hope God has forgiven all concerned. I think He has one poor sinner at least. I went into it as I go into everything else: to conquer. The result has been greatly favorable to the denomination at large. Rochester University is a verity and a power, with a theological seminary that no denomination need be ashamed of; and Hamilton in all its departments is a better institution than it would have been, had it not been stirred up with the "long pole" of rivalry. It is my constant prayer—God fill our land with educated ministers. I value education as a poor man does money: I feel the want of it. I sincerely pity any young man who attempts to preach the sublime truths of the Gospel of Jesus without at least a common English education. He ought to have, in this day of advance in all the sciences, a complete course in the best schools of the land.

When I look back over forty years of work, and reflect what I have gone through by way of self-mortification, and then how I have shamed the dear Church of God by my bad pronunciation and worse grammar, I have said, "If I were to spend my life over again, I would give at least five years of that time, no matter how old I might be to begin with, to securing the best preparation for my work within my reach." I think the council that ordained me would have done a far better thing in resolving themselves into an educational conference, and then called on the church, or churches, to have sustained my family and let me go to school; or set me at work at my trade to secure the means to support them, and then started me on my course of study.

I saw my need of education the first time I ever went into a pulpit to preach. While I lived in Rush, and had only just begun to talk in neighborhood gatherings, the pastor at Penfield wished to be absent a Sabbath, and sent for me to supply his place. I foolishly consented. Penfield was one of the most intelligent congregations in the Monroe

Association. So Sunday morning I took my horse and drove over fourteen miles; got there just in time for the morning service. The brethren met me kindly, as they all knew me, and some had known me before my conversion. I went up into the pulpit as I imagine a man would ascend the gallows, and took my text in Psalms xxxiii. 4: "For the Word of the Lord is right; and all His works are done in truth." I had given the subject some little thought, in my way of thinking, and got through better than I expected to when I began. So the devil suggested, "Hiram, you can beat that." So in the afternoon I took my text from Hosea x. 12: "Sow to yourselves in righteousness, reap in mercy." I had not proceeded far, when I used a common word among stage drivers to express *nothing*, so I said, "You can't get a *hooter* out of them." There was a Dr. C. in the congregation, who was looking me full in the face with interest, and I have no doubt now, with anxiety. As the word *hooter* came out, he buried his face in his handkerchief, and laughed till he shook all over. I stopped, ashamed and confounded, and holding up my hands, said, "Be dismissed," and pronounced the benediction. I went straight to the barn, got out my horse and started for Rush.

Fourteen years afterwards, when I was pastor at Warsaw and Rev. Daniel Barnard was pastor at Penfield, he proposed an exchange. I arrived at Penfield on Saturday, and called on Joseph Case, with whom I was to lodge. While he was in the barn, taking care of my horse, the deacon said: "Well, Brother Stimson, I am glad to see you. I hear good things about you. They say you have got to be quite a preacher, and are doing a wonderful sight of good. I suppose you won't say "*hooter*" to-morrow, will you?" I was half a mind to hitch up my horse and go straight home. The "*hooter*" was still after me. Fourteen years had not obliterated the little word "*hooter*."

Pardon this digression, and I will return to the narrative of my experience at Wheatland.

While the controversy was going on in regard to the University, and the prospect grew brighter of having it established at Rochester, a proposition was made to raise an endowment fund of one hundred and thirty thousand dollars; and after an effort had been made in the city, the next place that was expected to "lift" was Wheatland. Rev. Dr. Church, Deacon O. Sage and John N. Wilder, by my invitation came up, and in less than two days they raised over seven thousand dollars. I think this was the largest subscription from any country church in the State. While they had the wealth, they also had the disposition—a consideration still more important. They believed in education. They sent their children to the best schools the country afforded.

CHAPTER XV.

ADRIAN.

IN 1849, the church in Adrian, Michigan, sent me an invitation to visit them. I went and spent a month or more, and gave them encouragement that I might accept their call to the pastorate. I came home with that expectation, and did resign; but my church delayed action in regard to it until the small-pox had broken out in town, and my own family were afflicted with it. And for six long weeks all communication was closed. No meetings, except those occasioned by the funerals. Indeed, every day seemed like a constant funeral. As soon as we came together as a church, a memorial was handed me asking me to withdraw my resignation, signed by a long list of the best members of the church and society. I complied, and went to work as before. But, in the spring following, the church in Adrian renewed their call, and I accepted. In July, 1850, I moved to Michigan.

This was a sorrowful year to the family. One of our dear children sickened and died, in less than a month after our arrival, of a disease superinduced by the small-pox while at Wheatland. Soon, the other children were attacked with the chills and fever common to that climate. And then came my turn. I was seized as if by an armed force. So, out of the fifty-two Sundays of the year, I was only able to attend church thirty-three, and then with more shakes than Gospel.

The church had just closed a long series of meetings, under the supervision of that extraordinary man of God, Morgan Edwards. Already about *two hundred* had been baptized into the fellowship of the church, and the first Sabbath after I arrived I baptized twenty-four more. Thus the church had a mushroom growth from about one hundred to about two hundred and fifty; and the man who had led the vanguard had left the forces scattered and without a leader. All classes were thus gathered into the church, without much system or unity of belief. Of course, we do not blame Brother Edwards. It was not his place to systematize and educate. Some of the converts had not been near the church after being baptized, and did not intend to come. All they wanted was to be baptized. One man, who had been received, came to me and wanted me to sprinkle his children! He intended to have it done before he left "Hingland," but had neglected it. "But," I said, "your children are not believers, are they?" "No, indeed they are not; and that is why I want them christened. Me and my Bettie, ye know, were christened hinto the Church of Hingland, ye know, and then we were come to Hamerica, and have been baptized by Brother Hedwards. Now, we's want our children in has good standing as we are." It was with great difficulty that I could make him understand the nature of the ordinance of Christ's house—in fact, I did not explain it to his entire satisfaction, for he and his "Bettie" went and joined the Methodists, who would accommodate them to almost anything they wanted in a so-called religious way. They doubtless felt far more "at home" among the Methodists. We felt relieved. This was an extraordinary case; but many were singularly, if not similarly, affected.

It was here the story was started that I ran horses at a State fair. It grew out of the fact that I had a good horse and carriage at the time the State fair was held at Adrian, that I had brought with me from Wheatland. The animal was well broken and thought to be the best of any in the community, and I was invited to "enter" him for a prize. I agreed to, and before the fair came off I trained my little boy, fourteen years old, to drive. The horse needed no training. I told the boy to just sit up straight and mind his own business, and pay no attention to others. I thought he was trained all right, and I could trust him to enter the ground with the horse and carriage. The time came to exhibit this sort of property, and the boy drove into the grounds with a long list of others. But the cracking of whips and the rattle of wheels scared the boy,—not the horse, for it hardly knew what a whip meant. The fear he was under caused him to drive over the chains, and I saw that something must be done to redeem this mishap, or I should lose the premium. So, a friend, Mr. S. W. W., said: "Elder, you go, drive your own horse." I did so, and *of course* took the first premium for the best-trained horse in a single carriage.

In a few days, one of our Adrian merchants went East and fell in company with two clergymen of my own denomination, who inquired very curiously about me. He replied: "Oh, yes; I know him very well, and a very clever fellow he is, too. He has just had a streak of good luck." "Oh, indeed!" says one of the ministers; "in what way?" "Oh, he won five hundred dollars at a horse race!" "*At a horse-race?*" inquired my dumb-founded friends. "Yes, at a horse-race. I was there, and saw it myself." The story went all over the land as on the wings of the wind. The merchant has had many a hearty laugh over it at my expense. This is my first and last experience with agricultural horse trots. If it was so then, it is certainly so now, that one can't participate in them with horses, in any way, and not run great risks of losing his good moral reputation.

I saw that the condition of things was such in the church at Adrian that it would take years to get all into good running order. Careful discrimination was necessary between the "chaff and the wheat." Many that had been brought into the church under the great religious awakening, were genuine Christians, and evinced an earnest disposition to live godly lives, but they needed instruction, and constant watching for a time. Others, of whom we stood in some doubt, might in time be saved to the church, and be made of some value to the cause. Others still, if saved at all, would have to be saved "so as by fire." So all the next winter the pastor and church toiled to effect a healthful "circulation" in the extremities of the patient's system. But there was an organic disease that neither "cholagogue nor quinine" could reach—intermittent chills and fever, day chills and night sweats. These bid fair to bring on quick consumption. To *individualize* the figure a little, many had become so prostrated already, that they could not say "Shiboleth," one of the last words given up. A patient is very sick that can't speak this; and very well, that won't speak it. Some of the members had become ritualists. They didn't read off their part in the covenant meeting, but committed and repeated it. "I hope you will pray for me, that I may hold out faithful, and when I die, that I may meet you all in heaven"—about as much evidence that a man is a disciple of Jesus, as looking out of the east window in the morning is, that he is a Persian fire-worshiper.

But, there were some old staunch men and women, and a number of young people, who, like Caleb and Joshua, were bound to stand by the truth; who loved the Church and its ordinances, and felt themselves bound to see the body restored to its former health and efficiency. Among this number was a Mrs. M., a very intelligent and useful body, the wife of a lawyer who had been a man of some importance in the State. But he had become so dissipated and lost to respect that he had lost place and power as a politician, and was a kind of "hanger-on around town," getting his liquor where he could sponge it. One of our brethren said to him one day, "Squire M., why don't you go to meeting with your wife and hear our minister?" He straightened himself up, and in a pompous manner said, "Well, Mr. W., I will tell you. When I go to church I want to hear a man preach who has not been a stage driver, and never was drunk," and then set up a hearty laugh at Mr. W.'s expense. Some one who heard this conversation and was quite indignant at it, came and told me about it. A few months after, one Lord's day morning, there came into the house of God, this same Squire M. and his wife, his face all radiant with poor whisky. His eyes looked like worn out button holes. I was discoursing that morning from the words: "As ye go, preach." I was enforcing the importance of all preaching, and preaching everywhere, by example, character, and conversation. "It isn't all in all that you should be learned or eloquent. The first disciples were poor, and mostly illiterate, but they preached pretty effectually. Suppose a man has been a shoemaker, a poor sailor, or a stage driver; when he is sober and in his right mind, can't he preach, and do as much good as a miserable, drunken lawyer?"

The sensation all over the house was apparent. All eyes turned involuntarily towards Squire M. The next day he met brother W., and said: "W., that was a home thrust your Elder gave me yesterday, and my wife thinks it is good enough for me. I kind of like the fellow. I believe I'll come and hear him again. He is not afraid to speak what he thinks."

The continued sickness in our family, and my own imperfect state of health, with the vast amount of pastoral care demanded in this church, induced me to consider a call I had received from the church at Penn Yan. Our "anniversaries" met that spring in Boston, and I was advised to take a trip East, in company with my physician, John Cadman, and attend the Boston meetings. On my way home, I called at Penn Yan, and spent two Sundays. The church had been without a pastor some months, and were quite desirous of the speedy settlement of a pastor.

After my return home, I laid the matter before the church at Adrian, and resigned, after a short and trying pastorate of one year. But little had been done for the conversion of souls, most of our efforts having been put forth in behalf of those who were in need of greatest care and nursing, and to save the church from shipwreck;—all under the distressing influence of chills and fever.

CHAPTER XVI

PENN YAN.

THE Baptist church in Penn Yan stood high among the churches in that part of the State as an old and efficient body of Christians, numbering at the time three hundred and twenty-eight. They had not enjoyed a revival for a long time, and had now been destitute of a pastor altogether too long. Formalism had eaten out some of the joy of salvation from their hearts. But they were a united people, and believed in every good work, and in love to all mankind. If the temperance reform was to be pushed, they were ready. If "abolition" was to be agitated, they were found in the front rank. They believed in the largest liberty, and in the highest state of religious life. God was with them, and in them. During the first summer, about all I could do was to encourage the young, comfort the aged, and marshal the forces for a future onset upon the powers of darkness. This latter work, we think, by divine grace we succeeded in accomplishing.

Many ministers make a failure on this point. In time of declension they talk and preach depressingly, and so make depression more oppressive. What would we think of a man in dark and cloudy weather, who should come out upon his door-steps and begin to lament in this manner: "Dark day! a very d-a-r-k d-a-y, r-a-i-n-y and c-o-l-d. We are g-o-i-n-g to h-a-v-e a s-t-o-r-m-y n-i-g-h-t. We s-h-a-n-t r-a-i-s-e o-u-r b-r-e-a-d t-h-i-s y-e-a-r. I n-e-v-e-r s-a-w t-h-e l-i-k-e in all my e-x-t-e-n-d-e-d e-x-p-e-r-i-e-n-c-e. T-h-e-r-e-'-s n-o u-s-e of t-r-y-i-n-g." Any common-sense person would say he was sick with the blues. So far as he had any influence over his neighbors, it would be injurious.

I consider this continual croaking in the church, and the fault-finding spirit, productive of the very evil which it is intended to overcome. Come out with a good sermon on "Hope thou in God." Get the people to look away from themselves, and exalt the Lord in their hearts. Get them into the habit of taking cheerful views. In a covenant meeting, where croaking and mourning were the order of the day, an old lady, the last one to speak, arose and said. "Why, brethren and sisters, you distress me. Jesus is the same yesterday, to-day and forever. His promises will not fail. Don't let us any more entertain each other with this kind of cold victuals. I always set the best I have in my house before my company, and when I am alone, I eat the crusts in silence, thanking God for the warm meals I have enjoyed." This little talk of the aged sister entirely changed the tone of the church; the minister felt relieved, and he and his people changed all their social religious habits, so that God renewed them.

Early in September, I began to apply the truths I had been preaching during the summer, and to increase the number of our prayer meetings from one to two, and then to three a week. Instead of a sermon on Sabbath afternoon, we often turned it into a conference talk, the meeting taking this turn naturally, and not by previous notice. Never advertise any such change, nor be afraid of taking the liberty of making it. This was like the "nine and twenty knives," spoken of in the Scripture. By October the church was in a good working condition, and it was plainly to be seen that a change had come over the spirit of their dreams. Family altars were reconstructed. Old heart-burnings were healed. The frivolity of the youth had given place to sober thinking and prayer. Men of the world were becoming more attentive in the house of God. By November, we were "protracting" our meetings, and hardly knew how or when the extra interest began. I think it often gives the devil a favorable chance to rally his forces and oppose, to advertise long beforehand the intention of the church to hold extra meetings. Things went on in glorious majesty for ninety-seven days and nights, and there was not a dog to yelp against it. Sinners were constantly pressing to the inquiry meetings for advice and prayer, and the outlet of the beautiful lake was visited every Sabbath to introduce the new-born souls into the visible kingdom of the Captain of their salvation.

And now came the tug of war. A number of the youth that had been in the habit of attending the Congregational church, and some of the members of that church, came into this work. Some were converted, some were revived, as the case might be. As soon as they felt the need of a higher stand in religious living, in the simplicity of their hearts they went to their pastor, the Rev. Mr. C. for instruction. He inquired of them where they first began to be exercised on the subject. They told him, "in the meetings at the Baptist church." "Well," said he, "my advice to you, my young friends, is to keep away from those meetings. We never had any such meetings down in Stockbridge, in Massachusetts, where I came from. And I understand that Elder Stimson has been a *stage driver* and a *hard* case, and used to get intoxicated and turn over the stage; and my impression is, that he will upset the Baptist church, and have them all in the mud before spring. Your best way is to come to our regular meetings, and let Stimson and the Baptists quiet be."

This was a *poser* to the unsophisticated youth. These young folks came into our next young people's meeting, and one of them, my son, a lad sixteen or seventeen years of age being present, asked a Baptist friend, with surprise: "Was Mr. Stimson ever a stage driver?" To which he replied: "I suppose he was." He told what Rev. Mr. C. had said. When seeing my son, they begged his pardon and the interview closed. But my boy could not forget what he had heard. He came home and inquired: "Father, have—you—ever—been—a—

stage driver?" "Yes. Why? What of it?" He related the conversation at the meeting.

The next Sabbath, I gave the reasons for coming to that place to baptize, instead of administering the ordinance with a little water in the house. And this was all I said. The next Tuesday, I met Mr. C. in the street, and after recognizing me, he said: "Mr. Stimson, the clergymen of the village held a meeting at my study this morning, and having heard what you said at the water last Sabbath, we have concluded not to extend to you the courtesies of the ministry any longer, and I was appointed a committee to inform you of our decision." "*Indeed*," I replied; "What have I said, and who is your informant?" "Well," he said, "it is on the street, and I will not extend our conversation any further. Good day, sir." He wouldn't tell, nor hear me tell, what I said, and passed along.

In the afternoon, I met the Methodist minister, and asked him to explain the affair. "Oh! Mr. C.," said he, "wanted a resolution he had written against yourself passed by our little meeting; and to show you, Brother Stimson, that I do not have any such feelings, I wish to exchange with you next Sabbath." I consented. The thing went over town like a prairie fire. I soon baptized five of his members and as many more from his congregation, taking the three best singers out of his choir. Mr. C.'s people asked him to resign. He refused to do it, and they closed the meeting-house on Sundays until his year was out, when he left for the West. The revival continued, and extended into the churches at Milo and Benton.

During this summer, I received an accident that came near costing me my life. I had been invited to deliver a fourth of July oration at Bethel. When in the middle of my talk the platform broke, carrying down thirty men some eight feet. I lay for nine long weeks a great sufferer, not expecting ever to preach again. After I was able to be about, I visited my old field of pleasant toil at Wheatland. Rev. Dr. W. W. Everts had succeeded me in the pastorate, and radical changes had taken place. The church had extended her enterprise in meeting-house building. A new house had been erected at Clifton, two-and-a-half miles to the east, and one at Mumford, two-and-a-half miles to the south. Churchville had already become an independent body and also had a meeting-house, making in all four congregations. The pet plan of Dr. Everts was to have them all one church, but four congregations, he to be the pastor, and the churches to employ the young men from the seminary at Rochester to supply them alternately, in his absence in going from one to the other.

To some the enterprise looked feasible, to others objectionable. About the time the new house was completed in Clifton and the one in Mumford in an advanced state, a decided opposition to the plan was manifested. He had warm supporters of his ideas, but on the other hand he had hearty opposers. The opposing sides were about equally represented by the leading men in the church. The determination to carry the opposing plans was about equally divided. Each side engaged in the contest to win. Church meeting after church meeting had been held, and yet the matter was unsettled.

The Clifton portion of the church had invited me to be present at the dedication of their house, and preach the sermon. A friendly conference was also held at the house of Gen. R. Harman, to consider what means were expedient in order to conciliate brethren who for years had lived and worked together in the unity of the Spirit, many of them from childhood. It was then advised to organize two churches, one at Clifton and one at Mumford, as it was evident these three parties could not work and walk together harmoniously in the old church at Wheatland.

Acting on this informal advice, these branches resolved themselves into independent churches and called a council for their recognition. The church at Clifton extended me a call to become their pastor, which I accepted. The same council which met for the recognition of the church, also recognized me as pastor. Rev. Dr. G. W. Howard, of Rochester, preached the sermon. This was in December. The next day the same council met at Mumford, and recognized that little band of disciples as a church. Sermon by Rev. H. K. Stimson, and hand of fellowship by Rev. Zenas Case, of Ogden.

Thus the old hive had, within the space of a little over three years, produced three swarms, and all of them comfortably hived—Clifton, Churchville and Mumford. And the mother hive was no less determined than ever, though somewhat enfeebled, to gather honey, to live and let live.

Dr. Everts soon resigned, and was succeeded by Rev. S. M. Bainbridge as pastor at Wheatland. At Churchville, Rev. J. C. Drake was elected pastor;

at Mumford, Rev. Chancy Wardner, and at Clifton, Rev. H. K. Stimson. The old church at Wheatland had given letters to all who requested, to join any one of the three without regard to location. One or two families living at Wheatland went to Mumford, but all the rest were within convenient distance of the church of their choice.

The Wheatland church still retained some of the best material in the community, Deacon Jirah Blackmer and his family, Ira Harman and family, Gen. T. Brown and family, Ariel Harman and family, Hon. Elisha Harman and family, Sylvester Harman and family, Martin Sage and family, the daughter and sons of Capt. E. Blackmer, and a very respectable portion of the outside society in and about the town. But things did not appear as they used to in the days of her prosperity. The dear old church had lost much of its former glory. The large congregation that used to fill the commodious house, had dwindled down to a small one. The ample contributions often made to benevolent objects, were now scanty in comparison.

Here are some figures showing the Christian liberality of the old church in 1847–48: For foreign missions, $565; for home missions, $127;

for publication cause, $112; education, $150; Bible cause, $85; other objects, $111—total, $1,150. And a year or two afterwards, they gave, while Dr. Everts was pastor, to the Bible Union alone, $1,000. The four churches altogether have not come up to it by one half any year since. We have not introduced these figures for the sake of invidious comparison. It was the community in which we spent the happiest portion of our ministry. Dr. Everts and myself were, and are, personal friends. But aside from all personal considerations, the figures ought to convey a lesson.

The church at Clifton numbered but fifty-two at the organization. But the Lord was with us, so that by the time the Association met, we reported a membership of eighty-three. This was the strongest of the new organizations, both numerically and in personal ability. It was composed of men of sound judgment, and good business habits. A number of them had long been steadfast workers in the mother church. And their children, brought up by such nursing fathers and mothers as were these true Christian men and women, became, at least many of them, similar ornaments to the Church of Christ. A large number of these I had welcomed into the fold, during my pastoral care of the undivided body. This made it very pleasant to resume pastoral relations with them. I knew them, and had perfect confidence in their piety and integrity.

In the winter and spring of 1853–54, the church of which I was then pastor was blessed with a powerful work of the Spirit. It had been manifesting itself all the autumn and winter by an uncommon spirit of prayer, especially on the part of the older members. My health was yet feeble from my fall, and not being able to endure as much hardship as formerly, I sent for Rev. R. C. Palmer—the pastor has the right to send off for an assistant, without submiting the matter to a vote of the church, though it may generally be expedient to take formal action first—who was a workman that needeth not to be ashamed. His coming was like the "coming of Titus." God was with him in the power of His great Spirit. He resorted to no *claptrap*. He got up no furor of passion. He was not known for making it "easy" for sinners to become Christians. He poured forth the living truth of God's Word, showing man's lost condition, and his only hope to be found in Christ. A large number believed, and gladly followed Jesus in baptism. They were of all ages, from the child of tender years to men of gray hairs; some of them long accustomed to overt acts of sin. It was a godsend to this young church, the stay of brother Palmer with us for five weeks, and the conversion of such a goodly number.

My health had become so impaired that physicians advised me to submit to a surgical operation. Accordingly, I went to New York, and after six weeks, the most of the time passed in severe suffering, I was relieved and came home much better, and renewed in my spirit. While in the city, I was made the welcome guest of a brother and sister Hoskins, who nursed and cared for me as for an own brother. This was the result of a simple incident in Providence. A number of years before, while up in the Alleghany country, I wished to find a place to pass the night, and called at the shanty of a lumberman, who could not entertain me, but directed me to a Mr. Hoskins, who lived down the creek about a mile, "close to the saw-mill." I hastened on, and found a snug little cottage, where I was hospitably welcomed and entertained. I found them to be earnest, humble, devout members of the Baptist Church. They were poor in goods, but rich in faith. Twenty years had elapsed. His pastor in New York I had baptized fourteen or fifteen years before. While they were in consultation one day, my name was mentioned. "I know him," said Hoskins; "he spent a night at my house in Alleghany, and if you ever see him tell him where I am, and if he ever comes to the city I wish him to call on me." They were now rich, but the same simple, unostentatious Christians. They have long since entered upon their bright reward in the Spirit land. Of course, my stay with them was as pleasant as it could be made in the midst of continual suffering. Drs. Mott and Parker, who performed the operation, charged nothing, as I was a minister of the Gospel. Their bill would have been a hundred dollars. There are some advantages in being a *poor* minister after all.

The next winter, I helped in special meetings with a number of churches. I was at Marion, assisting Pastor J. W. Osborn; at Webster, assisting Pastor Holt; then at Dansville, with Pastor Howell Smith; at Parma, with Pastor T. H. Green, and at Rochester, with Pastor Howard.

It was quite convenient to have the seminary so near as it was at Rochester. One of the students, Rev. J. C. Stevens, belonged to our church, and he helped supply my pulpit. He was a choice spirit. He is now with God. The four years spent at Clifton were not all sunshine. Death had his work to do. He entered our circle at the parsonage home and took a dear boy, who sleeps in the new cemetery among the sugar maples. In the church and congregation, too, death came. The young wife of Mr. Hosmer, a lovely Christian lady, was taken. Miss Phidelia Harmon, a blooming girl, who had just graduated from the seminary at Albion, was called upon to take her place among the white-robed above. Sidney C. Hosmer, a young man of much promise to the church and his dear family, left us for scenes of higher activity in God's great home. We could illy afford to lose any of these or of the others whom we might mention who were translated from the Church below to the Church triumphant. But the Master had need of them, and we had need of the discipline. It taught the younger portion of the church many good lessons to lose for time so many of their associates.

CHAPTER XVII.

MARION.

DURING the fall of this year, 1855, the church at Marion, Wayne county, New York, had parted with their pastor, Rev. J. W. Osborn, with whom I had held a meeting two years before. They at once desired me to consider a call to the pastorate. I had misgivings about settling with a church for whom I had previously labored in a protracted meeting, for the reasons that the sermons preached during such efforts are generally on a higher key than ordinary pastoral preaching. I intimated this to the committee. But they said it had already been taken into the account by the church. So I accepted, and as soon as I could resign and make due arrangements, I left my Clifton field and settled among them.

I found them a warm-hearted people, liberal and zealous in every good word and work, and, moreover, quite careful about their pastor's necessities.

We had come into the place late in the fall, and saw at once that little aggressive work could be done that season for the souls of the impenitent. The Congregational and Methodist churches had united and sent for an evangelist to conduct their union meetings. I was invited to come in and do the "police" work in the camp, while the brother evangelist should have command of the rank and file. Just at this time, I received a telegraphic dispatch—telegrams had not come into fashion then—from the Rev. C. C. Norton, pastor of the Sixth-street Baptist church in New York City, to come to his assistance at once, as a great work of the Spirit had begun in his church. I started that day. "The King's business requires haste." I was absent in the city seven weeks, and on my return found the union meeting yet in progress, but not a soul had been converted. The evangelist had become discouraged and left the place. The two pastors were still trying to push the battle to the gates of the enemy. But in their onsets, they spent most of their ammunition in attacking the Baptist stronghold. So apparent was this, that my people had retired from the field in good order. I called the day of my return at a store, and there met the two co-laboring, co-fighting pastors. The merchant, an old man, was an infidel. He had lived in the town about forty years, and had been acquainted with its history from the beginning. As we three stood by the stove, he said: "Well, gents, I am glad to see you all here together. I want to give you my advice—it's free; and it's this: give up your meetings to the Baptists. I have been here forty years, and in all that time all the revivals have been held by them. Others have tried, but have come out just as you have. The Elder has got home, and he's an old war-horse. Let the Baptists have the field. That's all; now do as you please, gents."

That afternoon, the two ministers called at my study, and wished to hold the meetings in the three churches, including the Baptist, rotating from one to the other. I replied that I did not think it best for me to go into any such arrangement. "But," I added, "when you get through with your effort, if my people think it best, we may hold a few extra meetings." They then proposed that our church take the meeting on Sunday night. To this I consented, on condition that I was to have the control of it without "let or hindrance." They consented. So, on Sunday evening all came to the Baptist church. I had asked the Methodist Episcopal minister to preach. He took for his text II Samuel iv. 4, and went on for awhile like the man in the Bible, lame in both his feet, not forgetting to make a few thrusts at the Baptists, and then said AMEN; and we all said *amen* and *amen*.

Monday evening, Rev. E. F. Crane, my successor at Clifton, came to my help. As he entered the meeting-house he commenced to sing, a thing he could do as few can. In the course of a few weeks, over *one hundred* were saved in Christ. Brother Crane staid with me in all five weeks. When he left for home, eighty-four had united with the church. As soon as the converts began to follow Jesus in the first ordinance of His house, these two loving, "liberal" clergymen were attacked with sectarian "fits," or rather *hydrophobia*—madness at the sight of "much water." The Congregational minister had to employ the "Christian" minister to baptize a lady who wished to join his church, but insisted on being baptized and not sprinkled, the follower of Jesus declaring that he would not "go into the water." It was suggested by some one "that it would bring on a spasm." It would seem as though Christ must have made a great mistake in one of His ordinances!

The church in Marion, with all their good habits, had one bad one. They would come late to meeting. The morning services were at half-past ten o'clock. They had a good bell, and it was punctual in its bland tones in calling them to the house of prayer. Most of the congregation were punctual enough; but there were a few who were forever dropping in all through the worship. I expostulated. No good. Late attendance was a part of their practical piety. At length I tried this expedient: I took a text from Ezekiel ix. 3: "And he called to the man clothed with linen which had the writer's ink horn by his side." I had gone on for five or ten minutes, and in came Brother E. and his wife and two daughters. I stopped until they had taken their seats and then quoted the text, "And he called to the man clothed with linen which had the writer's ink horn by his side;" and added, "We have proceeded some way in our subject, and have repeated the text for the benefit of brother E. and his family." All looked at them, but they looked down. On we went again, and in a few minutes more, in came brother S. and his wife. We stood still till all was quiet, and then repeated the text: "And he called to the man clothed with linen, which had the writer's ink horn by his side," and then said: "For the instruction of brother S. and his wife, we will say that the subject is thus far advanced, and we will repeat what we have gone over for your benefit." Again we proceeded, when in came brother J., who heard all about the "ink horn" and all the preceding part of the sermon. We persevered up to the seventh or eighth straggler, emptying the ink horn upon the head of each. *It was an effectual antidote.*

One thing to the credit of this town: they have had no grog shop in it for over thirty years; those who would get drunk had to go so far for the stuff, that as a rule, they got sober before reaching home. In the village is a fine collegiate institute of high order, under Baptist control, and largely patronized. The church has sent out a goodly number of ministers who were converted and reared there. Rev. J. H. Morrison, and Rev. H. J. Eddy, D. D., are among the number.

During this year, I visited my children and other relatives in Michigan, Illinois, Wisconsin and Minnesota. While on my journey, I fell in with an old friend who perpetrated a *sell* on me and others in the cars. It is generally a religious duty to tell a good joke. It was about the time that Blondin, the rope walker, was exciting the country with his exploits at Niagara. This friend and companion told the passengers, while I was absent in another car, that I was Blondin. When I returned, I was much annoyed by people flocking about my seat, and staring at me with an uncommon gaze. I was so much annoyed by it that I went into another car. But in a few minutes in they came like so many *harpies*, filling up every vacant seat and even the passage-way, gaping at me in the same unaccountable way. At length an old couple came in and took a seat in front of me. No sooner were they seated than the old lady, turning around and raising her spectacles, peered into my face and said: "Where are you going to perform next?" "I am going to Chicago, madam," I replied. "Is you going to walk the rope there? If ye du, we am bound to see ye du it." "*Walk a rope?* Why, what do you suppose I am? I do not understand you." "Why, ain't you that feller what's bin crossing Niagara river on a rope so many times?" "No! Who said I was?" "Why, we heard of it all along back in these 'ere cars ever so many times, and we kind o' wanted to see you, ef you was the feller. Hope you arn't ashamed of it?" I saw the *sell*, and went back to my old seat in the other car, where I found my friend shaking like a man with the palsy, his face covered with a newspaper.

We stopped that night at Detroit. The next day, taking an early train for Chicago, while my friend was in the smoking car, I asked a young gentleman near me if the Hon. Stephen A. Douglas would make a speech anywhere on the way to Chicago? "Is he on the train?" asked a number of voices at once. "Well, that gentleman in the smoking car looks like him," I intimated. Off to the smoking car went two or three in hot haste, and soon returned, scattering the news like wild-fire that Hon. S. A. Douglas was on board, returning from the Senate. Others went and looked. One or two said it was not Douglas, but others were quite confident that it was; they knew him like a book. The resemblance was quite striking.

We were to take dinner at Marshal, and arrangements had been made among the passengers to call him out for a speech. Lest I should be identified in the matter, I had gone and laid down in a vacant seat, getting up just in time to be prepared for the dinner. As the train neared the station, a big lusty fellow jumped out upon the platform, as soon as the train slackened up, and cried out at the top of his big voice, "Fellow-citizens, ladies and gentlemen, I propose three cheers for Hon. Stephen A. Douglas, of Illinois. Hip, hip, hurrah!" Our stout, short friend pressed his way to the wash-room, followed by the multitude, crying, "A speech! a speech! Come, now, give us a five minutes' speech." He rushed into the wash-room and looked at me, shaking his head in a significant manner, "Sold out, Blondin; I will pay for the dinner." His Chicago friends heard of it, and used to address him as "Honorable."

CHAPTER XVIII.

RACINE.

LATE in the fall of 1857, I received an invitation to visit the church at Racine, Wisconsin, having the year previous spent a Lord's day there while on a visit among friends in that city. Having consented to do so, I closed my connection with the church at Marion, and on Christmas day arrived in Racine. After a few weeks' stay among them, they extended me a call to the pastorate. I had already found out that the church and society were in quite a divided state. The previous pastor was a resident in the city, and had a large social influence in the church and community. He had been pastor there about six years, and as in all cases, he had his special admirers; also those who were not well pleased with him, his administration and manner of preaching. This being the condition of things, he had resigned. I saw that a new pastor would have a hard time of it, and so deferred an answer to their invitation. But I consented to stay two or three months as a supply, giving the church a fair opportunity to become acquainted with me, and me an equal opportunity of finding them out, and of satisfying myself as to my duty in the case.

After the holidays were over, there were evident tokens of good manifest in the church, by the Spirit's reviving the members to a closer attachment to the Master. Mutual concessions were made, and the impenitent were being stirred up to think upon their ways. Soon the city was paying more attention to religious matters than had been the case for a long time. I began to think that the old animosities and scandal had been absorbed in the precious revival tide that seemed about to sweep over the city. It looked as if we should have a free coast and a fair breeze. But in this we were sadly mistaken. The time we had set for deciding the question of the call had come, and that right in the bloom of the revival interest. So by the earnest solicitation of friends we gave an affirmative answer, and in April went East for my family, Rev. N. F. Ravlin supplying the pulpit. On my return I went to work in all good faith, supposing that everything was amicably settled. But as soon as the ardent spirit that manifested itself in the winter began to subside, the old scandals were revived and circulated with more *vim* than ever, if possible. I thought it my duty to have some of the common reports about prominent members investigated. But others thought the better way was to let it all alone, and it would cure itself in time. I have not changed my mind on the subject since.

At a "packed meeting," the question was agitated whether the pastor should be sustained in his purifying process in the church, and a small majority voted that the scandals should be let alone. The next evening I was informed of the decision, and at once resigned. A large number of the church were dissatisfied, and in a few days called for letters to organize a new church, to be called the "Harmony Baptist Church of Racine." It was organized with fifty-two members, and procured a hall in which to worship. The Rev. N. Barrel was chosen pastor.

I was at this time really unable to preach, owing to loss of voice occasioned by the lake winds. I was advised by the physicians to remove from the lake shore. Accordingly I went to Sparta, a small village between bluffs, in the western part of the

State. Here I found a small Baptist church destitute of a pastor, and much depressed in spirit. The landlady at the hotel informed me where one of the deacons lived, and I called on him. He proved to be an old acquaintance of mine from New York. He at once suggested the appointment of a meeting. I tried to plead off on account of my health, but he insisted, and the appointment was made. Without going into all the details, I staid in Sparta seven weeks, and preached every day and evening! The Lord worked wonders in the midst of the people. I baptized eighty-two, making a clean sweep in some families—merchants, mechanics, farmers, aged and youth. I returned at the end of seven weeks, much improved by my residence away from the lake shore.

About this time, Mr. Goble, the missionary to Japan, returned to this country, and I volunteered to assist him and the Free Mission Society in raising a fund for his outfit, that he might return to that needy missionary field. In Wisconsin, and in spite of my feebleness of health, I raised nearly fifteen hundred dollars; and then went to New York State, to present the same cause to the churches.

CHAPTER XIX.

RE-SETTLEMENT AT WARSAW.

IN the course of my rounds, I stopped at Warsaw, where I had labored with such delightful harmony seventeen years before. As a result of this transient visit, the church gave me a call to re-settle with them as pastor. After duly considering the question—for a re-settlement is a more difficult question to decide than a first settlement—I consented. This was in 1859.

I found the church in an altogether different state from the one they were in when I left them for Wheatland, in 1844. But few of the old members remained, and the church was rent with unhappy dissensions, that had greatly weakened their strength and disheartened their spirit. Yet there were a number of old, staunch friends of the cause, who were unmoved by the adverse influences about them. All the ministers in the Association had been removed, either by death or settlement elsewhere, except Rev. H. B. Ewell, of Pavilion. He still "staid by the stuff;" though as pastor of that church, but little could be done, except to "strengthen the things that remained."

The year following was one of alternate fear and hope. I spent the winter in laboring with the pastors at Wyoming, at Elmira, at Brockport, at LaGrange. At Wyoming, Brother A. A. Russell was pastor. This church had often received and enjoyed the Divine Presence in the salvation of souls. At Elmira, Rev. E. F. Crane was pastor; at Brockport, Brother E. Nisbet; and at LaGrange, Brother L. Brasted.

In the midst of these revival influences, the mutterings of civil war were heard in the distance, which turned the attention of the whole community in a new channel. My second pastorate at Warsaw was not long, and was much broken into by the evangelistic labors mentioned. Still, I trust something was done in the year I was with them at this time.

CHAPTER XX.

LAGRANGE—THE WAR.

THE church at LaGrange had invited me to become their pastor, and in April I was settled with them in that capacity. No sooner had I got fairly at work, than the call of President Lincoln came over the wires for seventy-five thousand men to defend the country in its hour of peril. I at once wrote to two sons we had living in Minnesota to enlist in their country's service, urging upon them the importance of the sacrifice, and stirring their patriotism by reminding them of the Revolutionary heroes. The younger son had already enlisted, and was at Fort Snelling when the letter reached him. The elder had a family, and hesitated for a time, but afterwards entered the service, and was with Gen. Sherman in his march to the sea. He received a wound and came home to die shortly afterwards, leaving a widow with three little children. I expected my younger son had fallen with the multitude of others in the Bull Run blunder and disaster; and, although I was then at the somewhat advanced age of fifty-seven, I had resolved to take the place of my fallen boy, if the Government would accept my poor person. I wrote to the Hon. Mr. Rice, M. C. from Minnesota, asking if it was a fact that my son was killed, and telling him my determination in case he was. He showed the letter to some friend, and the War Department at once sent me recruiting orders to raise a company of cavalry in Wyoming and Genesee counties. I laid this proposition before the church where I had so recently settled. They gave their consent with a hearty good will, voting to let my family remain in the parsonage and to furnish them with a living the remainder of the year. Twenty-seven in the community enlisted in one week, many of them my own members and personal friends; and in fifteen days I had enrolled over three hundred.

We went into camp at Westfield, where the regiment was completed and afterwards mustered into the service. My men were divided up into one full company, of which I was elected captain, and part of two companies, of one of which W. G. Bentley was elected captain, and the rest went into a company of which Capt. Tozer had command. In a few days we were transferred to Washington, where we went into winter quarters. On our way to the seat of war, our regiment stopped for one or two weeks in Albany. While there, Rev. E. L. Magoon, D. D., presented me with a cavalry sabre, supposed to be of genuine Damascus steel, that had been in service in Oliver Cromwell's day. Its scabbard had long since been lost. It was presented on Sabbath evening in the First church, of which he was then pastor. The large audience-room was crowded in every part, my company occupying the front center pews. The Doctor made a thrilling speech, as he very well knows how to. I wish it was in print. The next Sunday evening, I made an address in the Pearl-street church, on the subject of Bible Distribution, at a meeting of the A. and F. B. Society. The Baptists of Albany were sound to the core on the war question.

We left the next Tuesday for the front, having received our commissions, uniforms for the men, and for the first time we went into camp in tents in Washington. To sleep on the ground under canvas, to eat without a table, made a few hang their lips and look a little watery about the eyes. It began to look a little like war, and yet we had not seen blood, nor smelt gunpowder. This first night in Washington was an exception during our stay, for we soon had things in comfortable shape; our tents were pitched in order and looked like a village; we extemporized tables and chairs, and had little sheet-iron stoves. Our provision was abundant, and, as a general rule, good: beef, pork, sugar, coffee, tea, rice and potatoes twice a week, and first-class bread all the time. We were a happy family of men for being away from home.

Our chaplain had not yet come, so I occupied his place by the request of the officers of the staff. Respect and reverence, at least outward, were shown for religion by officers and men. In a month or six weeks our chaplain arrived, and I went to his tent at my earliest convenience to bid him a hearty welcome, and to say that I had acted as volunteer chaplain in his absence. I found him quite pleasant, and assured him that anything I could do to keep him in his position would be a pleasure for me. The next day was inspection. Out he came, mounted on a fine horse, with his orderly carrying his Bible and hymn book. The boys thought this was preparing rather loftily to preach the Gospel.

Inspection was about ten o'clock in the morning. At eleven, the religious services would occur. We had a full band, the most of them being Christian men, and had up to this time done honor to themselves in aiding the worship. At the time appointed, they were in their places and played "Old Hundred" in fine strains, and then out came the chaplain, mounted, and with his orderly bringing his Bible. The congregation, rank and file, was about four hundred, including the colonel, lieutenant-colonel and, I think, all the line officers. His text was, "Endure hardness as good soldiers of Jesus Christ;" and than gave the officers what the boys called "Hail Columbia;" expressed what he should expect of them, and what they might expect of him. He then talked to the men as though they were a mean, profane set of rowdies, closing up his introductory sermon by calling on me to pray. I felt like saying: "Good Lord, deliver us!" but I didn't, out loud. The colonel in going to his quarters, said: "Well, if ever I hear him again, it will be because he can run faster than I can." The next Sabbath was a fine day, and all at service, of rank and file and all, was about eighty; the next Sabbath, only fifteen. This was the last gathering of the regiment to hear him. The men would not come out.

In March 1862, we were ordered to march to Yorktown. We left camp in the midst of a rain and snow storm. By order of the colonel, I was to have command of the camp and the sick of the regiment, he also leaving in my care the commissary stores. We then had about two hundred disabled men, the measles having had quite a march through our camp. I was ordered to muster out of service all disabled men, pronounced unfit for service by the surgeon, and to return to the Department all stores on hand. I found I had a job on my hands. Every man who had the ear-ache or a sore toe wanted to go home. Some were really sick, and would be of no service. Others were *home-sick*, and nothing could cure them but the sight of mother, wife or sweetheart. So, we took them in squads, day after day, to the War Department to be examined, and if really unfit for the service, to be discharged. It was amusing, not to say anything else, to see how lame some of them were as we started for the city, about two miles and-a-half off. Some of them had provided themselves with crutches for the occasion, who the day before could run and jump. If mustered out, they would send back their crutches to camp for the next squad.

In about four weeks I was relieved of this disagreeable command, and took such of the number as were considered able-bodied, and started for Yorktown, down the Potomac. There were many amusing incidents in the mustering-out business, previous to our departure. In the office, the mustering-out officer was a strong Catholic, a Captain ——, a most profane swearer, and always indulging his profane tongue. On one or two occasions I had gently reproved him, citing him to the regulations of the army on the subject, being positively forbidden by war-department law. During one of these little interviews, a gentleman of my acquaintance came in and addressed me as "Elder Stimson." "Why," said the captain, "what are you Elder of?" My friend replied, "He is a minister of the Baptist Church, and highly thought of. I have known him as such for twenty-five years." To which the captain replied: "Oh, what a pity! you ought to be a good Catholic, and have your sins pardoned every day, as we do." "Yes," said I, "and then swear all the rest of the time, and get drunk and fight, mixing up in all the brawls in the whisky shops." He never tried again to convert me to the "*holy* Catholic Church. As we were ready to march to Yorktown, a young

Captain Doolittle, son of Hon. J. R. Doolittle of Wisconsin, was standing with me at the door of the mansion where we had taken breakfast, when his father said to him: "Well, my son, be faithful to your duty and your country. If you fall at Yorktown, be buried there. It's sacred ground; made so by the army of the Revolution and by the presence of Washington who defeated the British." Old Senator Preston King was standing by, and with a twinkle of the eye, said: "Yes, Henry, if you find yourself dead, tell them your father wanted you buried there." This remark changed all the faces of the bystanders.

This son of Senator Doolittle was a noble specimen of a young man. A graduate of a New England college, he had given some attention to military drill, and had been commissioned captain of cavalry by President Lincoln, by special order. He had just been appointed on Gen. Schuyler Hamilton's staff, and was going down to take his place. Gen. Hamilton and his staff were ordered to the "Army of the Cumberland," where Capt. Doolittle was taken sick, and from which he came home to die, respected and beloved by all who knew him.

While we were encamped at Washington, during

the winter of 1861–1862, the greater part of our time was spent in drill in the cavalry tactics. Our colonel was detailed on a long and difficult case of court martial, so that the command devolved on the lieutenant colonel, an ambitious and austere upstart who had only a smattering of military science, and was very severely afflicted with the disease prevalent sometimes out of camp as well as in, known as "big-head." In his case it assumed a malignant type. I had been for a long time detailed on another branch of duty, and had not been as much drilled in marching as I thought I ought to be. So I got excused by the colonel and went into the drill of marching with the other officers of the regiment, under the instruction of our young lieutenant colonel, who "magnified" his office as much as ever a "onct-a-month" preacher did by "holding on" two mortal hours at a time; or ever a new-fledged deacon did by giving his elderly pastor advice as to the best method of preaching, showing him a more excellent way. As I came out of my tent one day to fall into line, with my cavalry boots all polished up, one of the officers said, "Well, Captain, you look as nice as a new pin—boots all shining and white gloves on. The gloves may possibly come back all right, but those boots won't, after Lieut. H—— nas marched you through a few puddles, as he marches us every day. I'll bet you will be willing to make an affidavit, when we come back, that the boots are made of Maryland clay, and that you will never put them on again." Our parade ground was ornamented with a number of little sink holes. I replied, "Perhaps he will march me through mud holes, but I think not, if I can get around them, and I think I can. On we went to the parade ground, marching and counter-marching for an hour or two. Finally we were all formed into line in the form of a platoon, and after "front dress," "guide right," the command came, "march." After we had marched twenty or thirty rods, I saw right in front of me, one of those puddles. I said to the captain at my side, "File to your left when we get to that mud-hole." When we came to it we filed off to right and left. Just as we were in this harmless act of self-defense—at least boot defense—the lieutenant saw us being a little out of order, and cried out, "Steady, steady, there! Close up, close up! What kind of a movement is that?" Our line was again soon formed, and on we marched to our quarters. We were halted at his tent and formed into a semi-circle, as was his formal custom, to be dismissed, when he complimented the officers for the improvement they were making in marching. He also added, "As to Captain Stimson, if at any time he comes to a mud-hole and thinks he can't go through it, if he will just speak to me, I will take him on my back and carry him over." I doffed my hat and said, smiling, "Thank you, Lieutenant Colonel, I have one objection to that. We were promised horses to ride, when we enlisted, and I should be ashamed to be seen mounted on a jackass." All the officers threw up their caps and cheered most lustily for the "old captain." Did I say all the officers? I think the lieutenant did not. In 1869 I met the colonel in Troy, New York. After making a few customary inquiries, and finding that I was then living in Kansas, he asked, "Do you ride a jackass out in that country?" I replied, "Not much."

But to return to our embarking at Washington for Yorktown. We embarked at Alexandria on board the old "North River" boat the "Knickerbocker." It was crowded to its utmost capacity. We stopped opposite Mount Vernon, and had an opportunity to visit the tomb of Washington. The next morning we found ourselves at anchor at a place called Saint Mary's, the wind blowing a gale. The commander of the boat dare not enter Chesapeake Bay at the time, as the vessel was not equal to a heavy sea. So we practiced patience forty-eight hours, waiting for the wind to go down. The first day passed pleasantly enough, especially as the colored people brought fresh plump oysters aboard and sold them for twenty-five cents a bushel. But the next day the bread and butter part of our rations was almost minus. The darkies did the best they could to relieve our wants by peddling "hoe cakes." But cold "hoe cakes" and no butter were hardly atoned for by oysters at twenty-five cents a bushel. The decks and walks of that old boat were covered from stem to stern with oyster shells, and still we were not satisfied. The Captain was better contented, as the Government was paying him seven hundred dollars a day for his boat. He looked as though he didn't care how long we lay there. It's astonishing how patient some men are, and also what an intimate connection there is between money and the exercise of this virtue of patience! Job is certainly deserving of the distinction of the "patientest man," in view of the sudden loss of his great property. It's a crowning virtue to "take joyfully the spoiling of our goods." This loss tests the nerves that connect with patience, sooner than does the loss of friends. Poor people, who have conquered themselves so as to be habitually patient, have attained to the distinction of sainthood in the true sense.

On this trip, no one officer had command of all the men. They were in squads of from twenty to one hundred. Some were new recruits from New York and Brooklyn, and belonged to the class of "hard cases" in a metropolitan sense. A young man in command of them would have about as much control over them as a child would have in conducting a tribe of Comanche Indians on a buffalo hunt. Sunday morning came and found us in this sad plight: card playing, the singing of vulgar songs, dancing, swearing—everything that was disgraceful and mean in the eyes of an American citizen. The few officers there were of us called a meeting in a side place, and proposed to have order on board in some shape. It was then proposed to appoint an officer of the day, whose duty it should be to see that things were set to rights and order restored. A suggestion was also made to have religious services at eleven o'clock. Captain

H. Doolittle was appointed "officer of the day," with two assistants; and we agreed to sustain the captain in his command. The captain put on the red sash prescribed in the army regulations, and putting on his sword walked out on the deck, and in a loud and commanding voice said: "Attention, soldiers!" All eyes were turned to see where the voice came from and who it was who spoke with accustomed authority. "It is ordered and commanded that all loud talking and all playing now cease, and that this boat now be cleaned up. At eleven o'clock we will have chapel services conducted by Captain H. K. Stimson, of the Ninth New York Cavalry; and for this purpose, I appoint Lieutenant F. and Lieutenant B. to take charge of the upper deck, and Captain M. and Sergeant V. to take command of the cabin. These officers will detail a force sufficient to see this order carried out." The appointment of these subordinate officers was all arranged beforehand, they being present at the council meeting in the corner. Soon, men were busy at work clearing up the ship, and Captain Doolittle walked the deck and through the cabin with as much dignity as General Winfield Scott. A few of the New York roughs attempted to let off some of their extra steam by making a noise, but a prompt intimation from Captain Doolittle that the first man who disobeyed the order would be put in irons, made them as still as mice. At eleven o'clock, as many as wished came into the main cabin, and I talked to them a little while from the words, "Contend earnestly for the faith once delivered to the saints." The day passed off with less turmoil than we had anticipated in the morning. When we got to "Shipping Point," where we disembarked, the green lieutenant from Brooklyn was much disturbed when he found out about the authority we had been *assuming* for the sake of order on board the boat. But it was too late to make any fuss about it. We justified ourselves on the ground of military necessity! The next Tuesday, we joined our several commands at Yorktown.

After we landed at "Shipping Point," we were invited on board the "R. S. Spaulding," an iron Government steamer, the head-quarters of Gen. Slocum. Here we remained two days, waiting for an escort to protect us in marching to the Union army, as the rebel scouts infested the wilderness between this landing and Yorktown. While staying here, I had a good chance of seeing the workings of the war system. Professing to have some regard to honesty and fair dealing, I was not a little shocked at some things I witnessed.

Near by where we lay at anchor, was a cove made from the river, in which was a large bed of oysters, containing about four acres, owned by a rebel farmer, the main source of his support for a numerous family. Our troops had waded into the water, and by feeling with the bare feet, had robbed the poor rebel of all his oysters next to the shore; and when these were all exhausted, had gone to the old man, hearing that he had two or three oyster boats hid away in his garret, and proposed to buy them at a very high price. The purchase money was some counterfeit rebel currency that a Yankee, indeed, had manufactured for such emergencies, and which could be bought at wholesale for about twenty-five cents a ten-dollar bill. It was well executed, and none but an expert could tell the difference between the two counterfeits—the counterfeit proper and the "counterfeit" of which this was a counterfeit. There was quite a trade carried on by way of disposing of this false scrip. With this worthless imitation of a worthless currency, the poor farmer was paid for his boats. In these, the soldiers launched out into the deep portions of the cove, and "hooked" all the rest of the oysters, stripping the old man of all his dependence for a living, and robbing him of his boats besides.

We called at his house and heard his story, and saw the counterfeit currency with which he had been plundered. It was sad to sit and listen to his tale of sorrow. His wife was from one of the "F. F. V.'s," and was wrought up to good fighting condition while the old gentleman related the facts of the swindle and pillage. She wished all sorts of ills on the "confounded Yankees." If she had the power, she would "poison the whole race of them, and let them lie on top of the ground to feed the turkey buzzards." I said I hoped she wouldn't do it. That this act was contrary to General McClellan's order I assured her; and that they ought to have taken a receipt for the oysters, and at some future day the United States Government would have paid the bill. This so exasperated the old lady, that I acted at once on the maxim that prudence is the better part of valor, and left the house, bidding them good-day. We found that that system of "protection" did not work to suit the rebels, or to the securing of obedience on the part of the federal army.

We had a similar case at Yorktown, within two miles of Gen. McClellan's head-quarters. Near our camp was the large plantation of an old Virginia gentleman, who owned some twenty-five slaves, all connected by blood or marriage. The old man was a staunch Confederate, and had two sons in the Southern service as officers. Being only three miles from Yorktown, he had applied for protection from "vandalism" by our men. A guard was detailed every day for that purpose, consisting of six men. The thing was looked upon as a very desirable duty on the part of the soldiers. So that, at nine o'clock in the morning, when the detail left for the plantation, there was quite a strife to see who should be selected. I had a boy who acted as cook and table waiter. When it came my turn to be officer of the day, he came and said he desired to be detailed to serve on the guard at the plantation. I consented, and Orderly Sergeant Strong so appointed him. As he was leaving for his post, I asked him why he wished to be appointed to go and stay there twenty-four hours. "Well, Captain, we can get hoe cake and milk and other nice things there, and then we can instruct them darkies in some useful lessons for their benefit." He at once fell into line and marched off.

The next morning, the old planter came into camp with a sorry face, and made complaint to the colonel that eight of his slaves had run away the night before; and he wanted the colonel to order a larger guard for that day. It so happened that our colonel did not think very highly of "abolition." He did not come into the army to fight for "niggers," but for the "Constitution." But he was willing to fight for the "niggers" in the sense of their apprehension and return to slave-owners. So, he ordered the guard doubled. But the next day, back came the old planter, with the complaint that nine more of his "chattels" had departed, leaving only an old man and woman, the parents and grandparents of six little children, on his hands to be supported. The colonel heard his doleful complaint, and sent for me. As I came into his tent, he said: "Captain, what does this mean? This gentleman says his servants have run away. Do you know anything about it?" I replied: "I am not officer of the day. I was yesterday. How should I know anything about it?" The colonel, turning to the planter, said: "Well, old man, we can't keep niggers from running away, as long as General Wool is harboring them at Fortress Monroe. —— the black cusses; the sooner you are rid of them, the better it will be for you." "Oh, no!" said the planter; "they are my main dependence. Who can ever do our labor for us?" "Set your rebel sons at work. It will do them good, and be much better for them than to be in the fort at Yorktown in this —— rebellion." The old "F. F. V." planter left the camp without saying, "Good morning, sir." The colonel ordered the officer of the day to recall the guard, and let the "rebs" take care of themselves and their "niggers." It remains to be said that, in less than eight-and-forty hours the old man's barn couldn't boast a board or his fence a picket. And it was said by the boys, that his hen-roost was as silent as a graveyard. This closed up our guarding of rebel property.

The whole talk was that a great and terrible fight was about to come off, and that at least 30,000 lives must be sacrificed on our side, not to speak of the rebel loss. The wide circulation and deepening of this horrible expectation, and the prevalence of typhoid fever, which was carrying off the men by hundreds and thousands, had then a most depressing effect on the courage of our troops. Everything looked dark and threatening to them.

General McClellan was the "Napoleon," the chief captain of the American army. To lisp a word against McClellan, was a high crime and misdemeanor. The officer who dared breathe a breath of suspicion that he was not the greatest of generals, was ordered to report at the War Department at Washington, as was the case with Gen. Hamilton, and others. This idolization of Gen. McClellan, for a time was an American mania, and will form an interesting, as well as sad chapter in the future reliable history of the great conflict, that will not be written while the generation of men now living remains. In our opinion, he attained a greater and more sudden reputation, and on a smaller capital, than any other man ever has on the American continent. The point of space he will occupy on the page of permanent history will be exceedingly fine.

The order was for us to keep at work building causeways, so as to make an easy way for retreat, in case of battle. Thus things went on for a long time, till one day Mr. Lowe went up in his balloon, accompanied with Gen. Stoneman, to take an observation of the fort at Yorktown. They had ascended about five hundred feet, when the rebels threw a small shell in nearly a line shot at the balloon, bursting within a short distance of it. This was on Friday, about four o'clock, P. M. Sunday morning at sunrise, the news was in circulation that Gen. Magruder was vacating the fort at Yorktown, and all must be in preparation for marching orders at the shortest notice. We need not detain the reader in describing what followed. Two days afterwards, a part of Joe Johnson's division of the rebel forces were overtaken at Williamsburgh, Va., and another small conflict occurred at West Point. These were only preludes to the great "Retreat" of McClellan to Harrison's Landing; a military maneuver that well entitles its author to the distinction of the "Great Retreater." If he had only turned "right about face," and made provision as rapidly for *backing down* into the rebel country, he might have anticipated Sherman in his march to the sea, by at least two years. He never ought to have fought with his *face* to the enemy. Those in front of him had nothing to fear. He was dangerous only to those in his rear, as the Union cause can abundantly testify. What a pity that the Government did not understand his tactics, and insist on his setting out on a march to the North! But then it's the fate of great men to be misunderstood. Where is General George B. McClellan?

The fact was that the Ninth New York Calvary had not, up to this time, been fully mounted or equipped. An effort had been made the winter previous to disorganize *all* the mounted troops in the army. Senator Nesmith, of California, had made a long and discouraging speech on mounted soldiers, including more ridicule than argument. Senator Sprague of Rhode Island, wanted a larger amount of artillery. These mere politicians desired to give shape to the warfare according to their "parlor" ideas. As though they knew anything of how the campaign ought to be waged! That our cause succeeded in spite of such advocates and some such generals, is a proof beyond question that it was on the side of humanity and right. The leading, practical men wanted a larger force of mounted soldiers.

But at this early day of the war, politicians not only constantly interfered with, but positively controlled the military movements of the men who were tiredly waiting to redeem their country from its thralldom. It was not a little amusing, as well as a good deal provoking, to sit in the galleries of the Senate and see what strategy and prowess these brave political heroes evinced, and with what dispatch they were going to subdue the rebellion and make "secession" bite the dust. It often made me think of that brave command that "marched up the hill, and then marched down again." These would-be "leaders" had more to do with keeping the cavalry from being mounted, and with depriving the country for a long time of the valuable aid this important arm of the service could render, than all other persons and causes put together. Of course they had in the field certain officers who were their tools. Thus the military field and the political field were co-operative in a very ridiculous, if it were not so sad a sense. The purpose of some of these "loyal" men may be discovered yet, now that the discovery will do no good.

Efforts were continually made to induce the cavalry regiment to disband and enter the infantry service. I knew of one fine cavalry regiment, the Seventh New York, called the "Black Horse Cavalry," from Troy, that was disbanded at the beginning of the war. But our men disdained to be disbanded, and insisted on being mounted and equipped. They found out that they could not be forced into any other arm of the service against their will. Another fact most patent and injurious in its influence on the spirits and discipline of the men, was the comparative ignorance of both the colonel and lieutenant-colonel, of cavalry tactics. They cut a ridiculous figure on horseback. Of course they owed their promotions to political wire-pulling. So, when we went down to Yorktown, our men consented to be armed with Austrian rifles and go as an escort to Gen. Hunter's park of artillery. When we arrived at Yorktown, the men concluded that they had finished their mission as an escort, and laid down their arms, fully resolved not to take them up, but to hold themselves ready any moment to be mounted and equipped as cavalry. In this condition of things they remained at Yorktown without drill, the most of the staff officers using all their influence and intrigue to induce the men to be transferred to the infantry.

At this juncture, I was sent to Baltimore with the wounded and prisoners from the battle of Williamsburgh, with liberty to go to Washington on a sick leave of absence for two weeks. It was also suggested by all the line officers and a few of the staff, that while in Washington I should see Secretary Stanton about our regiment, if something couldn't be done to relieve us of the embarrassment in which we found ourselves in consequence of the deadening delay. After disposing of the wounded and prisoners at Baltimore, I hastened to Washington. On reaching the War Department, Mr. Stanton informed me that at General McClellan's request, the Ninth New York Cavalry were ordered to Albany to be mustered out of service for insubordination! I was surprised, mortified, indignant, and righteously wrathy. I denied the charge then and there as utterly false. I told the honorable Secretary that the Ninth regiment was made up of the best class of volunteers the State of New York could boast. And I added, "If the country and its officials think we are not needed, we can well afford to go home. But if it is on the charge of insubordination that we are relieved, we can never go home to look in the face our wives, our children and our fellow-citizens. We enlisted as cavalry, and as such, we are willing to remain in the service of the Government, and "fight it out to the bitter end," but we do protest against being transferred into the infantry, and thus break up our organization as cavalry."

"Well, Captain Stimson, you better go to Albany and see Governor E. D. Morgan. I will give you leave of absence, and a pass to Albany. If you start this evening, you can reach Albany to-morrow by noon." "Thank you, Mr. Secretary." He ordered my pass made out, and I called on two of our members of Congress, Hon. A. Frank and Hon. R. E. Fenton, who gave me letters of introduction to Governor Morgan. The next day at ten o'clock A. M., I was in Albany and obtained an introduction to the Governor personally by an old friend, George Dawson, editor of the *Evening Journal*. I presented my pass and leave of absence, and at once made known the object of my business. He appeared as much surprised as I was on hearing it, and said, "I will telegraph at once to Mr. Lincoln. You call to-morrow morning at eleven and I will let you know the result." At the appointed hour I was admitted to the Governor's room, when he read me a copy of his telegram to Mr. Lincoln. It was as follows:

"*Mr. Lincoln, President of the United States:*

"SIR: I am informed by an officer of the Ninth regiment of New York cavalry that an order has been issued by the War Department to muster out of the service said regiment. I *hope and earnestly request* that said order may be countermanded, and if the Government cannot mount and equip said troops, call on the State of New York, through its proper executive, and it shall be done.

(Signed), E. D. MORGAN,
Governor of New York."

Mr. Lincoln replied by telegram:

"*E. D. Morgan, Governor of the State of New York:*

"SIR: The order to muster out the Ninth regiment of New York cavalry is countermanded, and the regiment will be here soon, to be equipped and mounted at the earliest possible moment.

(Signed), A. LINCOLN."

Characteristic. No red tape. Direct. Independent. Eminently sensible. Hearty. Lincoln had a clear head; but he had also what, in the old Bible language, is called "bowels," a quality just as important as judgment, or justice. He was no petrified piece of last century's wisdom, having no interest in "personal matters," as Sumner once imperiously said of himself. Lincoln had a personal interest in "personal matters," and did not try to put himself above the Almighty, who certainly interests Himself in "personal matters."

My health at this time was much impaired, having had an attack of the typhoid fever while at Yorktown; and having a leave of absence of six weeks from duty, from the Secretary of War, I went home to see my family, then residing at LaGrange, New York. It was evident to my physician, at the end of my furlough, that I was not fit for active service. So he sent on to the Department a certificate of the facts, and I was granted a leave of absence for an indefinite time. Soon after this I was taken worse, and so continued for the next eighteen months. During the time, I suffered a shock of paralysis in my entire right side, so disabling me as to prostrate my energies for the next two years, not permitting me to leave my house for that length of time, with one exception, and that to vote. I was taken in a carriage on a mattress to the polls, and returned to my dwelling to remain there all winter. The longest sickness in all my life.

During this confinement and severe suffering, a few discontented persons, who had not been personally enriched or honored by the war as they had desired, commenced a series of mean acts, accompanied with meaner invective against me, the whole amounting to the cruelest persecution, being at a time when I was wholly unable to defend myself or rebuke them. In making up my accounts in the enlistment of my company, I had intrusted the keeping of the books to two men who had joined the company, who were evidently prompted by the lofty purpose of enriching themselves out of the spoils of the war. It is believed by some that there were other individuals of the same tribe of human jackalls "in the service of their country." These two men, in company with a hotel-keeper who had quartered some of my men and the band of musicians I had employed during the time of enlistment, had conspired to have me indicted before the grand jury of the United States Court holding its session at Buffalo.

The deputy marshal called and made a service of the warrant on me. But I was unable to be moved, and so let the matter rest. These pretended patriotic gentlemen were not well suited with the leniency of the marshal who had served the warrant; and so sent off to a distant part of the State and got their man, a perfect Nero, to do their dirty, cruel work. He came into the place and stopped at the hotel above mentioned; and after getting well whiskyed-up, he got an old coop of a hack, and two rowdy assistants to help him secure his prey. Up they came to my residence, and bolted in with all the courage of grenadiers, as if to arrest some monster guilty of sedition and murder. With great pomp and show of authority, he made known the object of his visitation. I was in bed, where I had been for months. I was not dressed, and had not been for a long time.

My wife and children were all amazement at this strange manner of address to a sick and, as they supposed, dying husband and father. They of course knew not what to say or do. I politely suggested that I would be glad to send into the village for friends to assist me. "No," he replied; "I can give you all the assistance you need. I will have you in Albany to-morrow." My wife said: "Why, sir, the man is not able to be moved; he has not been out of his room for weeks. I would as soon think of moving a dead man." "Can't help it, madam; he must go alive if he can, and if not, dead." So I was dressed and hurried into his rickety old hack, and driven to the depot.

At Batavia, we were obliged to wait three or four hours to make connection. The news was soon circulated that I was at the depot under arrest by the United States Marshal, and the people flocked in to see me and proposed to become bail for my appearance at Court. He said he did not know what the bail would be, and that he could not and would not consent. Neither would he allow me to go to a friend's house, near the depot, and stay while we were waiting for the train. "No, sir." A friend then asked him if he would furnish me with a sleeping-car berth? He said he could not do it. The friend then handed him the money to pay for a berth, and he took it in my presence. As soon as the train arrived, I was hurried into a crowded car, and seated with the marshal and two miserable drunken rowdies of the baser sort. I said, "Marshal, can't you get me a sleeping-car?" "When we get to Rochester, I may, possibly; but I can't now." It was now past ten o'clock at night, and I was much exhausted by the fatigue of waiting so long and the excitement.

At Rochester, he secured the berth. The night was cold, and I suffered all the way from the constant opening and shutting of the doors. A little after daylight, we arrived at Albany. He procured a carriage, and then asked me if I would like breakfast before he took me to prison. "Yes," I replied; "and I have friends in the city whom I would like to see." "*Friends!* Who in —— are your friends here?" I replied, "All my friends are not in that bad place." "Well, I will take you to a hotel to get breakfast, and then we will see about *friends*." We halted at a low, third-class house, and I was helped up stairs and laid on a sofa. I asked the porter to have the clerk call up where I was. He soon came, and I asked him to write a couple of short notes for me, as I was unable to write for myself. He wrote the following:

"*Hon. George Dawson:*

"DEAR SIR:—I am here at the —— Hotel, under an arrest by the United States Marshal. Will you call on me soon, and oblige,

"Yours in bonds,

H. K. STIMSON."

A similar one was also sent to Rev. J. D. Fulton, D.D. A boy was dispatched to carry them to their respective addresses. While I was sipping my coffee, and attempting to swallow a little breakfast brought up by a waiter, in came the "friends" addressed.

They both exclaimed as they entered: "Why Stimson, what has brought you here? we supposed you were dead, or near to it." I replied: "Not dead, and the way I came here, was by the force of the United States Marshal." At this moment he came in, and seeing Mr. Dawson sitting in front of me and holding my hand, doffed his hat and stammered out: "Good m-orn-ing, Mr. Dawson." Mr. Dawson at this arose from his seat, and said to the marshal: "Why, what in the name of common sense have you brought this sick and dying man here for? I would like to know." Mr. Fulton began by asking him: "Are you human?"

The marshal apologized, and appealed to me if he had not treated me well, and like a gentleman? If he had not secured a sleeping-car and a carriage? To which I answered: "As to the sleeping-car, a friend of mine in Batavia gave you the money with which to pay for it; as to the 'carriage,' I wish these gentlemen could see it, I think somebody in the 'hen business' would like to have it." The fact was, he had secured his appointment through the influence of Mr. Dawson, and now began to realize that his poor, sick prisoner had friends away here in Albany three hundred miles from home, whom he wished he did not know at all. He became exceeding clever to me, and would do anything for me.

Mr. Dawson said to him: "Well, go and find out what the bail will be and see that it is forthcoming." and Fulton said (how characteristic): "I will take him to my house, and if he isn't there when you come, then take myself and wife." He ordered a carriage, and soon I was in his pleasant home, under the kind, Christian nursing of his family. Soon a physician was sent for, and I was safely out of the protecting power of this specimen of a human brute, called a marshal. Mr. Dawson and his partner in business became my bail, and after a two weeks' rest, I was sent home in company with kind friends who volunteered their gratefully received services.

Two of the first lawyers in Western New York volunteered to defend me—Hon. L. W. Thayer of Warsaw, and the Hon. Sanford Church, of Albion, ex-Lieutenant-Governor of New York. At the next term of the United States Court at Rochester, the case was called up. Mr. Church addressed the Court by saying, among other similar things, that, "this case was an unheard-of transaction in civilized prosecution, legal or military." Hon. Mr. Thayer followed, by characterizing the whole affair, from beginning to end, as "unworthy of the cognizance of any Court," and moved that the Court enter a *nolle prosequi*. The Court so ordered.

The two men who had instituted these proceedings against me, were men to whom I had shown especial favor, and had them detailed for less severe service than the common soldiers. Yet they were the first to stimulate insubordination, and to embarrass me in my control of the company. They were clamorous for their discharge; but I was not able to relieve them from the obligations that they had voluntarily assumed—hence their venom. One of them, who had acted as my company clerk, and plotted my ruin, has since been found guilty of forgery. I am not able to say what has become of him. I still live to pity him, and those that so cruelly conspired with him against me.

Conscious of my innocence, I did not fear the result; yet, I was greatly distressed that I should be even charged with wrong doing; and being dragged away to prison is not very agreeable. There was, however, one pleasant feature in it, for it discovered to me friends whose sympathy and friendship is, and will be so long as I shall live, very sweet to me; and I want just here to leave this testimony of my gratitude to my comrades and brother officers in the Ninth New York Cavalry. Their letters came pouring in to the officers of the court, assuring them of my innocence, and were of great service to me. Through it all the Lord led me; surely "He that is for me is more than they that be against me."

During my long sickness, I had no way of making money, and I soon consumed what I had. I could not relieve my mind of anxiety concerning food and raiment, the means of providing which for my family I had none, except what was furnished by liberal friends of all denominations, added to what little my daughter could make by teaching a small district school. But we did not come to want. The church at LaGrange, nine miles off, time and again came down in force, and brought us supplies of provisions and money, and, what was worth more than these, showed a deep, fraternal love for us which greatly relieved the tedium of painful and protracted sickness.

I have read the manuscript of Captain Stimson, concerning his connection with the Ninth New York Cavalry, and the facts, as he states them, are known to me to be true. W. G. BENTLEY.

ST. LOUIS, February 7, 1874.

CHAPTER XXI.

HO, FOR KANSAS!

MRS. STIMSON had a brother residing in Kansas, who solicited us to come to this new State, where he thought there would be more advantages for our children in the way of securing positions in life, than in the older States. My physician's advice to seek some milder climate as the last hope of recovery, had already prepared us to listen favorably to the Kansas call—not church, but individual. We had a small place on which we were living, but there was an incumbrance on it that certainly we had no very bright hope of ever removing, under the circumstances of protracted illness and no income. After weighing the *pros* and *cons*, we concluded to join the army of emigrants for the far-off West, I expecting to find a grave in a short time among strangers. We left New York in April, 1864. I could not walk at the time without the aid of crutches.

We stopped in Kinderhook, Michigan, to visit a dear daughter, with whom we spent two weeks. Here I attempted to preach for the first time in nearly two years. This duty, if such it could be called, I discharged sitting in a chair. I could not stand in one position long enough to read the Scripture. We bade adieu to the dear ones in Michigan, and after a long and tedious journey through Missouri—the war at the time still raging and keeping all passengers in a state of constant fear—we at length arrived at Leavenworth, where our youngest son was taken sick, detaining us a week at the hotel, the landlord showing us the kindest attention. Here I had my first lesson of Kansas business matters.

I had found out that there was no way of going to the Neosho valley but by the round-about one of staging it to Topeka, and then across the country in a little two-horse hack, over a trackless prairie to Burlington, and at exorbitant prices all the way. While we were waiting for the recovery of the boy, some one suggested that our cheapest way would be to purchase an outfit of our own; that a pony team and a light wagon could take us and baggage with ease, and that the concern would sell at any time for about what it cost. So I began to look about for a bargain of the kind. While sitting in the office of the hotel one day, a decently dressed young man stepped up to me (wholly accidental—so many interesting things are accidental in Kansas) and asked me if I didn't wish to procure a team to go into the country? I told him I did, if I could get one at a reasonable price. He said he had a good span of ponies and a light wagon, and invited me to go with him to the feed stable and see them. So I took my crutch and limped off with him to the stable, some three or four blocks. He brought them out and hitched them to his wagon. I saw that they were larger and better than the average run of ponies. After we had driven around town for a while, mostly on the back streets, I suggested that he drive down one of the main business streets, and to the hotel. He said the "ponies were afraid of stages and covered wagons, not being used to them, and that we had gone far enough for me to judge." "Well, I like their movement; what is your price for the outfit?" "Well, I will tell you, stranger: I am in a hurry to go back to Illinois; my father is not expected to live; I will take two hundred dollars for the whole 'shebang.' The

wagon is a little worn, but the harness is new. I paid forty dollars for it last week." I saw it was a bargain, and just what I wanted. "Well, young man, you drive it to the 'Michigan House,' and I will take it." "Stranger, as I have told you, I don't like to drive them on the main streets; they are a little *skeery*." "Let me have the reins, then. I'll risk them. I never saw a horse yet I couldn't manage some way." But he objected, and put the team in the stable, and I hobbled back to the hotel, thinking what strange customs they had in Leavenworth, and what a singular breed of ponies.

He had not forgotten to say, however, that he would be around in the evening and close the trade, if I said so. I told my landlord what a fine rig I had found, and that the ponies were shy of the main streets. He replied, "Mr. Stimson, you will have to be on your guard against thieves. If that team and wagon are as you describe them, and can be had for two hundred dollars, you may be sure the fellow has not come honestly by them. I will go over and look at them." In less than thirty minutes he came back, saying, "Your team has just been called for by two men from Missouri. They have been after the fellow the last ten days. They were stolen in Clay County, Missouri. They have got the team, but the thief is minus." The ponies had got over their front-street fright. There are many plausible thieves in Kansas. The climate, or soil, or both—or something—seems to promote this quality of *plausibility* in all the somewhat numerous tribes of thieves in this promising, ambitious and destined commonwealth. From what high or low source they may have caught the contagion, the deponent saith not. But a smoother set of pioneer thieves never existed. They are so smooth that they can't be caught; and if they are caught, they are so smooth they can't be hung. But, thank God, they are dying out. That's the only hope.

We took stage for Topeka, and after a long day's ride, we were set down in that capital of the new commonwealth. The next morning, at three o'clock, all five of us were crammed into the little seven-by-nine hack, without having had any breakfast. The old rickety concern, we felt, might fly to pieces any moment. At eleven o'clock, we were set down to our breakfast of beans and flies, and it was hard telling which outnumbered the other. But we found good fare where we stopped for the night, at least it seemed so then. The next morning, we arrived at the county seat of Coffey County, the humdrum of a place we had had such glowing accounts of, destined to be a *live*, *wealthy*, *business*, *manufacturing*, *commercial*, *literary*, *political* and *religious* center. Kansas is a very prolific State in great towns. Cities germinate and grow, prospectively at least (a very slight qualification), with the utmost spontaneity and rapidity on Kansas soil. In some instances, the wild grass is not killed out of the avenues before the city attains its greatest dimensions. There is much in a name sometimes, as well as in the soil and climate. There are no villages or towns in Kansas. The use of the more expansive name of "city" may account in part for the marvelous dimensions of some of our places. This and the broad-gauged term "avenue," confer a metropolitan flavor most conducive to growth, prospectively at least. The name "Prairie City" may serve to elucidate our idea to some of our Kansas readers.

I wish I could describe my first impressions, and those of my family as we peered out of the woods, after crossing the Whistler's ford. "There," said the stage driver, "is the town of Hampden. That box house is where the printer lives, and that is the office on the high ground; and that long low building is the court house, and those logs piled up there is a blacksmith shop, and that is the carriage maker's place of business." It consisted of a shanty for hens, and a small barn. I believe I have catalogued the town; if not, Colonel F. W. Potter will correct me. As the girls put their heads out of the stage and took a view of their new home, I thought I heard something like a sigh. I don't think it was a laugh. They were speechless.

I stopped at the printer's, and found our relatives glad to see us, that is, they said so. And we settled in the city of Hampden, county seat of Coffey, Neosho Valley, Kansas. The valley, as a valley, is all right. That still remains, and is a rich farming country, destined some day to be highly cultivated; but all independent of Hampden as a county seat. I soon saw that the political cast of the place was democratic, and that nothing but pure democracy would be tolerated as a general thing. Negers were to have no sympathy, and abolitionists must keep mum. The war was a failure, Lincoln was a babboon, George B. McClellan was to be the next president, and the man who denied it was a fool and a knave. Such was the political and moral complexion—for the two are similar in such a case— of the city of Hampden.

I did once venture cautiously to express my humble opinion on certain great questions of humanity and national policy, and was at once chided as being out of order at the centre of business; "it would not do at the county seat." If a man wanted to talk that way, he could cross "Whistler's ford" and relieve his mind, but he could not do so and remain in "Hampden, county seat of Coffey."

There was one slight drawback, Hampden was a very dry place. Water could be had by going to the river, or at Denicke's well. It seldom came down from above, and it could not be obtained every time by any means, by digging. Water was worth something at the "city of Hampden, county seat of Coffey." Water being an important element in my religious, moral and sanitary creed, and free-thinking and free-speaking a cardinal right in my political creed, I concluded it was best for me to leave "Hampden, county seat of Coffey." Some thought we had "missed it." They were correct. We "missed" about four hundred dollars, all of our this-world's property, which we had spent in the flourishing city of "Hampden, county seat of Coffey." Good-by, "Hampden!" may there never be your equal this side the millennium. I am sure there will not be afterwards.

CHAPTER XXII.

A KANSAS "FIELD."

THE A. B. H. M. Society had sent me a commission as their missionary for the Neosho Valley, with our head-quarters at Humboldt, Allen County. Our instructions were to explore the whole valley from Council Grove to the Indian country. In October, we moved to Humboldt.

My health had so far improved that I was able to preach once a day on the Sabbath, and occasionally twice, and ride in a buggy from twenty to forty miles a day. There were then no bridges. The people had not at that early day invented county bonds. The accommodation for travelers was not equal to what I had seen in some parts of the United States. I can't speak for Europe. Altogether,—including the extent of my field, brought to mind past infirmities and the permanent hold disease had on me, by exposure to storms, by fording of the streams, and often by swimming the ponies and carriage, and by the exactions of the Society calling for just so much labor, whether it was entirely practicable or not,—I was soon brought nearly down to my sick self again. I must say, too, that the compensation I received for these labors was not such as to keep a man's spirit in an undue state of exhilaration, taking into account the fact of a large family and also the fact of war prices. For example, I paid ten dollars for a hundred weight of flour, thirty-five cents a pound for bacon, fifty cents a pound for coffee, two dollars and fifty cents a pound for tea, and for other things in the same proportion. We had lived all winter in a room eight-by-fourteen feet. We were compelled to set our table and chairs out of doors to make room to go to bed. For this, including the out-door room, I paid fourteen dollars a month rent. These every-day facts were looked at in the light of wealthy Eastern churches, with good comfortable parsonages, the members there not taking the deepest interest in the pioneer work and workers.

[Talk about heroism! If you can find those who endured hardships more manfully, who crucified the flesh more heroically or who labored more abundantly and with a more Christly spirit than some—we do not say all—of these early pioneers in the employ of the Home Mission Society, you may deny the propriety of our language when we call them heroes, who belonged to an heroic age. Their fields were sometimes as extensive as half a dozen Methodist "circuits." They were often away from home twice as long at a time as the ordinary "circuit rider." The Methodist system is substantially one of "circuits," even the pastors staying in a place but for a limited time. So that the early "circuit rider" was not cut off from the sympathy of the Church at its great centers of influence. Of course he endured hardships. Let no one undervalue his work or his personal character. But much depends on how hardships are encountered. He encountered them backed up by the whole influence of a powerful organization that was making and had always made a chief glory of abounding in his very kind of labor; that considered itself especially called of God to a pioneer work. And then his work was personally reviewed every year by his bishop, and his promotion was in proportion to his self-denial and labors. It is difficult to conceive of a more congenial atmosphere in which to perform early missionary labor, than that which continually surrounded the pioneer Methodist "circuit rider." The case of the appointee of the Home Mission Society of the Baptist Church was quite different. He was, in a measure and to a greater degree, isolated. His work could not be adequately represented to "those in authority" who seldom or never visited the field in person, and often it was uncharitably compared with work done far away and under totally different circumstances. The spirit of the Church then and now is more properly spoken of as a *foreign* missionary spirit. The home missionary servant was often well-nigh forgotten, and his toils were comparatively unappreciated, while the appointee of the Missionary Union was kept in the warmest remembrance and his work most highly prized. The sympathy felt for him was active, practical and cordial. So that we believe the statement correct, that of all men who helped and are helping to subdue this Great West to the sway of Messiah, the comparatively isolated appointees of the A. B. H. M. Society are worthiest of the name of heroes.—Ed.]

I think, if I had my life to live over, I would do more for the home missions than ever I have done. I would labor more to bring the wealthy men and churches of the denomination into deeper sympathy with the men and families on the frontier who are enduring well-nigh all things, in some cases, for the Master's sake. But, thank God, these inconveniences and privations did not deprive us of His power at Humboldt. Amidst the clangor of war and the constant fear of the cruel "bushwhacker," which was only another name for murderer and plunderer, and whose foul deeds were being perpetrated nearly every day all about us, the Spirit was given and souls were converted to Jesus and became obedient to the faith. The place had been sacked twice and burned once by rebel Missourians. It was now a military post, with altogether too small a protection to the remaining citizens, what few there were of soldiers being much given to drinking. With two saloons in full blast every day, Sunday not excepted, and the click of the billiard-balls to be heard at all hours of the day and night, I made an attempt to preach a free and full Gospel to the few who came and listened. The larger part of the congregation was made up of troops from the post. Among them, I found a young man who was a Christian and took part in the devotions. He made no special claim of talents, but I soon saw that he had them; and I learned from the officers that he had been ordained, and preached yet occasionally.

Coming to Kansas with his father's family, consisting of two or three brothers, he told them on the breaking out of the war that they ought to have a representative in the army of the country, and if no one of the others would be that representative, he should be himself. He enlisted in the cavalry service. I at once encouraged him to engage again in the ministry, but he declined, as he said he did not intend to preach until he had secured an education. I made an effort to get him a discharge from the army for that purpose; but soon peace was declared, and he arranged his affairs and spent some time at our State University at Lawrence, and then completed his course in the Theological Seminary at Chicago, with great credit to himself and instructors. He is now one of the honored and beloved ministers of the State. No church need be ashamed of the Rev. R. P. Evans, pastor at Olathe.

God poured out His Spirit at Humboldt in the midst of all the depressing and distracting influences at work. The place was very wicked. No sooner were backsliders reclaimed and sinners alarmed, than it seemed as if all the emissaries of the pit of perdition were sent there on a special embassy of ruin. But truth triumphed, and our Jesus conquered as He rode on "mighty to save." No opposition could stop the work. Profane swearing, drunkenness, lewdness, lying, thieving—all had to give way to the Spirit's work and the power of God in answer to prayer. The place we held our meetings in was crowded every evening, and in the day-time Christians of all denominations would come together for supplication and exhortation. God was with us in mighty power.

Soon, there was a disposition on the part of a number of the converts to follow the Master in the ordinance of baptism. The officers at the post gave us the use of a tent which was spread at the water's edge for the accommodation of the female candidates. On the Lord's day, I baptized fourteen—all adults. Thus the work went on to the praise of Christ.

The man who kept the main saloon and billiard-tables of the place, was the son of a "hard-shell" Baptist of southern Illinois; and among the officers who frequented his place, was Capt. Kendall, who had been well brought up, a man of fine abilities and education, but who had given himself over to drinking and gambling. A young man, not a Christian, had conceived the idea of making a donation to the "poor missionary;" and in carrying out his idea, he called at the different places of resort, as well as business. This saloon was visited, among the other places. There he found Captain Kendall, playing billiards. The young man stepped up to the bar, and handed his paper to Mr. Saloon-keeper. He at once rejected it, with an oath! "No, not a —— cent. My father is a Baptist minister, and has preached these forty years and never received a dollar for it, and is a man well off, with a good farm; and I don't believe in these missionary Baptists, nor their protracted meetings. I won't give 'nary red.' Let them go to work, like honest folks." Captain Kendall, hearing this reply of Mr. Saloon-keeper, said: "Well, your father must have been a —— old fool, and his son is a chip off of the old block. Here, John, put me down for fifty dollars; and call at my tent to-morrow, and I will pay it."

A donation day was appointed. The largest place in town was jammed, all the officers and boys in blue vieing with each other to see who should do the most. I received over two hundred dollars. It was a timely gift, as all things were at war prices. Spring had come, and we were obliged to get out of our little "seven-by-nine" room where we had wintered and suffered. As there was no vacant house in Humboldt, a kind-hearted brother at Iola offered us a part of his house as a gratuity, and as this was in our field, we of course took with delight his offer and moved. We have all felt ourselves under great obligations to Brother and Sister Weller, of Iola, for their Christian sympathy and generosity.

CHAPTER XXIII.

CLOSING THE WAR IN MISSOURI.

DURING this spring the war came nominally to a close, and yet all along the borders of Kansas and Missouri the skulking "bushwhackers" were committing fearful depredations. Men ran great hazards in venturing out to any distance from the settlements. An old gentleman, with his wife—friends and neighbors of ours from New York—had come into the country to visit his children, and was taken sick and died. The widow requested me to accompany her with the corpse back to her old home in New York. I consented, and we had got as far as St. Louis and there I met our brother Jesse Stone, of Topeka, on his way to Boston. He was going through Rochester, and would take my place, giving me the privilege of attending our Anniversaries at St. Louis, which were then in progress. At the close of the meeting, the Missouri Pacific road had tendered free passes to all members of the convention to the end of the line, then at Warrensburgh, Missouri. A large number of the Eastern brethren accepted the proffer, among them Rev. William Michels, D.D., of New York City, U. D. Ward, Esq., of New York City, Rev. S. Graves, D.D., of Norwich, Connecticut. Some of the number were going through to Kansas. As soon as we were well under way, stories were put in circulation about the sad havoc the guerrillas were making in Missouri, so that at Warrensburgh they all concluded to return by the next train. But as my home was in Kansas, I must go on. We arrived in Warrensburgh about nine in the evening. The stage left at ten. An old man and myself were all the passengers to take the stage for Independence, Mo., about one hundred miles. The driver had a bottle of whisky, and was quite "tight" to begin with. The night was exceedingly dark. The road ran most of the way through the prairie.

As the stage moved out of town, the driver halted and took on a boon companion, of like disposition and condition with himself, being under the delusive influence of bad whisky. They sang bad songs, and used bad language without stint. After traveling five or six miles, we met the incoming stage with a full load of passengers. It stopped long enough to convey the news of the massacre at Holden of several of its citizens. We were to change horses at Holden. I saw this sad tale excited my aged companion in travel, now almost *travail*, and he suggested for us to return to Warrensburgh, and get a conveyance to take us through by daylight. But I said; "No, that will not benefit us by way of protection from guerrillas." So on we went in the dark.

Between midnight and one o'clock, the coach stopped, and I heard the driver say: "We are out of the road; here, you hold the lines, while I get off and look for it." After a long reconnoissance he came back, and reported he could not find it. The old gentleman and myself had got out of the coach, and observed that the man he had left to hold the team, was sound asleep on the box. I asked of the driver: "Where did you leave the road-track?" He replied, with an oath, that he didn't know. I asked him to let me have the coach lamp and I would go and see if I could discover it. As I took the lamp, the old gentleman opened the stage door and took his satchel out. So we started off together. And a fruitless search it was. We came back to find both men in a drunken sleep in the stage, occupying the seats, one of them having taken my satchel and shawl for pillow and covering. I went to the boot of the coach, and got the bottle of whisky and emptied it on the ground, and then threw the bottle as far as I could out on the prairie. I set the lamp in its socket, and waited for day. Nothing could be seen but the dim horizon in the distance. Not a star shone through the thick clouds that made the night so densely dark.

I saw all this time that my aged friend was much excited, though he said but little. As daylight broke the spell of darkness, I could discover in the distance, men walking back and forth with glistening muskets. It was not light enough for me to see the dress of the men. The question that arose to me, and well nigh choked me was: "Is the color grey or blue?" I soon saw that four of them were approaching us, and I called up the boys and told them to hitch up, as we wanted to be moving. As the men neared us, I saw that they were soldiers in BLUE! How blessed was that blue! I felt better, as well as I can remember. The fact was, this drunken driver had been out on a waste prairie four or five miles, and these were the United States troops on the lookout for the raiders on Holden. They saw us by our stage light, and had kept us in view for hours, expecting that the bushwhackers would make their appearance, and pounce upon us as their prey. The sergeant of the guard directed us to the main road, and at eight o'clock we arrived at Holden. We were due there at four o'clock, A. M. The town was panic struck. Six of her citizens had been murdered in open daylight, and in cold blood, by a band of lawless devils in human shape, who, although the war was closed, were pushing their fiendish work of death for plunder's sake.

I informed the stage agent of the conduct of his driver, and went before a notary public and made affidavit to the facts as above related. The hotel was demoralized and broken up by the murders and subsequent panic, so that no breakfast could be obtained there. A stranger informed us that just out of town, on the stage road, was a boarding house where we could get something to eat. So my old companion and myself asked the stage agent if he would have it stop for us at the place. "Well," said he, "I am not certain that the stage will go to-day, as the military will not furnish any guard. You do not want to go without protection, do you?" There were some railroad contractors that had been waiting for the stage ever since it was due in the very early morning, and were very anxious to get to their men on the job, six or eight miles ahead. They said they "*must go.*" Railroads are generally built by men who talk in that way. They could defend themselves "a little." One of them, turning to me, said, "Stranger, have you any revolver?" and to my companion: "Old man, have?" I told them I had none. "Well, here is one I will lend you as long as we are together." I thanked him and took it. The old gentleman said, "I should not know how to use one if I had it; I never shot a gun in my life." "Well, said I, "call for us at the small house on the hill, and we will walk along." The lady gave us corn cake and bacon, and bitter coffee, made worse with sorghum. I saw the old gentleman kept his satchel in his hand all the time, and after our meal he said, "I will walk along and get in when you come up."

An overgrown specimen of a "puke," who seemed to be general hanger-on about the house, said, "If you have got anything valuable with you, you had better leave it with me, for I doubt if you ever get to Pleasant Hill alive, if you don't have any escort there. Them —— bushwhackers are in the bush between here and that place." I saw this excited the old man afresh. As we walked along, and as soon as we were out of hearing of this individual, who had all the latent symptoms of a bushwhacker himself, my companion said, "I suppose you are a good, honest man, and I will tell you my condition. It is this. I am going to Kansas to see my sons at Emporia, or near there, and I am carrying them money to buy land with. I have got *twenty thousand* dollars in this satchel. I live in Pennsylvania, in Crawford County. I am a member of the Presbyterian church, and I hope, a Christian. I had no thoughts of any such trouble as this. If I had, I never would have started. I have never been away from home much. I thought I would hide the money somewhere in the woods, and then if I could, go to see my children." The tears came in the old man's eyes as he spoke. I said, "Now, this is your best policy. Keep quiet. Act careless about your money. Treat your valise as though there was nothing in it. Throw it down anywhere. Keep your eye on it, but appear unconcerned about it. Don't get excited when men talk. That man saw you were anxious about something, where we took breakfast."

Up came the stage with the railroad contractors and one lady aboard. The old man threw in his rubber cloth satchel, and on we went. One of the passengers informed us that our greatest danger was about five miles on. Then we would be out of harm's way until at the Osage River, a few miles this side of Independence; but the probabilities were that we should have an escort of cavalry from Pleasant Hill to Independence. We arrived at the former place about two P. M., and found that the troops stationed there had just returned from a long and weary scout for bushwhackers. They were wearied out, horses and all. The captain of the guard said he could not send a protection until the next day; but finally said, "If the men will volunteer, I will consent." And the old man said, "I will pay them something." So the bugle sounded a "call," and up came the men. He made known to the soldiers the facts, and added that some of the gentlemen had promised them a present if they would go to the crossing of the Osage River. The old gentleman said, "Yes, I will give each man a dollar that will go," and twelve volunteered. We were safely escorted to the river, and before dark, we were in the city of Independence. The railroad was completed from there to Kansas City. On this of course we gratefully, and with much relief, rode into the "village at the mouth of the Kaw." Here my old Pennite concluded to stay until the next Monday morning. He proposed to give me twenty dollars for aiding him. I thanked him No, I didn't wish to be compensated for doing right and using my wits. I went on to Lawrence to spend the Lord's day.

Soon after returning home, the Kansas State Convention of Baptists was to hold its third annual meeting in Paola, June, 1865. Paola had been a military post during the war, and long barracks had been constructed for the quartering of the troops. The commanding officer of the post had given the use of these buildings to the Convention, and had arranged them as well as he could for the holding of the meetings. There was a good representation of officers and men in the meetings. The delegates of ministers and others from the State were fully as numerous as could be expected. Rev. J. B. Taylor, appointed to preach the opening sermon, was considered, doctrinally speaking, of the "hard-shell" stamp. If there were ever any doubts entertained before of the propriety of the epithet as applied to him, they were all effectually scattered by this sermon. It was antinomian "hard-shellism" hardened. The Association received it kindly, charitably, and in a way that spoke volumes for their common sense, by letting it pass without note or comment. That brother's effort was destined of course from all eternity to fall upon ears that were dull of hearing, and so to drop into well-earned oblivion. Inconsistency is woven into the very texture of the lives of men, individually as well as into that more complex life of associated men—mankind. That in this day of steam and electricity and personal achievement, any one could hold to such ideas as those mildly called "hard-shell," belonging only to the "sleepy hollow" age of the world, if to any, is one of those phenomena that prove beyond controversy that the "fall" made men liable to become fools as well as knaves.

All was moving on with the best of feeling, until the last day of Convention, when the committee on the state of the country reported a series of resolutions, among which was one on the death of President Lincoln, expressed in terms of lamentation, and adulation of him as a Christian President, etc. The room was crowded with United States officers and soldiers, as well as of "citizens." No sooner had the resolutions been read, than the "hyper" brother arose and moved that "so much of the resolutions as referred to Mr. Lincoln as a Christian President be stricken out;" and then went on to make a most violent speech, denouncing the President for being in a theatre when he was assassinated. He ought to have taken it into account that he was "foreordained" to have gone there! You might as well undertake to put out powder when it is once ignited, as to have kept that audience, so largely made up of the "boys in blue," still. I being in the chair, called, "Order! Order!" But more than a dozen men were making efforts to get their hands on him. One had his bowie-knife drawn, to kill him on the spot. But two brethren, Major H. A. Dean and Sergeant R. P. Evans,* interfered, and saved the man from sudden death at the hands of United States soldiers. He was spirited away and secreted until night, when he left for his home in Lyon County. The resolutions were passed without opposition, except as above noted.

---

*Now, Rev. R. P. Evans, of Olathe.

I have related this unhappy affair, simply because great injustice has been done the brethren who were prominent in the Convention, by charging them with being the instigators of intended violence to the person of Rev. J. B. Taylor. To me, it was said, in the city of New York, that "I, as the presiding officer of the body, and others connected with me, put the officers and men up to it." All present at the time know that I tried to keep the meeting in order. I but speak for the brethren of the convention, when I say that the charge is false.

We then had a noble band of brethren in this new State. We were far from each other. Our ministerial meetings were few and far between. The churches were small and poor. There were but one or two finished Baptist meeting-houses in the State—one at Atchison and one at Manhattan, I believe. There was a frame up at Neosho Rapids. Leavenworth, Lawrence, Topeka, Junction City, Paola, Fort Scott, Ottawa, Emporia—not a Baptist church edifice in any of them, and all growing; towns of importance in anticipation, with all the elements to make them fulfill the expectation.

I am astonished at the advance made by us, in

every respect. Our Sunday school system was in a disorganized condition. The schools were feeble, poorly organized and irregular in attendance. We had a few young ministers of education and ability. Now, we have them by scores; and the above-named towns are supplied with able men, and with church buildings that are ornaments to their respective cities. The summer and autumn of 1865 marks a new era in the history of the churches in Kansas. The war having come to a close, Christian men began to think of doing something for the Master. Quite a number of the men who had gone into the war and a few of the ministers returned to their homes, to preach Christ and serve the churches. While they thanked Him for victories in the field, they thanked Him still more for the victories of the Cross over sin and depravity. Immigration came in like a flood, and towns that had been in a stand-still condition during the nation's conflict, sprang into new life. God was in Kansas, notwithstanding some "jayhawking" citizens.

CHAPTER XXIV.

"OTTAWA UNIVERSITY" AND LEAVENWORTH.

IN October, 1865, the trustees of the Ottawa "University"—Rochester and Harvard forgive the mark!—invited me to move to that new "city," and take an agency of the institution, on a salary of one thousand dollars per year, and traveling expenses paid. I consented to do so, and at an early day moved my family to the place, and commenced my work as I was directed by the chairman and secretary of the board. The Baptist church at Leavenworth had begun to build an edifice, and the pastor, Reverend Winfield Scott, invited me to be present at the laying of the corner-stone; and, by the consent of the board, I went. Soon after, Mr. Scott wrote the board, asking them to permit me to enter their service as agent to collect funds for the carrying on of their great project. Consent was given; and I went East for that object, and spent the spring and summer of

1866 in the New England States and New York. I first stopped in Quincy, Illinois, collecting about two hundred dollars. Next, in Chicago, I raised the same amount. In Coldwater, Michigan, I raised one hundred and thirty-four dollars. I then went to New York, Boston, Hartford, Providence and the lesser towns and cities, and returned to Ottawa, having been absent from my family from the ninth of February to the eighth of October. During this time I was sick in New York City six weeks, but able a part of the time to supply some of the vacant pulpits, the pastors being away on their summer vacations, the compensation for such services to be applied to the church in Leavenworth towards their building fund. I went to New London, Connecticut, and spent ten days with an old fellow-laborer, Rev. Jabez Swan, whom I had not seen in thirty years, and with him went to the Stonington Union Association, and heard him preach to the hosts of New England Baptists. It was "a feast of fat things" to hear him expound the Word of God and describe the revivals he had witnessed in that old Association, and what he had accomplished in his early pastoral work in New York and other States. I saw that a few of the younger brethren in the ministry thought he was a little too rough in his manner of address. But the large majority of these representatives of the New England churches had the greatest faith in his integrity and piety. Thousands upon thousands all over the land were his epistles known and read of all men. Many of them were present in this meeting. In his first pastorate in New London he had, by his plain, truthful dealing with error, so exasperated the Universalists that they, in their hot zeal, had gone on and built an expensive church, going far beyond their means, hoping blindly to be able to meet their coming liabilities. When this new and elegant house was dedicated, many of Swan's brethren said, if he had been a little more mild, that society would never have built such an edifice; it grew up into form and beauty out of his imprudent and rash course towards them. Brother Swan hearing this a number of times, replied: "Brethren, the day will come when you or your children will see that meeting-house dedicated and owned by the Baptists in the city of New London. Now, mark my words." Brother Swan was soon called as pastor of the State-street church, in Albany, New York. During the two or three years of his settlement in Albany, the debts on the fine Universalist house in New London began to press upon them. Sixteen thousand dollars must be raised, or the house would be sold under the sheriff's hammer. No relief came. Three or four of the wealthier Baptists went to Albany, and said to Brother Swan: "If you will come back to New London, we will buy the new Universalist meeting-house, and have you installed as pastor in it. He consented; and in a few weeks a sheriff's deed was made out to the Baptist church and society, and Jabez Swan installed as its pastor. There he remained, enjoying the fulfillment of his prophecy, until age had disqualified him for active labor as a pastor in the place.

Rev. Jabez Swan was an outspoken man in all his private and public ministrations. As a man in social life, he was as mild and quiet as a child, and as tender in dealing with inquirers after truth as the beloved John. In the pulpit, he was like Paul—logical and truthful. In prayer, he was a power with God. He could prevail. While pastor in Albany, he was called upon, as the custom was in that State at the time for the resident ministers in Albany, to act in turn as chaplain of the House of

Representatives and Senate. The Speaker of the House at the time, Hon. E. Litchfield, was a Baptist. When Swan's morning came to officiate, Litchfield called the House to order and said: "The Reverend Jabez Swan will address the Throne of Grace." Swan commenced in the usual way of formality, but soon introduced the practical matter of supplication, making time and place and subjects as pointed and personal as possible—something like the following: "Oh, thou Almighty Savior of sinners, here in this congregation are such as need salvation, and of every imaginable class. Here, O Lord, are men steeped in iniquity, in bribery, in drunkenness, lies, licentiousness and debauchery; bold blasphemers, men who fear not God nor regard the interests of man—men who are reprobate to all that is holy and good. Now, Lord God, make known Thy mercy in saving them from the power of the second death, and sustain Thy servant who is called to preside over them, that he be not contaminated by this herd of thieves and robbers. In Thy name we ask it. Amen and amen." Honorable Mike Walsh, of New York City notoriety, an eccentric fellow, arose in his place at the conclusion of the prayer, and moved a question of privilege. When the chair had announced his name as having the floor, he continued: "I move that a copy of this prayer be spread upon the journal of the House, for it's the most appropriate prayer I have ever heard in this place."

While thus acting as agent of the church at Leavenworth, I was permitted to witness the Spirit's power in the salvation of sinners, in a number of places where it would have been delightful to have remained and assist the different pastors, had duty permitted me to do so. But I had a special object in pursuit. And I have always acted on this principle: never to do two things at once. "This one thing I do," said Paul. I did depart from this rule for a short time at Coldwater, Michigan, where I found the church in a divided state, and where it seemed to be duty to remain a few days and assist in the Christian work of reconciling brethren. After a week's stay, not without its good results, I trust, I went on, stopping at Detroit over one night. In this city, the churches were at the time embarrassed with debt; and so I hastened on to New York State, where I was born and where my youth had been spent in folly and sin: where the Spirit first revealed to me the deep depravity of my nature;

where God, for Christ's sake, forgave my sins and led me to the cross for hope of eternal life. As I came to some of the places where I had lived as a sinner, I could not suppress my tears of mingled grief and joy — grief, when I remembered the blindness and hardness of my heart when a youth; joy, when I considered my great deliverance from the power of sin.

One sad reflection came upon me like an armed force. It was this: Many of the old ministers, and those who were my companions in the labor of the Gospel, had gone to the Better Land to rest, and were waiting for the resurrection of the just. The time was when I knew nearly every Baptist minister in the State from Lake Erie to the east end of Long Island; from 1840 to 1857, I had commingled much with those in the western and southern portions of the State. Among them, were men of choice spirit. But now, their places were vacant or filled with the young men who had been raised up in the churches and educated in our schools, nearly all of them strangers to me. It was, however, a cheering reflection that upon many of these sons of the Gospel the mantles of their ascended fathers had fallen, and the Elishas of to-day were doing the very work of the Elijahs of yesterday. It is a source of joy and pride to see what the schools of the prophets have accomplished for the Baptist churches and their ministers in the last quarter of a century. Forty years ago we had in all Western New York, but few educated ministers, and now nearly every church in the State is supplied with a pastor whom no church would be ashamed to have stand before any audience as the ambassador of Christ. I could but exclaim, "God bless these dear young men with the power of the Spirit!" The most of them gave the best of evidence that they were taught of God, as well as in the Seminary.

I found only one exception, and perhaps what I criticized in him was a mistake more than a fault. A young brother was to preach the opening sermon at an Association. His text was Isaiah lxiv. 6: "We do all fade as a leaf." After an introduction by way of urging upon the assembly the importance of a *chemical*, *agricultural* and *scientific* understanding of the processes of nature in the growth of vegetation, he announced his theme, "The Fading Leaf," and then set forth the doctrine of the text, (he said it was the doctrine) First, "The process of fading and falling;" Second, "The use the leaf is put to by nature, after it fades and falls." The sermon had one grand feature. It was just twenty-seven minutes long. At the conclusion, all said *Amen*. I was invited home to dinner with an old friend who asked me, with a twinkle of the eye, as we walked along, "What agricultural society did that young man say he belonged to?" There was not a good round sentence in it, from beginning to end, for Christ and the salvation of lost men. But this case was an exception to the young men generally. He had more learning than good Gospel sense.

I have given my views in a previous chapter on the subject of an educated ministry, so that I will not trespass again upon the time of the reader to enlarge upon the subject at this point. Everywhere I went I was hailed with a most hearty welcome by old and young, friends and strangers. After the meeting of the anniversaries in Boston, I came to Connecticut and spent the time till their annual State meeting in the city of Hartford—a meeting long to be remembered. It was a grand sight to see those New England Baptists who had contended so earnestly for the faith once delivered to the saints against ecclesiastical domination and the authority of a law of persecution, and to hear the reports from the churches they represented, showing how much material and spiritual prosperity attended them in all their religious enterprises. Such devoted men, laymen and ministers! Such liberality as was evinced for every good object! Such fraternal respect for each other, and for the opinions of others! There was no great "*I*" and little "*you*," as I had witnessed in some places. The doctors of Divinity did not put on airs, or betray any symptoms of having that bane of human greatness, "the big-head." Every man's hat fitted his own head. One evening of the session was given to a social and simple supper in the large edifice of the First Baptist church. At this supper a number of gentlemen, not members of the denomination, were called upon for speeches, among them Hon. Mr. Hawley, Governor of the State, and son of a Baptist minister in the State, who had toiled when Baptists everywhere in New England received "*cold-shoulder*," and Baptist ministers small salaries in addition. I was called upon to represent Kansas and the needs of the Baptist church at Leavenworth, and in response to my plea for the latter, received nearly seven hundred and fifty dollars. All the pulpits of that State were open for the presentation of the wants of the needy. Well, Connecticut is a grand old State! It's a good State to be in. It's easy work to praise it.

At Danbury I found a noble band of Christian men and women. Here I was invited by the pastor, Rev. D. M. Stone, D. D., now of Milwaukee, Wisconsin, to present the claims of my object. Also at Norwalk I received the same invitation from Rev. C. N. Swan, son of Jabez Swan, of New London. The church at Stamford is a grand specimen of what a church ought to be. This church, Rev. Edward Lathrop, D. D., pastor, good and true, treated me with New Testament consideration and liberality. I then came back to New York and took the line of churches up the Harlem road to Westchester, Putnam and Dutchess counties, and attended the two Associations composed of the churches in that wealthy region of hills and dales which well nigh flows with milk, the farmers furnishing this article in the greatest quantities for the New York market. From these hills the water also for that mighty city is furnished. The Croton River is here turned into two or three reservoirs, from which it flows in underground acqueducts about eighty miles to the city, costing millions of dollars. I did not wonder that so many of the people in that country were of Baptist proclivities, water being so valuable an article, and so highly prized. I heard no complaints that it was "dangerous to health," as we hear out West.

While in Rhode Island I received a telegram requesting me to go to Washington, D. C., to meet a friend, and to attend to business relating to the "University" at Ottawa. Having complied with this, I returned to New York, where I resigned my position in connection with that enterprise, and then hastened to my home in Ottawa, Kansas. As their pastor, Rev. I. Sawyer, D. D., had resigned, the church invited me to supply their pulpit until they could obtain another pastor. Mrs. Stimson was acting as matron of the Indian Department of the school. I accepted the position of supply until the next autumn. I then went to Lawrence, and commenced a meeting in connection with the pastor of the Baptist church in that place, Rev. E. D. Bentley. This was about Christmas. I only expected to remain a few days, and then return to Burlington to spend the winter with my daughter and her family.

Perhaps it will be of sufficient interest to the

reader to detail somewhat the precious work of grace in Lawrence during the winter of 1867–1868. It was Wednesday evening, the time for the regular prayer meeting of the church. Pains had been taken by the pastor and others, to give notice that there would be preaching in the lecture room. At the hour appointed there were seventeen present, all told. I talked to this handful from the Word of the Lord in Nehemiah iv. 6, "For the people had a mind to work," introducing two simple thoughts: First, The magnitude of our work; Second, What is our individual work as Christians? At the conclusion, I suggested this as a test of our willingness to enter at once upon the work, that each one bring a friend with him, or her, at the meeting the next night, and that would make thirty-four. Thursday night came, and there were over one hundred present, and soon we had to go into what was the main audience room at the time, and before January was out, all the churches in the city were in a full blaze of revival spirit, and multitudes of the impenitent were heard to inquire, "What must we do to be saved?" It was estimated that in all, four hundred had submitted to Jesus, and hoped in his saving power.

I remained in Lawrence until June, and then went to Atchison, to supply the desk until Dr. Sawyer, pastor elect, should assume his position in the church. I spent the remainder of the year in preaching in destitute communities and in asssisting pastors in protracted efforts, as opportunities offered. During the time of holding these meetings, we experienced great inconvenience for the want of proper places in which to hold them, and the suffering to the people was great from what are called "basket meetings" held in the woods. These annoyances or sufferings proper were two: First, The chills and fever attacked the people, because of the miasma that arises from all unsubdued lands in the Western States, especially from low-wooded lands. Second, The flies, of which we have large swarms in this country, annoyed the horses and mules so badly that it was almost impossible to keep the animals in camp. Besides these, the heavy rains, so common in the forepart of the season, might be mentioned.

CHAPTER XXV.

"THE BAPTIST TABERNACLE."

AT one of these out-door, afflicted gatherings at LaNape, Brother Winfield Scott and myself suggested the idea of a large tent, such as we had both seen in the army, and the practical utility of which we both knew. If we only had this, we could go on to the open prairie, where it would be healthier and pleasanter, and could also be protected against the hot sun and the dews, the rains and the flies. When the thing was named to the multitude, it was hailed as the very thing needed, and a resolution was passed that if possible one be obtained, and that Brother H. K. Stimson be requested to solicit subscriptions for the purpose—the tent to be called the "Baptist Tabernacle for Kansas." Early in this winter, I started out on this mission for a temporary meeting-house that could be easily moved from place to place, as circumstances should demand. I found the Northern winters in the sections of country I wanted to visit for the purpose so severe, and my health so feeble, that but little could be accomplished until the spring should open. Meantime, I had gone on East and made a few collections. In April, I left New York for the West. At Chicago, I had the tent constructed, seats and all; and, by the advice of brethren, set it up in that city, the friends there contributing towards the expense. We held meetings in it for four or five days and nights, with large audiences filling it to its utmost capacity. It would hold, comfortably seated, about sixteen hundred persons, and by crowding it, twenty-five hundred could be got inside of it.

When we were ready to move it, the Chicago, Burlington and Quincy Railroad Company, and the Hannibal and St. Joe Company, volunteered to convey it to Leavenworth, free. The Reverend L. P. Judson, of Stillwater, New York, accompanied us and took charge of the tent as far as Leavenworth; and there, with the assistance of that ever-ready and industrious Reverend Winfield Scott, we pitched the Tabernacle for dedication. Large crowds assembled from day to day and from night to night. We next moved it to Ottawa, where there was to be a Sunday school celebration, and where we were persuaded to erect it for the accommodation of the large meeting. From there, we went to LeRoy, Coffey County. At this place, the small church gave us the best accommodation in their power, under the circumstances. At this place, my health gave out, and I was obliged to desist from further personal labor during the season. The brethren at Burlingame, Osage County, had proposed to send teams for the tent, in which to hold the meetings of their Association. But failing to come to time, we put the Tabernacle into winter quarters at Burlington.

This tent enterprise aroused a good deal of opposition from the enemies of religion, and, I regret to say, a few of the professed friends of the Master in Kansas. Why they should oppose it, I could never know. It was *suggested* that it grew out of the fact that they did not get it up, and that there was no money to be made out of it for their pockets.

[This somewhat famous tent might have been as successful, practically, as it was bold and original in conception, if it had not been for two mistakes—one of which Father Stimson was not responsible for, under any circumstances; and the other was a most natural mistake to make for a man ambitious of doing the most good. Too much cannot be said in praise of the idea of such a tent. It showed a more thorough comprehension of the situation than anything ever devised in a religious way, even in prolific Kansas. The first mistake was in making the tent too large. It was not too roomy for some places where it would be advisable to erect it. But it was designed for pioneer work, for towns and communities where there were no church buildings or public halls, and where one-half the room would accommodate all the people that could be induced to attend public worship, even in so novel and inviting a place as a tent. The canvas, seats and poles were a full load for four horses. It was a great job to move it from place to place. If it had been half as large, an ordinary wagon and span of horses would have been all the equipage necessary for its removal. The work of erecting it would not have been half as much; and in every place it would have been entirely full—and others, besides public speakers, know the inspiring effect of a full audience. The second mistake was in erecting it in places where it wasn't really needed. In Chicago, where it was gotten up, it was well enough to spread it for an opening meeting. But, even there, it ought to have been with the square promise on the part of responsible ones that every cent of indebtedness on it should be paid off at the time. It never should have been erected in Leavenworth or Ottawa. These towns had certainly passed beyond the tent period. If a tent that would comfortably seat five or six hundred had been kept in the infant towns of Kansas from the time this monster canvas first made its appearance at Leavenworth, and had been manned by Brethren Stimson and Scott, it is safe to say that the number of conversions in the State during the time would have been at least five thousand greater.

I would rather be the author of a grand failure, than to live forever like some old parchment-skinned conservative, whose main characteristic consists in equivocating so as to avoid every square, vital issue, and whose religion consists in not doing anything that will have the least appearance of being out of the ordinary beat. Such men, however much they may cry "Lord, Lord," hardly belong to the race of heroes smitten with the power of the Spirit until wherever they go the cry is: "These that have turned the world upside down, have come hither also." If they ever keep company with the apostles and their spiritual successors, the Lord will surely have to shake the easy-going, damnable conservatism out of them. I would rather be Sir John Franklin, though the unknown region of the Pole is never pierced by the prow of any human navigator, than to be old Sir Parchment Conservative, with my money bags and blessings, the fruitage of other people's enterprise, and for whose daring and skill I had only sneers. I would rather be the child of the man who devised for God and humanity this tent, though it was too large, and though it was set up at first where it was not needed, than to be obliged to call any of the full-favored persons, or those afflicted with the dry rot of conservatism, who ridiculed the enterprise, my father.

It was my good fortune to be present a short time at Fort Scott, during Brother E. P. Hammond's stay in that enterprising city, when the old tent vindicated the wisdom of its originator. It was during his great religious campaign in Kansas, in the year 1872, when God so signally blessed Atchison, Leavenworth, Topeka, Ottawa, Paola, Fort Scott, and last, but chiefly, Lawrence, with His saving grace, and the name of Hammond became a household word with thousands who previously cared for none of God's fellow-laborers. All these places except Fort Scott, had church buildings, or halls large enough to accommodate the multitudes that crowded the meetings of this wonderful man of God. Here there was no place that would hold the half of them, until the active ones thought of the tent, and brother Hammond with his quick insight for expedients urged the brethren there to secure it. I went as a special messenger in behalf of the church at Ottawa. I arrived at Fort Scott after ten o'clock at night. I hurried up town; delegates from other places and for the same purpose being aboard the same train. I found the tent jammed with human beings, and the backless seats in the open, chill air outside, all full. It was estimated that from five hundred to a thousand were outside the tent each night. People had come from long distances in covered wagons to attend the meetings. If it had not been for the big tent, Fort Scott would not have enjoyed the labors of the great evangelist, which resulted in such "showers of blessings." If the tent had never served any useful purpose before, and never shall again, its service in the great meetings at Fort Scott has vindicated its making many fold. —Ed.]

At LeRoy, after we had got the meeting in operation, one of the lawyers of the place, an old acquaintance of mine, met me in the street with the remark: "Ha! Elder, I understand you have gone into the circus business, and are now performing in our city." This was said with a leer in the expression of his face, that expressed his hatred of religion. I replied: "O, yes, Squire J., and I am out now to look up a babboon to put into the concern, and you are the very one for the place; come right along, I will do well by you." He turned on his heel and left. As a general thing, our efforts with the tent were treated with due respect by all classes.

CHAPTER XXVI.

KINDERHOOK—WHEATLAND.

MY feeble and failing health demanded rest and quiet. So I went East to Michigan, to stay a while with a daughter in that State and recruit for the spring campaign. But I was advised by physicians and friends not to think of exposing myself to the fatigue and hardship of such exhausting work, especially at my time of life. At Kinderhook, Michigan, where my daughter resided, was a Baptist church without a pastor. In fact they had never enjoyed the regular, consecutive labor of a pastor; preaching "onct" a month, or "twict" at best, being the rule with them. The church numbered about thirty or thirty-five. They had built a snug little meeting-house, and had a good congregation. An invitation was extended me to become their pastor, which I accepted. I at once moved my family there, and found them a good, common sense people, quite consistent in their daily walk, and willing to do what they could to sustain the cause of Christ, and hold up the hands of the pastor and make his position secure and comfortable. So the first year passed off agreeably, and with evident tokens of good in prospect.

Our Sunday school was a union school. No sectarian sentiments were to be taught in it, as is the common rule in such cases. Not even a book was admitted that had a tendency in that direction. In the year 1870–'71, we had quite a religious awakening, and a number of hopeful conversions to Jesus. On one Lord's day, a regular teacher in the school was absent, and her place was supplied by the wife of the Methodist clergyman of the place. In the lesson the subject of baptism occurred. A young lady in the class asked a' question on the subject. The teacher at once protested that baptism was not by immersion, and that Jesus was not baptized as an example, but as an introduction into the priest's office. When I returned home, I found quite a fermentation working on the subject, and thought, as it was a union school, these things ought not so to be. The next Sabbath, the said Methodist lady came with her husband to frown me down, and to choke off all utterances by way of protest on my part. Wishing to counteract the mutually interdicted influence then and there, in my own house of worship, as it was manifesting itself in the pew away in one corner, I said, "If you wish, Mr. H——, to discuss these questions at a proper time and in a proper spirit, I hold myself ready to engage in the discussion. But just here and now, I am not ready to enter upon it, and for the present, I protest."

But the spirit of war was diffusing itself like leaven in the meal. In June, Brother A. P. Graves came and labored four or five days with the church, and the revival spirit of the previous winter was renewed and increased to a large extent. The meeting closing on Friday, the next day was our covenant meeting. I gave notice of the same, and Mr. —— gave notice that he should be there and preach at five P. M., and if any wished to join his class, an opportunity would be afforded. Saturday came, and to my surprise nearly every convert was there. And as they presented themselves, one after another, for baptism, a number of the Methodist brethren and sisters made the request to be admitted, and among the number was the man who had been a class leader, and a strong supporter of that church for years. He arose and said: "You all know me and my course of life. I want to be *immersed*, and become a member of this Baptist church." Ten or twelve united and were baptized the next day in Silver Lake. It was a grand day for converts and the church, and the old pastor never felt better in his life.

The Methodist minister lived opposite my house, and as he returned home to attend his five-o'clock appointment, his good wife sat in the doorway, waiting for him, and I sat in my door. As he drove up to the gate, his wife rose, and walking with rapid strides, threw up her hands and exclaimed in upper tones, "John, they have all gone, George —— and all, into the Baptist church!" Mr. H—— hung his head, and sat silent for awhile. He then went and put out his horse. This broke up the sweet union, so much talked of by certain ones—union as long as they can have their say and way.

Just in the midst of this revival, the old Wheatland church extended me a call to visit them, and re-settle with them as pastor. I went down to New York and spent two weeks with them, and gave them encouragement of accepting their invitation. They expressed a great desire that I should, and offered me many inducements, pecuniary and other. But when I returned to Kinderhook, and found what the Spirit was doing, and the state the church was in, and how much the young converts needed the fostering care and counsel of a pastor, I wrote to the friends in Wheatland that it would be impossible for me to leave at the particular juncture. For some unaccountable reason my letter and other letters did not reach them, nor their communications reach me. So the negotiations between us ended. Perhaps it was all for the best. In a human view, it did look as though something might have been accomplished for that old wealthy church and people. I can imagine that an effort at that time would have resuscitated the cause in that once very flourishing field of religious power.

On the other hand there would have been many things against such a success. The two young churches on either side of them were anxious to secure the wealthy and active members still remaining in the mother church. Mumford and Clifton were like the "daughters of the horse leech." And then again, I was much older, and somewhat impaired in health. As I said to an old friend, H. K. Stimson of 1850 was not the same man in 1871. A large majority of the members remaining knew me only when they were children, and the elderly ones would say, "Well, we heard that clattering voice a long time ago, but now it has lost its ring and vim." It may all have been for the best as it was. I meant to do right. The other too churches had good, reliable pastors, and are working in harmony serving God. I wish we had more such here in Kansas, and more such meeting houses with their bells in many of our new and rising towns.

The old cemetery in Wheatland is a sacred city of the dead to me. There are the remains of a multitude of dear old friends, in whose names and memories there is a sweet fragrance. They were, many of them, my counselors and supporters, in the days of my residence among them. These hands helped to smooth the dying pillows of some of them, and over the cold bodies of many I said, "Dust to dust." And, a dearer tie than these—a large number of them I buried with Christ in the baptismal tomb. One little cherub lies in the sacred enclosure of that cemetery whom we deposited there during the first year of our residence in Wheatland. Oh, what a glorious day that will be when the graves shall give up their dead, and we shall greet each other in the Celestial City! God hasten it in His time; and let us be prepared to meet Him and each other with joy, and not with grief.

CHAPTER XXVII.

BURLINGTON, KANSAS.

IT was a strange Providence that brought us back to Kansas again. But I can now see that it was a Providence fraught with the weightiest considerations, as all His dealings are. Our children who remained here were constantly writing, urging us to return to Burlington; and the remnant of the Baptist church here held out inducements to me, pleading that something might be done to resuscitate the fallen cause of the church in the place. Their late pastor had deserted them and joined another denomination, and left the church in a distracted state. He had gone off largely in debt, to his own disgrace and their shame; and if something was not soon done, all would go to ruin. Through his mismanagement, a small dwelling-house had been purchased with a tax-title against it and a mortgage of two hundred dollars. They had already paid more than the property was worth or would bring in market. On arrival, I found things even worse than represented, and the church few in numbers and poor. I did not expect to settle as pastor with any church, but to rest with our children and do such missionary work as might present itself, especially among the poor and destitute communities in this county. But soon the church extended me a call to become pastor; and although they could not promise a competent support, they would do all that in their poverty they could to sustain a pastor. Under these circumstances, I accepted the position and set myself at work. We had no place in which to hold our meetings, only an old dilapidated school-room in an upper loft—dirty, dingy, inconvenient, uninviting. The Sunday school was about the only redeeming feature of the concern, and that greatly retarded for the want of an attractive place in which to collect the children. Many of the parents did not wish their children to go up into the old stone building. The school had been kept together by Brother I. Mickel, who was doubtless the best superintendent in the city. In the course of the winter, the Episcopal chapel was vacant, and the wardens of the church invited us to occupy the house until they should be supplied with a rector.

We accepted their kind offer, and at once entered the chapel with our Sunday school and congregation. Both were soon largely increased, and things moved on for awhile with a degree of prosperity. But soon some of the feminine members of that church began to put on "high church" airs, and thought it an outrage on the sacred place for an "unconsecrated and unordained" man to preach there, polluting their "sacred and holy sanctuary." And then, "if this old Baptist Elder and his little church can get up a Sunday school of seventy-five or eighty children and a decent congregation, why can't we?" who are the regular succession. The good brother, the rector who had preached to the church and was expected to return in the spring, was a true, evangelical, Christian gentleman, and had suggested the matter of our occupying their house in his absence. Soon, however, we were notified to vacate the premises, and were again turned out upon the "cold charities" of the world.

Some of the most lovely and devout Christians I have ever seen, were members of the Episcopal communion. They were "low church," though, you may be sure. Such cared much more for Christ than for "church," and for his true members than for mummeries. As for "high church" people, Simon-pure, I have the same feelings and respect for them I have for the high-priests and Pharisees mentioned in the account of the murder of Christ. They belong to the same category. They have great regard for the "outside of the cup and platter." They have much more respect for the vestments than the character of the men (or men and boys) who "minister" before them. They never could have endured John the Baptist. His "vestments" would have been shockingly wanting in length and in all regard for the sacred proprieties. They would prefer to do without the Messiah, rather than receive Him at the hands of such a "Forerunner." A Gospel that could be preached in the wilderness, or on a lake in a fisherman's dirty boat, and that was glad news to tax-gatherers and harlots, is altogether too rough a thing for them in their soft silks. How such "high church" grandees are ever to endure a heaven of equality, to keep company with redeemed Magdalenes and poor people with bad antecedents, and to worship Him who "exchanged visits" when here on earth with families that did their own work, is a matter of strange interest to me. Women seem to have a "fatal facility" for soaring (or sinking) into this hyperion of double-rectified religion. It must have been invented to suit their superlative notions. There is something so select about it. It doesn't bring them into contact with females who presume to worship God with last year's bonnets on their plebeian heads, and who manipulate the "prayer-book" with ungloved hands. It's the nobbiest thing out, this genteel, gilt-edged, high-toned, Fifth-avenue, carriage-and-four, F. F. V., superlatively refined improvement on the religion of the homeless, wandering Son of the Nazarene carpenter.

Notwithstanding we had no place in which to meet except an old dingy Court-room, our Sunday school kept up its interest. We were very kindly offered the use of such meeting-houses as were not used by the respective churches worshiping in them—a kindness appreciated by us all. At this time, the mortgage on the property of the church became due, and the parties holding it were pressing its payment. An effort was made to cancel the claim; but the old patrons of the enterprise were unwilling to contribute any more, and there the matter was likely to hang. Just before this, a brother and sister had come among us from the

Second church of Rochester, New York. They proposed to assist in the payment of the mortgage, on condition that an effort be made to build a house of worship; in which case, they would also purchase a lot on which to build it. After much pleading and a little ill-feeling on the part of some, the mortgage was paid, by Mrs. Stimson giving fifty dollars of money especially belonging to her. This offering did not come out of our two hundred-dollar salary, not yet all paid. We shan't cry if it's never paid. This Brother Wigston, from Rochester, New York, procured a suitable lot; and it was decided by the trustees and church that I should go and solicit assistance in erecting a suitable house of worship. Accordingly, on the ninth of April I started out on my mission; and after spending a few weeks in Michigan, where I received a cordial greeting and material contributions to my object from both pastor and people, I hastened on to Western New York. Many of these Michigan people will be held in refreshing memory, and will have the lasting gratitude of the little church in Burlington, for their liberal, practical sympathy, manifested to them in their poverty. I have often said when alone, "God bless the pastors and churches in Michigan."

CHAPTER XXVIII.

OLD MEMORIES.

I ARRIVED in New York just in time to witness the proceedings of the Niagara Baptist Association at Akron. It was in this Association that I was ordained, and in which many of my youthful ministrations were bestowed. Here I met a few of the veterans of the Master's cause, but not one of the old ministers. All were at rest. Hon. Burt Van Horne was a child when we labored in this Association. I remembered well the house and home of his devoted father and mother, who were pillars in Zion; and the day he was baptized in one of those precious revivals in Newfane. He was moderator of the Association, a position he has held for a number of years consecutively. And a capital presiding officer he makes. I spent the next Lord's day in Lockport, and the next week in attending the Orleans Association at Shelby. Here I met a large number of old friends, but not a minister that I knew when I was young. I was led to ask: "The fathers, where are they? and the prophets, do they live forever?" Here, I met the widow and family of one of the Wheatland members I baptized in 1847, and was made the guest of the family during my stay there. I was offered a collection, and was invited to visit their churches in the Association.

I then went on to Rochester, and spent a long time with old friends and with the churches in and about that goodly city. The land-marks in many places had been moved, and in not a few respects radical changes had taken place—some for the better and some not for the better. Rochester is a grand little city, in which I, in common with the whole Baptist brotherhood, feel a degree of pride. How different now from the first time I saw it in 1819! Fifty-four years had changed it from a little village to a prosperous, literary, religious city of eighty thousand inhabitants—the influence of which is felt to the ends of the earth through the educated sons of its institutions of learning. I went there to live in 1824. Then its streets were not paved, except with black mud. I remember that in Buffalo street, between State and Sophia, I got "stalled" with an empty coach in 1826, and had to send back to the hotel for help to get out. There were some things I remembered as I revisited the localities, that I wished I could forget. I will not enumerate them; "of which I am now ashamed." They bring a blush to my temples as I think of them. I will allude to only this one, of the lighter sort. This is hardly a specimen of many that were much more disgraceful. The village had then just organized a police force, and had for a place in which to confine violators of the public peace, the basement of the then new court-house, long since given place to the stately edifice that now graces the city. In this room they had just put new cricket-bedsteads, and nice rose blankets, so that the city criminals could have rest of body, if not of conscience. These sleeping accommodations had not been used. I knew the man on duty that night; only one at a time was required. His name was "Constable Beach," as we called him. It was court week, and every bed in the "Eagle Hotel" and "Mansion House" and "Clinton Hotel" was full. Mr. Ainsworth, the keeper of the "Eagle" had given the beds in the attic story, that were usually occupied by the stage drivers, to some of his court guests. So we were called to lie on the floor in the bar-room, or sit up, just as would suit our tastes best. After yawning out our stories and getting tired of our entertainment, and feeling the need of rest, I saw Constable Beach pass along the street, on his round of duty. At once I thought of the new beds under the court-house, and suggested to the boys a plan for lodging for the remaining short hours of the night. The plan was this: we would go into the street and get up a sham fight among ourselves; Beach would come along, arrest us and put us into the new rooms and clean beds of the city "boarding house." Out we all went, five or six of us, and began our row, then clinched. Up came Beach in great haste, arrested all of us, and hurried us over to the court-house bed rooms. "There, boys, you can lie down there if you choose. In the morning I shall take you before Squire Warner," and he locked us in. In the morning he came in and said: "You will all want your breakfast. I will go over with you to the 'Eagle.' I suppose you all board there." He saw us laughing as we were straightening up, and asked: "What was the fuss among you last night, boys?" So we told him a plain, unvarnished tale. "Well, go and get your breakfast, I will let you off this time, but you must not do it any more, boys." I told him if there was any damage done, he must get it out of Russ Ainsworth, and put it into the public fund as "lodging money." Thurlow Weed was then publishing in the village a small weekly paper, and made a note of the affair, under the caption of: "A Joke on Constable Beach; Cheap Lodgings at Corporation Expense."

During my stay in the region, I visited the town of Mendon, where my childhood and youth were mostly spent. An old friend invited me to make my home at his house while I remained there. And a brother in Rochester, formerly a resident of that place, Mr. S. F. Kimball, accompanied me, having sent on an appointment for the Sabbath. We were met at the depot by Mr. Daniel Allen, who conveyed us to the village of East Mendon. This little village has been left out by the railroad some three miles to one side, which slighting has appeared to dry up all the sources of business enterprise in this once enterprising little burg. In our days of staging, it was what we call out West a "right smart place." Two or three daily lines of stages changed horses, and breakfasted and dined here, so that a ready market was found for the hay, grain and hotel provision the farmers of the region had to dispose of. It contained four stores and two good hotels;—now, only one little store and one third or fourth-class hotel. But this was not the most disheartening change visible. The religious decline was more depressing to me than all else. The two meeting houses were standing nearly empty every Sabbath. The Baptist house, where crowded congregations used to meet, was now sparsely filled, and the same was true of the Presbyterian. I met but few that I recognized, and less, far less, that were members of either of these churches in 1828–1831. What few there were that remembered me in my youth, had some romantic story or frivolous trick of mine to relate, to my chagrin. Some of them were false, only made up to perpetuate a bad record of youthful folly and nonsense. Some of them told me of my pranks in youth, that their fathers and mothers had been cognizant of.

On Sunday my congregation was composed of Baptists, Presbyterians and Methodists, who had come out to hear "the man who once was the fun-making boy of Mendon," now an old Baptist minister. They gave me a fair collection for the object of my mission, and seemed to do it heartily, as to the Lord. On Monday, I called on a number of old friends, and then returned to Rochester. My temporary home while in the city, was in the families of A. and J. A. Hibbard, where I experienced as much kindness and attention as I could expect from my own children in sickness. No better nursing and care could be bestowed on an own father. Long shall I cherish a deep sense of gratitude to God for these dear friends, and many others in the "Flour City."

My stay in Mendon, though brief, brought to mind frequently the person and character of one who "being dead, yet speaketh;" one who occupied a large place in the hearts and thoughts of the people, and who waged so successful a warfare against sin and the devil, in this and adjoining places. I refer to Elder Weaver.

CHAPTER XXIX.

ELDER WEAVER.

ELDER Weaver—"Elder" was the much more common designation of ministers then, specially Baptist ministers — was a power wherever he preached. He was a farmer when he began preaching, and was, strictly speaking, self-educated. What he acquired was acquired from few books, and without all the aids of the modern school system. He had very noticeable peculiarities. He was a large, bony, angular, rough-looking man. He was what we boys used to call "cock-eyed," not exactly cross-eyed, but the opposite of that, so that while he seemed to be looking in one direction he would really be looking in another. His complexion was exceedingly dark, and his bushy whiskers as black as a raven. These chin appendages were a source of complaint on the part of his friends. Whiskers on a ministerial face were not as orthodox then as now. His heavy black hair he used to wear quite long. He often preached with his coat off.

His praise was in all the churches. He was eleven years pastor of the Mendon church. When he settled there the church numbered twenty-one, and worshiped in an old school-house, called the "boiling spring," because they always had such powerful devotional meetings. What temporary place of worship receives any such epithet now, on account of the meetings in it? This "boiling spring" fact is as high praise, well-nigh, as could be bestowed on a church. Brother Weaver was a young man when he came to Mendon. He was their second pastor, and this was his second pastorate. The first was Jesse Brayman, who afterwards apostatized to the Universalists, and met his end by going into a well which caved in on him. Elder Weaver was ordained at Lysander, Onondagua County, near Syracuse, a much larger place than Syracuse at that time. He was settled there as pastor a couple of years.

There were seven years of continuous revival during his eleven years' pastorate at Mendon. There were five years in which additions were made to the church by baptism at every communion. This was stated in his farewell sermon, which I went seven miles—from Rush,—to hear. I shall never forget the opening hymn, on that day:

> "Lord, what a wretched land is this,
> That yields us no supply.
> No cheering fruits, nor wholesome trees
> Nor streams of living joy."

He was a great singer. Description would utterly fail to give an adequate idea of him as a singer. They used to say he sang everybody into the church. His singing might not have been called "fine" by the musical critics, but it was fairly weighed down with *soul*. Negatively it was not faulty, but positively it was heavenly to every devotional soul.

He went down to New York to help the pastor of the Broome-street church, Israel Robords, in a protracted meeting; and pulled off his coat like a workman in fact. During the series of meetings, the young men would say to one another: "Come, let's go down to Broome street to meeting. There is a man there who preaches like a man a-mowing. He pulls off his coat."

He used to indulge at times in flights of real eloquence. One instance: The galleries of his church were crowded with young people one evening, when a number of them kept up a constant whispering and tittering. Turning towards them, he said, in a manner and with tones that cannot be described any more than they can be forgotten: "What an astonishing evidence of human depravity, that while the man of God is declaring the way of salvation by the Cross, young gentlemen and ladies in the gallery should be making sport of the very means of their salvation from sin and death—while, peradventure, God's recording angel stands ready to write 'eternal damnation' on their hearts." The result: a number were struck with conviction; among them, Miss Sally Roberts, afterwards the first wife of Hon. H. E. Smith, of Rochester, formerly of Fowlersville, New York, and Prince Benedict, known to hundreds.

During his pastorate at Mendon, people, young and old, came on ordinary occasions to hear him from Victor, West and East Bloomfield, Perrington, Pittsford, Henrietta, Rush, Lima and Avon, varying from six to ten miles distant. Dr. Comstock, pastor of the Baptist church in Rochester, used to say, in pleasantry, when many of his congregation would go fourteen miles to hear Brother Weaver: "I guess we had better move our church out to Mendon, you like to go there to meeting so well, and so have but one pastor."

All his associates loved and respected him, though they were not blind to his faults and did not indorse all his methods. The following are among his cotemporaries: O. C. Comstock, father of the missionary; Robert Powell, Philander Kelsey, Norman Bentley, I. Roberts, Marvin Allen, Ichabod Clark, David and Jesse Corwin, Alfred Bennett, John Peck, cousin of J. M. Peck; Horace Griswold, Aristarchus Willey, Joseph and Jesse Elliott, Zenas Case and Martin Coleman. These men, all ministers, and mostly self-educated, were raised up by God to meet the then-existing state of things. They did their pioneer duty faithfully. Their fragrant memory is a rich heritage to the Church. Let their names forever be embalmed in grateful hearts — among them, let Weaver be remembered gratefully as long as any. He was their equal.

CHAPTER XXX.

REFLECTIONS—HOME AGAIN.

THE friends and churches in Rochester responded cheerfully to the wants of the West. The new interest, called the East avenue church, did a noble thing, also the Lake avenue church. Both of these had but recently been organized. The pastors of the First and Second churches were absent, but promised to help in the future. At a prayer-meeting of the latter church, I took up a collection of thirty dollars, and a brother from Richmond, Virginia, gave me twenty-five dollars. I attended the Monroe Association, and then left for my Western home, expecting to make short stops on the way.

In looking over this tour and visit, it is one of the most gratifying to me personally of any I ever made—as I was permitted to have more time in the immediate communities where I had labored most and longest, and as I went over the same ground where I had spent the days of my youth and the vigor of my manhood, and where I had a degree of success under the good Master's guiding hand and the influence of the Spirit.

This reflection constantly impressed itself upon me, "What Divine goodness has followed you all the way in your life, even in the days of your guilt as an openly profane sinner and thoughtless wanderer from, a despiser of Jesus and His love to a lost world!" The only regret was, that I had made such poor improvement of the unnumbered blessings showered upon my pathway for over forty years of Christian life and public ministry. I had no good reason to complain in other respects. I had been kindly cared for, as a general rule. The brethren had always treated me with the greatest kindness and, in many instances, with needed leniency and Christian liberality. As I passed out of New York, I thought that, in all human probability, I should never see this land of my nativity again, until I should see it in its renovated condition, when "purified by fire" and our Jesus shall have come "the second time without sin unto salvation." I am now an old man, and cannot expect to come back again to this goodly old State, I thought, that gave me birth and a field to labor in; and so I said "Farewell," as I gazed on her green hills to enter Pennsylvania on my homeward-bound journey to Kansas.

I spent one Sabbath at Coldwater and at Kinderhook, and arrived safely in Burlington in time to vote for Ulyssus S. Grant. The contract for building the church edifice was made and the work commenced, to be completed in the February following, but the severity of the winter prevented.

The first week of January, 1873, was observed, as is often the case, by a union of all the churches in the place in a meeting for special prayer in behalf of sinners. Some indications of the Divine presence were manifested and the meetings continued. About this time, I went to Junction City to attend a public religious meeting; and being earnestly solicited by Brother Greene and his church to remain and assist in conducting some special services, with a view of awakening an interest in the things of salvation among the impenitent, I consented. The meetings were protracted, day and night, for three or four weeks, with good results to many of the church and to a few impenitent persons, when my health became quite impaired, and I felt it my duty to return home.

[The preaching was most faithful and spiritual, and yet the results were not what we all had expected to see. There were some visible causes to prevent the accomplishment of the greatest good. The weather was, most of the time, severely cold. The house could not be made comfortable. Many, who would otherwise have been glad to come, remained away in consequence. The hidden causes of defeat in the case were undoubtedly still more potent, if possible—at least, it was not for lack of able, faithful preaching and personal effort at the time, that scores were not converted. May the seed sown in that inclement time yet bring forth a rich harvest.—Ed.]

On my return home, I found the union meeting quite disturbed by a spirit of sectarian selfishness, quite out of character with the loud professions of love of "union" when the protracted effort was begun. One element of discord grew out of the views of one class of Christians in regard to the doctrine of personal holiness, this being made the "all in all;" and another bone of contention was the control of the meeting, which was assumed by one denomination. This had alienated the other churches till it was thought best to separate, and let those work together who could in the spirit of the Gospel of peace. The work then took a new impetus, and continued till late in the spring. A large number were reclaimed who had become very remiss in religious duty, and a number of the impenitent converted to Jesus.

Just as the meeting was at its height, I received a telegram from Central City, Colorado, urging me to come to the assistance of Reverend D. S. Bowker, up in the mountains of gold and silver. I responded in person. The great meeting in Denver, under the management of Reverend E. P. Hammond, had been in progress some time when I arrived there, on my way up to Central. I stopped only long enough to take the next train, but long enough to see that God was in the place in very deed, doing great things, whereof all Christians were glad. Denver had not entirely recovered from the "hardness" it had acquired during the early gold fever days; so that a protracted meeting could not be expected to have such sway as it would in a more moral and church-going town.

However, in proportion to the organized religious forces in the city, undoubtedly as much was accomplished in Denver during the weeks of Mr. Hammond's stay as in Keokuk, Iowa, in Bloomington, Illinois, or Lawrence, Kansas. The city was shaken from center to circumference. The largest hall in the place was hardly sufficient to hold the crowds that pressed to hear the Word of Life preached and sung. The meeting held by special request of the proprietor in the most spacious and notorious dance-hall in the place one Sunday afternoon, when it was estimated that of the thousand present fully nine-tenths arose in response to the different invitations for prayer, is one never to be forgotten by those who had the privilege of being present. Mr. Hammond himself regarded it as one of the most solemn and powerful meetings he ever attended. He was in the best of spirit for conducting such a strange meeting, being fresh bodily and being sustained by many earnest, praying Christians. The out-door meetings in Denver also were remarkable, many of them especially so in point of numbers and interest. Being present at nearly every meeting of the whole series during Mr. Hammond's stay, having been invited by Bro. Scott to assist in the meetings, I know that, under the circumstances, speculation and gambling being rife in the city and a general spirit of worldliness pervading society, the revival of 1873 was a great success. Hundreds were renewed in spirit, and became new men and women in Christ.

[The revival spirit extended to Georgetown, Central and Golden, high up in the mountains, and to Boulder, Evans, Greeley, Colorado Springs and Pueblo, on the lower level. When we went to Central, we found Brother Stimson hard at work, with all the elasticity of spirit and hopefulness of a young man, in a series of meetings at the new chapel of the Baptist church, Brother Bowker pastor. Whoever has labored, even for a short time, in a mining town, knows something of the hardness of the field. A mining town differs from all others. Of all difficult places to impress religiously, such a town is the most difficult; so conceded by those of wide experience. Anything for the greatest good, that is lawful and right, being Father Stimson's motto, he consented to the plan proposed of discontinuing his meetings in the Baptist house, and going in, for the time of his stay at least, with Brother Hammond. So, although the field didn't seem entirely clear, he took his place as a "high-private," and worked with all the simplicity and earnestness of a young convert.

After Brother Hammond's short stay in Central was over, Father Stimson had so endeared himself to the people and commended himself to the leaders, that he was invited to remain and conduct the union meetings. This he did as long as they continued "union" meetings proper, much to the satisfaction of those responsible in the conduct of the effort, and to the awakening of sinners and the edification of the saints. The number of the latter in proportion to the population was not very great, and consequently their edification not a very long work. The awakening of the sinners was a much more tedious process. At the conclusion of the union effort, Brother Stimson began meetings again in Brother Bowker's chapel, which he conducted for a number of days, accomplishing no little good, and leaving a memory most fragrant among all good people. Mr. Hammond spoke to us in the highest terms of Father Stimson, whom he met for the first time during this winter's campaign in Colorado. He liked his spirit and admired his ability. It was on his strongly expressed advice on the subject of a suitable leader for the meeting in Central, as he was about to go, that Father Stimson was unanimously selected.

From this lofty mountain town Father Stimson descended to the plain, and again found himself in Denver, where he was at once comfortably housed in Brother Scott's hospitable home, and where he found a most congenial atmosphere in which to work, side by side, with his young co-laborer of other days in Leavenworth and Kansas. The great union meetings in the evening at "Governor's Guard" Hall, had been discontinued on Mr. Hammond's departure for the mountain region of Central; but Brother Stimson found a good state of revival interest in the meetings conducted by Brother Scott in his new lecture room just opened for worship. Here he remained and labored with great acceptance, pleasure and profit, for more than a week. The interest in the meeting increased during his stay. To the fact of this experienced help from Brother Stimson, both timely and cordially rendered—whoever saw him when he wasn't ready to work in a revival?—and to the fact of the Christian shrewdness of Brother Scott as a leader, is largely due the great additional strength acquired by the Baptist cause in Denver during the winter and spring of 1873. His coming to Brother Scott at the time he descended from Central, was like "the coming of Titus."

After staying some days, and helping most efficiently in gathering up the crumbs that nothing might be lost, Father Stimson returned home with the consciousness of having helped the Denver pastor do successfully that most difficult work,—close a long and deeply interesting protracted meeting, in a way to counteract none of the good accomplished, and bearing with him the blessings of hundreds who had met him for the first time during this working visit. He began at once to complete the meeting house at Burlington, and to make the arrangements for dedication. A few months were sufficient, and the neat little structure was added to the monuments of Father Stimson's zeal, enterprise and faith. To build a little house in a little place is often more of an undertaking than to build a large edifice in a large place. There is so little capital to work with—there are so few really independent workers—the pastor has often to create and sustain all the enthusiasm, besides doing three-fourths of the planning and engineering, not to mention the actual manual labor. The enterprise at Burlington was no exception. It's no reflection on the one or two male workers and the six or seven poor widows in the church, to say that if it had not been for Brother Stimson, or if his place had not been supplied by some equally hopeful and courageous pastor, the church would not now have a house of worship or any immediate prospect of one. And in the midst of hard times the outlook would not be very cheering. A fitting close of an earnest, practical life, is the beautiful little chapel at Burlington, an account of the dedication of which we copy from the *Kansas Evangel*, a paper which in its infancy has done much for the cause in Kansas, and which is one of the brightest stars of hope for the future. —Ed.]

The new Baptist meeting house at Burlington was dedicated on Sabbath, July 20th. It was a lovely day, and every arrangement was complete. No apologies for failure had to be made. A novel plan was hit upon, which we will charge up against Brother Stimson, pastor, for conducting the services. We will say to begin with, it was a success. It was understood by all the denominations in the place (and they have as many as any town in Kansas,) that the Baptists would monopolize the whole Sabbath services of the town. Accordingly, appointments were made for two services at the same hour, both morning and evening, one at the Methodist Episcopal church, and the ministers to alternate in the services. Brother Gunn, of Atchison, and the Topeka pastor were the preachers. The congregations were large, and Brother Gunn's sermons, at least, were good.

The new church is a fine, proud structure, 32x55 feet in size, with arched ceiling and well furnished and located. A new organ, chandeliers, a cosy orchestra, fine pulpit, baptistry, and carpets for the aisles, make up some of the furniture. It is, in brief, the neatest church in the place. The church membership is only about twenty, and none of them wealthy; the most of them poor. As we listened to the story of their struggles to build this house for the Lord, we could but thank God that He had given to His cause there such noble representatives.

Brother Stimson, though having reached his three score years and ten, is still brave as a warrior, and is hardly conscious of his failing strength. Through his efforts, principally, the work has been done. What he could not get others to do, he did himself. The high esteem in which he is held by the community gave him courage, and enabled him to succeed.

We must mention in particular, among other faithful workers, Brother William Wigston, a mason by trade, who was Brother Stimson's right hand man. Before he came to Burlington, he took the contract to build the abutments of a bridge across the Ohio river. He then promised the Lord that whatever he made out of the contract, above common wages, he would give to Him. The Lord blessed him. After finishing the job, he decided to come to Burlington. Before reaching there, he sent forward a beautiful Bible, hymn book and communion set. True to his promise, when he arrived he at once put $500 cash into this meeting house, besides building the foundation and putting in the baptistry. He is now sexton, and delights in giving much of his time to the service of the Lord. Would that our churches had more of such men.

At the close of the morning service, the pastor read a statement relative to the financial condition of the church. It was found that the house had cost $2,800, and that a balance of $800 remained unprovided for. Collections and pledges were taken sufficient to reduce this amount to $500.

We left this little band hopeful, having received a fresh inspiration to work from the example set by the Burlington Church.

CHAPTER XXXI.

MY VIEWS OF THE INDIANS—MISCELLANY.

BEFORE I came to Kansas, I had an exalted idea of the character of the American Indian as a noble specimen of human nature. In some respects he really is so; as for instance, in his native condition, as a muscular and well built animal, capable of great endurance, and a "good feeder." He has intellect sufficient to be cunning, and to make a first-class tyrant in any situation where he has the chance. With an Indian, "might is right." Hence all the females, in every tribe I have seen or heard of, the mothers, wives and daughters are the most abject slaves, compelled to do all the drudgery in the wigwam and on the hunt; see to all the ponies, bring all the wood and water, dress all the game, tan all the buffalo hides, and take care of the papooses besides. A professed Christian Indian acts like all the rest in these respects. The Osage Indians are doubtless the best developed specimens in a physical point of view, of all the tribes in Kansas. And they are an unrelenting, revengeful set of savages, never forgiving a real or supposed injury.

I once had occasion to be among them three or four days, and got perfectly cured of all my notions of Indian superiority, Fenimore Cooper and the Quaker peace agents to the contrary notwithstanding. I shall waste but few more tears over their condition, at my time of life. I hope they will all inherit "happy hunting grounds" when they are through with the chase here. Only I am thankful that I am not called to labor to prepare them for the enjoyment of those grounds. I don't think I ever had the faith to work forty years and see no fruit of my labor. The Modocs are no exception to the general Indian rule.

A gentlemanly Indian agent had invited a number of friends to go with him and his escort to the Osage Reserve, as he was going to pay the annuities. So, several ladies and gentlemen of us started on a pleasure trip. Probably none of them will ever want to go on a similar pleasure excursion, especially the ladies. If you refuse to eat with an Indian when he has made a feast, he won't forgive the insult without a large present of some kind.

The feast on this occasion was dried buffalo meat, strong coffee, and biscuits made of the best of flour and baked before the fire on sheet-iron pans. These biscuits were the only thing we relished, and we ceased to relish them after we saw the squaws mix them up. We never took a second meal with as much appetite as the first. The dried meat is cut into fine pieces, put into a kettle and then boiled in water, thickened with flour till it is of the consistency of soup. This is turned into a large pan, around which all the company sit on the grass, and help themselves by dishing out the mixture with their spoons. No plates. Indians, white men and women, compose the company. No squaws. The coffee is dipped off as you need it in little tin cups. After the Indians (squaws are simply squaws) and the guests are served, the squaws and papooses have their meal, if there is any left—and by eating all, including coffee-grounds, no matter how much is left. Then the dogs come up and wash the dishes, and all is ready for the next meal.

I wished to post the ladies of the company on all the facts of Indian life, and told them of the assistance the dogs rendered at each meal. They at once begged to be excused from appearing at table a second time. We excused them; but if the Indians did, we never knew it. They inquired for the "*Can a mah popo*"—the pretty women. One of the party told a lie by saying that they were sick in the wagons. At which the chief said: "Eat too much, ha?" Our friend nodded "*yes.*" I forgave the lie, and that was just as well as if Father Schoemaker, the Catholic priest, had done it. The women certainly were sick at their stomachs whenever they thought of eating with the Indians.

This Father Schoemaker has been among them over forty years. He is a quaint character, old but vigorous. He belongs to the Jesuits. He has given names to streams and other natural objects in the region of the Mission, and has built some very substantial buildings for the uses of his church; but, although the Mission has been established forty-eight years, and every possible appliance has been used to civilize and educate and Jesuitize this tribe, yet, up to this time, not the first son or daughter of the Osages has been converted to Christianity, or even to Catholicism! I mean a full-blooded Osage. A few French traders have been adopted into the tribe, and have married Osage women. Their children have become Catholics, but not civilized. If the gray-haired monk of a priest who hums his Catholic songs about his secluded home in the forest, takes any comfort at the retrospect of a long life spent among the Indian tribe with the results such as I have indicated, he is not begrudged it by me. I wouldn't disturb his dream. The Government has been induced to give this old man a section of land for his services at the Osage Mission, now in Neosho County! It is understood he began his labors among the tribe by telling them that Jesus was a great war Chief, and his apostles "braves," who accomplished great exploits in the slaughter of their enemies. The results have been little or no more cheering where the Gospel has been preached to them, I am compelled to say.

Efforts have been made to educate them in the rudiments—reading, writing and arithmetic; and yet, not one in five hundred can do the simplest example in addition or subtraction. Still, this old Jesuit must be made a beneficiary of the Government to the amount of several hundred thousand dollars in all! I blush to say that the effects of the Protestant labors among the Indians have not been much more encouraging. The mission among the Sacs and Fox tribes by the Methodists, and the Delawares by the Baptists, have been a little more successful than such efforts generally. Rev. G. W. Pratt, now of Leavenworth, accomplished a good work in the latter tribe, as long as he remained among them. The same is true of the Ottawas, for whom Father Meeker, a godly man, labored for thirty years.* But, as the white man came in with whisky and its fore-runner, beer, the whole tribe apostatized to drunkenness and a life of laziness; and, although the Baptist denomination and the United States Government expended great sums of money to civilize and Christianize them, all that remains is the remnant of the school property at Ottawa and a little quarter-blood Indian girl, who hears her voice echo through those halls of "literature and science."

If the missionaries now in Kansas, working industriously and self-denyingly among the enterprising immigrants in our new cities and settlements which will soon be an honor to the nation and humanity, were to make no more permanent, prac-

* The press that S. S. Prouty used in printing the *Neosho Valley Register*, in 1859, was brought to this country by Father Meeker, forty years ago

tical impression on the white inhabitants, the societies they represent would withhold all support. They don't come far short of it, in some cases, now.

The philosophy of the Indian nature, I do not attempt to explain. I do know this much:

First, The Indian has no relish for intellectual improvement or moral advancement. He loves whisky, tobacco and all such vile stimulants.

Second, He will not work, under any circumstances. Even those who have been claimed as partially civilized, will not labor.

Third, The large majority of the Government agencies among them have only tended to increase their savage, hopeless life.

Fourth, The exceptions found to the above estimate of Indian character are persons who have some white blood in their veins, like Eli S. Parker, a noble man. Show me an exception among pure-bloods! In view of all I have seen and learned of the Indian, I am half inclined to believe in Darwin: at least I should not have blamed him much if he had come into personal contact with the Indian before bringing out his "development theory."

Fifth, Gratitude is not found in the Indian's vocabulary, nor is it an element of his nature. An

Indian never considers himself under obligations to any one.

I have entertained Indians in the most hospitable manner I was capable of under the circumstances, giving him the best my home afforded, and then in a few days called on him and remained over night, and in the morning have paid a bill of two dollars and fifty cents for the entertainment.

THE MAN WHO FOUND OUT THAT HE COULD ANSWER HIS OWN PRAYERS.

Deacon W——, of B——, in Western New York, a good Christian man, but somewhat formal and prolix in his family devotions, was more orthodox than practical in his christianity. One morning while at family prayer, there came to the door a poor man with a bag under his arm, to get from the deacon a small grist of wheat for his needy family. It was a time of great scarcity in breadstuffs. While listening to the deacon's supplication, which included among other good things, a request that the Lord would remember the poor in the place that were in want of bread, his courage and confidence grew apace. His soul was filled with gratitude and hope, as he stood and listened to the words of the deacon: "Now, O Lord, open thy hand, and in thy ever liberal Providence, supply the wants of the needy, feed the hungry and clothe the naked. Thou canst do it, Almighty Father, as giving dost not impoverish Thee. There are many in our community sick, and many poor that are suffering for bread. O, Lord, supply them in the riches of thy fullness, for Christ's sake. Amen."

Poor Mr. J——, who had stood at the door all this time, could but weep as he heard the words of the deacon, a member with him of the same church, and he said to himself, "I shall get the wheat;" at the same time thanking God that he belonged to a church that had such a sympathizing deacon. He rapped on the door and was admitted. After answering kind inquiries about his sick wife and little ones, he made known the object of his visit—he wished to get a grist of wheat. "Well, well, Brother J——, I should like to accommodate you, but wheat is two dollars a bushel in Rochester, and I think I must raise some money in a few days. I am sorry I can't help you in your time of great want while your family is sick; but I wish you could get it somewhere else." Mr. J—— went away with a heavy heart, having suddenly lost his confidence in the deacon's sincerity.

A little fair-haired, black-eyed grandson that had been kneeling with his grand-parent and heard him pray for the poor, looked up in his face and said, "Well, Grandpa, if I could have answered my prayer this morning as easy as you could, I would have given Mr. J—— a bag full of wheat." "Would you, Charley?" inquired the old man. "Yes, I would, because that is what you asked the Lord to do." "Call him back, Charley." Mr. J—— returned, and the deacon handed him the granary key and said, "Go to the barn and fill your bag, Brother J——, and if you want anything while your family is sick, come here and get it. I have just found out that I can answer my own prayers, and shall endeavor to do it the remainder of my short life."

On Sabbath he arose in his place in the meeting house, after sermon, and asked the pastor if he could have the privilege of speaking. Of course consent was given, and he related the facts as above stated, and concluded by saying, "I have just learned by this incident that God has so arranged His divine economy as to enable me and others to answer our own prayers in five cases out of eight."

A SHORT WAY WITH A SKEPTIC.

An old infidel asked me once to explain the reason why God made the children of Israel travel forty years in the wilderness, when they could have crossed to the promised land in four days and a half? I told him I would think the matter over, and call on him with a solution of the matter in a few days, and then, turning on my heel, said I would also give him a question to answer at the same time, or now. "It is this: Anatomical professors tell us that the canals in the human body are about nine yards in length. Now, I want you to explain to me why they should be crossing backward and forward through the chest and abdomen to twenty-seven feet in length, when one straight canal about twenty-two inches long would have answered?" "Well, Elder, you have got me. I will quit if you will."

THE EFFECT OF A PERSONAL APPLICATION OF THE TRUTH.

I went to assist a Brother S—— in Western New York, where a deacon had struck a neighbor's hog and killed it; but he would not confess it or pay the damage. The pastor and best members of the church were greatly grieved, all being confident that he was guilty. But it could not be proved, as two trials had been held—one by the church and one by a legal court—all to no purpose. The deacon was quite officious, always in the front seat, ready to exhort, to sing or pray; and every time he would begin to speak or pray, the man whose hog the deacon had killed would get up and go out, along with a number of personal friends who sympathized with him in his hatred of the deacon. By and by, when the deacon was through, they would all come back and take their seats. I had heard of these movements before from a minister who had been there on a visit, and gone away mortified at the ill success of the effort made, and indignant at the obstinate deacon.

I got there on Saturday afternoon, and took a survey of the situation at the evening meeting. I was satisfied from what I saw, who the man, Deacon S——, was. That night I found the pastor and his wife all weighed down like a cart with sheaves, on account of the state of things in the church. Sabbath came and passed, with about the same results. The evening was approaching, and the thought of having one man block up the way of salvation to a church, while sinners were looking on with a degree of triumph over the inconsistency and open wickedness of one of the members, pressed upon me with great weight. The question had become a serious one with me, "Can I do or say anything to make this faulty brother do right, and remove this awful stone of stumbling? What shall I preach about?" I finally fixed upon this passage in the fifty-first Psalm, verses 10, 11, 12 and 13: "Create in me a clean heart, O God, and renew a right spirit within me. Cast me not from thy presence; and take not thy Holy Spirit from me. Restore unto me the joy of thy salvation; and uphold me with thy free Spirit. Then will I teach trangressors thy ways; and sinners shall be converted unto thee." I went on to show what a wicked man David was on one occasion, even after God had called him "a man after His own heart." I was about to close and saw that the deacon was as unmoved as a stone, although the rest of the congregation were manifesting the deepest interest. "Is it possible," I thought, "that I must close this sermon and meeting this evening and the deacon remain impenitent for his wrong, and the man he had injured go to hell over his obstinate conduct?"

I leaned over the high desk and addressed myself personally to the deacon thus: "Now, Deacon S——, as you love the salvation of your neighbor A—— from eternal perdition, and as you killed his hog, and you know that all your brethren believe you did, go this minute to him and confess your sin, and ask his forgiveness. Don't let one miserable swine keep you from the smiles of Jesus, and Mr. A—— out of the blessed Kingdom." And while I was yet speaking, he arose and went to A——, took him by the hand and made a full confession of all, saying, "Neighbor A——, I killed your hog and I am sorry for it. I hope you will forgive me. And if you will come to my house to-morrow, I will pay you the full worth of the hog and the cost of the suit." A—— broke down, acknowledged himself a sinner, and was soon believing in Jesus as his Savior. This was the starting point of a great work. I staid and preached day and night for five weeks. The pastor baptized more than eighty who were converted during the meeting; and the church was restored to harmony.

TAKING A MAN AT HIS WORD.

When I had returned to reside in Warsaw the second time, there was still living in that community an old friend, who was addicted to coining jokes on the ministers, if practical jokes, all the better. I met him in the village one day, and asked him if I could get some hay of him, it being haying time. "Well, yes, Elder, you come up with your wife and make us a visit, and I will put in all the hay you can carry home in your buggy. I don't expect to get anything out of ministers for hay, as they hardly ever pay for anything of the kind, even if they agree to." "Well, Mr. B.," I said, "I hardly think Mrs. Stimson would be willing to ride with a bundle of hay, but I will come up with a one-horse wagon and get a "bundle" when it is cut. When shall I come?" "Next Monday, if it don't rain."

So I went and got a large one-horse lumber wagon, and put on a common two horse hay rack. I had a heavy, stout horse that weighed about twelve hundred. So off I started with a boy to help me load. The hay was all put up in the nicest order in the meadow. I had loaded on eleven big bunches when Mr. B. came up, and after surveying the whole establishment, said: "That's what you call a buggy, is it?" "It's a one-horse wagon, Mr. B., and that's what I told you I should come with." So he took hold and helped me. We turned to the next row of bunches, and put on eleven more, making twenty-two in all. "There," said he, "go ahead; but you will never get home with it, and if you don't, you shall pay for it." When I got to the village, I had it weighed. It made just twenty-two hundred and fifty weight. Mr. B. has not yet heard the last of the "bundle" of hay in a one-horse wagon, and has concluded to "come" no more dry jokes on poor ministers.

I HAVE OBSERVED that there are two things about which the mass of mankind are determined to be humbugged, Religion and Medicine.

A religion of fanatical incantations, Mormonism, Spiritualism, Universalism, Heathenism and Devilism, all cater to the vitiated tastes and depraved desires of poor human nature. And men naturally appear to prefer any one of these to a knowledge of the "Truth as it is in Jesus," that is pure and undefiled, and that is consistent with good common sense and sound judgment.

The same is true in regard to Medicine. Men will employ quack physicians, and take quack nostrums, much sooner than take really useful remedies. I heard a doctor of the quack school tell a family that had a sick daughter, that her complaint was of the heart, *i. e.* "the heart-string had become so relaxed and elongated, that the heart had fallen down below its proper place, and as it swung back and forth like a clock-pendulum, it struck on the sides of her chest and produced a soreness;" and as a remedy he prescribed what he called "pucker root" and alum, sweetened with honey, to contract the heart-string. The dear family thought he understood the case exactly. The next week the poor sufferer died, and I attended her funeral. I thought he ought to be classed with "Dr. Terrible," who, it is said, bled the devil, using a pickaxe for a lancet.

I HAVE OBSERVED, and am convinced, that rich ministers are, as a general thing, a drug upon the church and congregation. If they are able to preach to the church for nothing, they become indolent, penurious and sleepy. I never knew of a church that paid their minister up promptly, that was not happy and prosperous. A church that is always pleading as an excuse for not giving to charitable objects, that they must pay their minister first, but that are constantly in debt to him and the sexton, is a church the poor in which are obliged to take care of themselves, or go to the poor-house.

Persons that come late to church are the first to complain of long sermons; and those that sleep in sermon time are the first to detect the defects in the discourse.

ELDER JACOB KNAPP IN ROCHESTER.

I was present in the meeting at the First Baptist church in Rochester, New York, that Brother Knapp was conducting, and as many have regarded the "lightning" story as an exaggeration, I feel called upon to confirm the facts as related in his autobiography, edited by Dr. R. Jeffery. It is true in all its particulars. The first volley of brickbats had been thrown at the church. The pulpit then stood in the end next to the street, with a large window behind it; so that the mob had a fair chance at the person of the preacher, whom they hated with a cruel hatred. The most blinding lightning that I ever remember to have seen, flashed at the very moment, flooding the whole of Fitzhugh and Buffalo streets with a blaze of light, accompanied with the most stunning thunder-burst. The mob fled in such haste that not ten of them were left in the street in five minutes' time. To saint and sinner it was evident that God had interposed to defend His truth, and the preacher from violence.

PASTORATES.

I have been pastor of fourteen churches in forty-three years, and have had a salary all the way from one hundred and fifty dollars to sixteen hundred dollars per year. I have never been able to discover the difference between a small one and a large one. Each would come out about the same. Perhaps the large one was a little more gratifying to my family.

WHAT GOD HAS DONE FOR ME AND BY ME IN FORTY YEARS.

I have preached over ten thousand sermons, such as they have been. I have baptized eighteen hundred and eighty-seven professed believers in Jesus, the Savior of sinners; among that number, fifteen ministers, three of them Pedobaptists, two Methodists, and one Presbyterian. I have attended six hundred and thirty-four funerals. I have solemnized four hundred and twenty-eight marriages. I have been present at one hundred and fifty-four ordinations and organizations of Baptist churches. I have voted for President of the United States from General Andrew Jackson to Grant, nine in all. I didn't vote for all that were elected! I am thankful for that. My sins are so many less, as there have been worthless men among the nine. I have assisted more than three hundred poor fleeing fugitives, from the house of bondage of Southern slavery into Canada, and in many instances at the risk of being imprisoned for the violation of the fugitive slave law, for which a wicked, pro-slavery congress was guilty. And I would do the same thing to-morrow, under the same circumstances. So much for repentanee on that subject.

I HAVE TRAVELED in twenty-two of the States of the Union, in both the Canadas and in "New Jersey"—in all, miles enough to girdle the earth four times. I have preached in them all, except

Texas—and there I was not permitted to remain long enough, as the rebel "bushwhackers" cared more for our horses and watches than for our Gospel. We thought, as the lame captain expressed it, "Doubtless there is to be a great battle, and as we shall have to retreat in the end, therefore, as I am lame, I will go now." So we left Texas as soon as good horses would convey us out safely into Kansas. What I saw of it, convinced me that it was then not a good State to be in, except for cattle and horse-thieves. And I have had no special desire to return.

A MODERN ZACCHEUS.

In one of our precious revivals in Western New York, a time when all the community were spell-bound by the Spirit of God, a case occurred similar to the one when Jesus was on earth, recorded in Luke xix. 5–6:

"And when Jesus came to the place, He looked up, and saw him, and said unto him, Zaccheus, make haste, and come down; for to-day I must abide at thy house."

"And he made haste, and came down, and received Him joyfully."

A young gentleman, of high standing among his friends and the wealthy, was an attendant upon the meeting in progress. He became quite affected and solemn, but for a long time made no effort to come out boldly and confess Christ. One afternoon, just after the meeting had opened, he sent up to the desk a short notice, requesting the pastor to go with him to the study, as he wished to see him on important business at once. I left the meeting in charge of a deacon, and retired to the study, as requested. He commenced by saying, as soon as we took our seats: "Mr. Stimson, the facts I am about to divulge will ruin me for this life and perhaps for the life to come. It is this: I was a clerk in a store in the city of ——, State of Michigan; and while there employed, I was guilty of purloining some very costly silks and satins, which I have now in my trunk, as I have never had an opportunity of disposing of them; being, too, under the constant impression that I should be detected if I offered them for sale. Now, God, by His Spirit and the truth, has arrested me, and four long weeks I have been like a man on coals of fire. Now, I ask you, as my pastor, what to do; and I will do it, if it disgraces me and my family, and I have to lie in the State's prison for years, I will do it; for to live under this burden of mind, I cannot any longer. To me it is a living death, by day and by night." I was overwhelmed and amazed at the confession of the young merchant, as he was then a partner in a thriving business in the village. I locked the door, and then engaged in a moment of prayer with him. When we arose from our knees, I said: "Now, my young friend, you go and get your trunk, with the goods in it, and start for Michigan at once; and when you arrive at the place, call the firm together, and, without gloss or guile, confess your sin, and throw yourself upon their clemency, and be prepared to take what follows." He at once said, "I will do it." At his request, I wrote a letter to the parties wronged, stating the circumstances of his confession and of his relations in life and business standing. I then sent him with a boy to drive my buggy to the depot, four miles away. The next day he arrived at the place of his destination, restored the goods and made an unvarnished confession, and received a full pardon from the parties. These Christian gentlemen, for such they were, wrote me a most cordial and Christian letter, in which they expressed confidence in the deep repentance of the young man; and said that they had not missed the goods, and never should have known of his thieving, if he had not confessed it. He soon came before the church, related his experience, expressing himself as a great sinner against God. To this day, he is an exemplary, honorable Christian man in one of the Eastern cities. How much better and wiser the course of this young man, than that pursued by many, who, rather than expose themselves and their fellow-men, go on with a canker constantly eating away at their souls; feeling every moment that God is against them, being cognizant of all the facts of their wickedness, and Jesus continually inviting to come down and give them entertainment in the homes of their hearts. Those who comply, find pardon and peace.

Near twenty years have passed, and *no one* has ever known the above facts but the parties concerned. I can keep a secret, if I never have joined a secret lodge.

CHAPTER XXXII.

SERMONS—ALMOST A CHRISTIAN.

"Then Agrippa said unto Paul, Almost thou persuadest me to be a Christian.

"And Paul said, I would to God, that not only thou, but also all that hear me this day, were both almost, and altogether such as I am, except these bonds."—ACTS XXVI. 28–29.

MAN is a religious being. Religion is an inherent principle in his nature, raising him above all other animal tribes. His instincts and aspirations place him on an altitude above all the residents of earth. Being a religious intelligence, he is possessed of all the endowments of immortality. He is responsible for his conduct to the remotest limit of its influence. If it were not for his upward instincts, his degradation would be hopeless. If he didn't care for immortality, he would be beyond moral reach.

Men are compelled unwittingly to pay tribute and respect to the Christian religion, even when they know nothing by experience of its real merits. Thus, Agrippa, his heathen conscience stirred by Paul's masterly defense of its great fundamental truths, cried out: "Almost thou persuadest me to be a Christian." Men have only to let go their hold on sin and let their principles, which are at best but little better than sins, fly to the winds, and multitudes would be led to make the same exclamation, and to look at the cross by faith, which would result in making them Christians altogether.

Let us proceed to notice:

I. What constitutes a Christian in reality.

II. What is it to become almost a Christian, and yet fail.

III. Persuasion for all men to become Christians in fact.

1. A Christian is a regenerated sinner. The Holy Spirit regenerated him. There can be no substitute for regeneration. Very many are deceived by human substitutes. As one says: "I am a Christian by birthright. My parents had me baptized in my infancy. I have learned the catechism and keep the law of our church, and have been confirmed as a true child of God by the bishop or priest." All this gives no claim to being a Christian,

and is a trap of Satan to deceive and ruin the souls of men. There must be a radical change of his entire moral nature. He must be born again, as John says, i. 12, 13:

"But as many as received Him, to them gave He power to become the sons of God, *even* to them that believe on His name:

"Which were born, not of blood, nor of the will of the flesh, nor of the will of man, but of God."

Jesus taught the same doctrine to Nicodemus (John iii. 3, 4, 5):

"Jesus answered and said unto him, Verily, verily, I say unto thee, Except a man be born again, he cannot see the kingdom of God.

"Nicodemus saith unto Him, How can a man be born when he is old? Can he enter the second time into his mother's womb, and be born?

"Jesus answered, Verily, verily, I say unto thee, Except a man be born of water and *of* the Spirit, he cannot enter into the kingdom of God."

This, beloved, is the only way of making a Christian in reality. This work of the Spirit will manifest itself in repentance of sin, by faith in the Son of God, and in obedience to the law of His Gospel. This will make a man a Christian in fact.

He will be a new creature. "Therefore, if any man *be* in Christ, *he is* a new creature: old things are passed away; behold, all things are become new." (II Cor. v. 17.) He will be a Christian in reality, and not by any mummery of human invention.

2. A Christian is controlled in his conduct by principle and not by emotion. Multitudes act from the emotional part of their nature, and deceive themselves by thinking that this emotion is a ground of belief that they are Christians. Nothing is more delusive and destructive of their present and eternal interest in Christ. Religion is a *principle*, and all the duties of a religious life must have their base in it. Emotional religion is a prolific source of apostacy from Christ and the Church. Many ministers of Christ contribute to this state of things seen so often in the declension of those who "did run well," by saying, in substance, "get up your feelings, and then go to work for God." Thus, many are waiting for the tide of their emotion to rise and their zeal to be inflated, so that they can float into religious enjoyment; when the great effort should be to get down upon the solid rock of pure Christian principle, of "Christ in you the hope of glory."

Far be it from me to say anything against emotion. It acts upon the Christian as a fair breeze does upon the ship; it helps it into port. With a favoring wind he sings:

"Homeward bound, Homeward bound."

But if his ship is unsound in the hull, every increasing breeze only makes her creak, and hastens its destruction. It is a sorry case to have the wind blow fair and to be constantly crying to the men at the pumps: "Heave ho! boys, heave ho! boys, we shall all go to the bottom if you don't work the pumps." So it is with your sentimental professor, who is void of true principle, based on Christ's finished work of atonement.

3. A true Christian applies himself to the work of Christ in doing something and all he can to extend His Kingdom among men. He will seek out opportunities to develop the power of the Gospel. To him the world is the field, and while he is in it he will find something to do in the private interview, in the family, in the Sunday school, in the prayer-meeting, sowing beside all waters. He will get good by doing good. The best proof of one's Christianity, consists in applying one's self to Christ's work.

We have now seen what a Christian is in reality. Let us ask,

II. What it is to be almost a Christian, and yet fail?

A person, having his birth and being in a country where the Gospel is proclaimed in all its fullness, and where he has enjoyed the constant means of salvation, being still without hope in Christ, the Savior of sinners, may be said to be "almost a Christian." A stranger to human depravity and to the obstinate state of mind to which the sinner is habituated, would say, in looking at the sweet, heavenly influences by which they are surrounded: these, who hear oft-repeated invitations to embrace Christ, who are the objects of the wooings of the Spirit of God, surely are all Christians. But, what is the fact? Only *almost*, not quite yet possessed of a good hope, not quite yet destitute of a good hope. They can say, the land that gave me birth is denominated a "Christian" country; and yet, the truth remains they are "without God and without hope in the world"—almost Christians, but making the sad failure of neglecting the one thing needful in the very midst of the richest privileges. Not to be able to say, "I know that my Redeemer liveth," is to make the fatal mistake of all time, is to come short of the end of creation.

2. There are very many who acknowledge the cardinal truths of the Bible, the reality of heaven, the awful existence of hell and the propriety of a coming judgment day, in which all the world are to be judged; they attend upon the ordinary and even extraordinary means of grace, and yet have never yielded to the claims of the Gospel, and are only almost Christians. "His Spirit has striven with me by day and by night, His people have prayed for me, and companions that loved Him have invited me, my Christian parents have wept over me, I have had my foot on the very threshold of the Kingdom of the blessed Church of Christ, and yet I have no abiding evidence that I have been regenerated by the Spirit of God; no comforting assurance of connection with Jesus; I am only almost a Christian. I have only desired heaven as a refuge into which to escape from the storm of indignant wrath that will one day overtake me; a retreat to keep me out of perdition. I have no relish for the society of the pure in heart that surround the throne of God and the Lamb. I was almost a Christian once, but I have made a sad failure, an eternal fail-

ure." This, doubtless, will be the regret of many. They will have to appropriate the language of one of old, 'The harvest is past, the summer is ended, and I am not saved.' Procrastination and the love of sin have kept me in the state of being almost a Christian.

Pauline Colburn was a young lady brought up under the most sweet influences of a kind and religious family, and often the subject of deep impressions of her condition as a sinner out of Christ. Constant in her place in the house of God; every Sabbath joining her voice in the songs of worship; she often told me as her pastor, that she meant to yield to the claims of the blessed Jesus. So tender were her feelings, that one would think she was not far from the kingdom of God, only not quite ready to offer herself up unto the Master then and there. She was in the gallery on Sunday, and sang as sweetly as ever. She wept while in conversation, but hesitated, and went home. On Monday morning she arose from the breakfast table, and retired to her room, exclaiming: "I have been almost a Christian, but never loved Christ; now I am dying," and in *five minutes she was a corpse.* Almost a Christian! Poor girl! Almost a Christian!

But let us conclude by noticing:

III. The Persuasions presented for all men to become Christians.

1. Sin in its very nature and tendency is destructive of all human happiness, present and prospective. God hath said: "There is no peace to the wicked." How true this is in all the history of sin and sinners! We have a way of graduating sin. "Small sins," "little sins," are every day spoken of among men. It is well to remember that: "Sin is the transgression of the Law," and the Law is a transcript of the perfections of Deity. Sin, then, is the violation of God's own rights as our King, Law-giver, Father and Redeemer. So then, he that sins is contending against the Almighty. Beloved, do not let us talk about "little sins." No one ever became an outrageous sinner at once. It is sinning by degrees that augments us into incorrigible sinners.

In the British navy a ship was ordered so constructed that every timber in it should undergo a strict inspection, and no stick should be used in this war structure that was the least defective. A carpenter was at work on a huge oak beam, into which he thrust the point of his scratch-awl. He at once called the attention of the inspector to the defect. He came and examined it, and turned away, saying, "It is nothing but a little worm hole. It never can do any damage." The noble ship was completed, rigged and furnished with every appointment for a long voyage, with a noble staff of officers and seamen. But when far out on old ocean, she was found to be weak in an important place. Search was made, and to the astonishment of all, it was found out that the timber with a little worm hole was now perforated through and through with worm holes, and was but little better than a stick of sand. It was so placed as to receive the greatest strain. Orders were given to steer for the nearest port. But soon a storm came on, and the two combined forces of wind and wave grappled with it, and the new ship, staunch and strong as all supposed, was conquered. It became the victim of the sea. It went to the bottom, carrying all on board but three, to tell the sad tale of the disaster caused by the little worm hole. Precious lives and costly freight go to the bottom continually in the great world from just such insignificant causes.

Sin that may at the time be but little, if not repented of will bring destruction like a whirlwind, and send the sinner to the bottom of the great abyss beyond the hope of recovery. Little sins and great sins are of the same family. One has grown to great proportions. The other is growing. Then be persuaded to break off your sins by turning to Jesus, in whom alone all true happiness and all safety are found.

2. All men are persuaded to become Christians by the consideration of what Christ has accomplished. The love of God in giving the Son of His love, is an incentive of the highest order. It not only claims your attention, but it demands your admiration and homage. God *so* loved the world of sinners. "*So*"—that little word "*so!*" Oh, sinner, I wish you and I understood it! So loved the sinner as to give His only begotten Son, that whosoever believeth in Him might not perish but have everlasting life. And then, in addition to all this, consider the appliances and influences set at work to persuade you to yield to the claims of the Gospel: "For the love of Christ constraineth us; because we thus judge, that if one died for all, then were all dead." The love of Christ urges you to stop and think how much Jesus has suffered for you. Were there ever love like His? "For God is love." (i. John iv. 8.) All His perfections and procedures are but so many modifica-

tions of his love. What is His omnipotence but the arm of His love? What is His omniscience but the medium through which he contemplates the objects of His love? What is His wisdom but the scheme of His love? What are the offers of the Gospel but the invitations of His love? What the threatenings of the law but the warnings of His love? They are the hoarse voice of His love, saying, "Man, do thyself no harm." They are a fence thrown around the pit of destruction, to prevent rash men from rushing into ruin. What was the incarnation of the Savior but the richest illustration of His love? What were the miracles of Christ but the condescensions of His love? What were the prayers of Christ but the pleadings of His love? What were the tears of Christ but the dew-drops of His love? What is this earth but the theater for a display of His love? What is heaven but the Alps of His mercy, from whose summits His blessings, flowing down in a thousand streams, descend to water and refresh His Church, situated at its base?

Stop a moment, and consider what the Spirit is doing for your enlightenment to make you see the depravity of your nature. Unnumbered influences at work to lead you in a way you know not! Praying friends are daily and nightly weeping at a mercy seat, saying, "Spare, O Lord, O spare my son or my daughter from going down to the pit!"

And then think of what's only a little in advance for you to meet—one of two vast considerations: a heaven of light and uncreated glory, where Beauty and Purity, Holiness, Goodness, in fact everything to increase one's happiness with the good of all ages; and the consideration of being without any interest in Jesus, without one assurance that you have accepted the proffered pardon. You will have to say, "I must be deprived of the associations of all Christian friends, and never see the face of the Crucified One."

3. The vast future in which all your interests are concealed. Eternity! Eternity! There your best friends have taken up their abode. Perhaps your dear old mother, or your father, has long been employed with the sainted hosts of God's dear children, and with celestial voice and fingers skilled in divine art, has been swelling the song uninterrupted,

"Worthy is the Lamb that was slain for us."

Do you not desire to join in that song? or do you still choose to vacillate and hesitate and turn a deaf ear to the Sweetest Charmer? Hear Him: "Unto you, O men, I call; and my voice is to the sons of man. O ye simple, understand wisdom; and ye fools, be ye of an understanding heart."

Two inferences :—

(*a*) Is it not wisdom for you to be a Christian in reality, at whatever cost? Do you not feel that it would be highest attainment of wisdom to be able to say,

> Jesus, I my cross have taken,
> All to leave and follow thee.
> Naked, poor, despised, forsaken,
> Thou from hence my all shalt be."

(*b*) Do not be contented in being almost a Christian. Contentment while in this state is as fatal as contentment in the most open and rebellious condition. Contentment in any condition short of personal union and fellowship with God through Christ, is a trick of the devil. Contentment in being almost a Christian is the stupor that leads to eternal death. Arouse yourself from it. Shake off the fatal spell, and not debar yourself from all that's good in time and eternity.

II.

THE DISPLEASURE OF GOD WITH THE INDOLENT.

"Curse ye Meroz, said the angel of the Lord, curse ye bitterly the inhabitants thereof, because they came not up to the help of the Lord, to the help of the Lord against the mighty."—JUDGES V: 23.

It is evident that Meroz was so situated that it could have rendered important and essential aid to the cause of Israel, in their conflict with the enemy, if it had been so disposed. But Meroz, assuming the same sentiment and position of very many of the present time, thought it *prudent* to be neutral in this conflict for right and for liberty. How many there are who study the devil's dictionary to find a comfortable definition of the word *prudence*, and they and their friends laud them to the skies for their wise forecast and "prudent" conduct, in not being identified with the radical and revolutionary Spirit that is stirring perhaps the entire nation to the depths, in the interests of humanity and justice! It was so a few years since in the agitation against American slavery for over forty years. The same has been true in the temperance reform. Men and ministers have stood and looked on with stoic indifference, while drunkards have been made by law, and thousands have gone down to drunkards' graves within their personal knowledge.

They see these friends and acquaintances go down to a drunkard's undone eternity, and then with a linen handkerchief they wipe their mouths with as smooth grace as if they had been to a banquet. If prompted to speak, it has been to say, "Well, these hot-headed cold water men are responsible for this. Moderation would have been far better. By their hot haste they have driven men to sell it, and men that love it will drink it, if they can get it." This is morality with a vengeance, taking the side of Belial against Christ and humanity. These are your men who pride themselves on their great prudence; conservative souls that are not fit for the Kingdom of heaven. Christ has no need of men who think more of how to retreat than advance; who wait to see which way the wind blows before they start; who have no idea of standing for the right till the right is popular. God wants revolutionists.

This ode of Deborah was chanted at the celebration of the victory, and while honorable mention was made of such as had distinguished themselves by deeds of valor, Meroz is referred to in terms of execration, and burning, blistering reproach. There is another day of celebration yet to come, and an ode to be sung by far excelling all that was ever heard on earth. The question is, What mention shall be made of you in that last day? Shall it be "Curse ye me those that have stood neutral, while virtue and sound religion and humanity have been calling for help?" Or shall it be in approval, like that of Deborah and Barak, and those with them in the conflict?

In this discourse we propose to notice:

I. The Conflict going on.

II. The Help Demanded.

III. The evident Results of the Conflict.

I. The Conflict now in Progress.

1. Error has waged a war against Truth, and has aroused all her minions to overthrow it, by every possible strategy known to a barbarous and savage warfare. Its most common attacks, are to assume the garb of Truth. But it is Truth perverted for the sake of advantage. "For the wrath of God is revealed from heaven against all ungodliness and unrighteousness of men, who hold the truth in unrighteousness." (Romans, i. 18.)

A few specifications. "All men will be saved, no

matter what their sins or character may be. Salvation is sure." "Jesus was a good man, but not divine, nor equal with God." Carnal will substituted for divine obedience and submission to the Gospel of Christ; human merit for Christ's suffering and atonement. These all hold the Truth in unrighteousness, and are the scouting parties sent out by the devil to reconnoiter the outworks of Zion's fortress, while Truth stands in her white uniform, bidding defiance to these sons of Belial, and near by her, within bugle-sound, are encamped these "wise," "discreet," cowardly, chicken-hearted professed friends of *both parties*, with their field-glasses taking observations. Many of them members of the church, and at the last election voting for the captain of this same squad to sell strychnine whisky, or are renting some low dance-house, or gambling-hell, or its twin sister, a gay shop where drunkards are finished up in the latest style for perdition. This is Meroz, that takes no part in the conflict now going on against Zion. No marvel that God's angel should say: "Curse ye Meroz."

2. The conflict is waged with superhuman effort to make the avowed friends of Jesus subserve the wicked purposes of the enemy.

The young convert of Christ is attacked in his weakest point. With blandest smiles the enemy says: "Let all your religious actions be with the greatest moderation. Keep cool, quite cool, on all matters of a spiritual nature. Join with the world in its social recreations. No harm for a Christian to play billiards; why, our minister keeps a billiard table in his house, right adjoining the study; and his wife said she would dance, if it were not for the speech of some of the members of his church who think it not right. Why, you look fatigued; won't you take a glass of wine?—it will not hurt you? Our minister drinks it at his table every day. Oh, how I wish you could have been at Mrs. Snodinglove's party, the other evening. We had a very pleasant time indeed. You know she is a member of our church, and she thinks it no harm for Christians to go to the theatre or circus. She is very fond of dancing too."

Thus, by the time this gabbling daughter of Jezebel has finished her tittle-tattle to a convert just espoused to Jesus, if he is not well on his guard, ten chances to one if he is not taken captive at the will of the devil, so that when sister Light-minded has her "levee," he is there to subserve the cause and machinations of these enemies of God and His anointed. Joined in affinity with the world, his religion has become cool indeed. No more deep solicitude for their young companions to come to the cross. No more singing in the spirit, and with the understanding:

> "Nearer, my God, to Thee,
> Nearer to Thee;
> E'en though it be a cross
> That raiseth me.
> Still all my song shall be,
> Nearer, my God, to Thee,
> Nearer to Thee."

"Ye did run well; who did hinder you that ye should not obey the truth?" (Gal. v. 7.)

"As ye have therefore received Christ Jesus the Lord, so walk ye in Him." (Col. ii. 6.)

Thus they have joined the neutrality party; and they too think our religious sentiments and convictions should be expressed with great "coolness." "Coolness" means coldness toward Christ when rightly interpreted.

II. The help demanded in this crisis of the conflict.

To help the Lord "against the mighty," is the key note of the conflict.

1. The duty of the ministers of Jesus to expose the falsehood and sophistry of every lying spirit. Not only is it the duty of the servants of Christ to defend the Truth and Zion in her possession of it, but to carry the war into the enemy's camp, showing no quarter to a rebellious foe. Throw everything at the devil; like Luther, throw your inkstand at him, if you have nothing else; or like Whitefield at the Moorfields, preach Christ and Him crucified, to the surging mob; or like John Knox at Saint Mary's, in the face of armed soldiers threatening him, "stand up for Jesus," and proclaim "the acceptable year of the Lord," and "the day of vengeance of our God." Christ, Paul, Peter, John the Baptist, all set the ministers of after generations a good example in this line of ministerial duty. We venture the assertion that full one-half of the declension in our churches is caused by the cringing, sycophantic, cowardly conduct of the professed ambassadors of Christ,—mere men-pleasers; God-dishonoring representatives of the highest calling on earth. "I use great plainness of speech."

If all the evangelical ministers professing the doctrine of salvation by faith in Jesus, were to come out in the spirit of the Gospel, and make an onslaught on the powers of darkness, as they now array themselves in the land, Romanism with all its idol mummery and anti-Christ priestcraft, Universalism, Unitarianism, and polished skepticism would all evaporate like the rank vapors before the rising sun. We have a few who have the moral courage to enter the lists, and declare the whole counsel of God, to a lost and depraved world of sinners. We have a superabundance of *lectures* and *essays* and pretty nonsensical gibberish, without point and effect upon man's moral and religious being. Some think these efforts have warmth. But the vitality is only galvanic, and the heat that of a corpse warmed by lying in the sun. No vital connection with Christ and the Spirit, and consequently no stir of the soul! The demand is for God-fearing, Christ-loving, and sinner-reclaiming, reformation preachers, of a free and full Gospel, and that now come "to the help of the Lord against the mighty."

2. The demand is also for all the people of God to "come to the help of the Lord."

All, both male and female, can find something to do, and that to good advantage, if they only had the disposition. The women of our churches have always been more efficient, according to their sphere, than the men. Here, in this contest, "Jael, the wife of Heber," struck the final blow:

"Then Jael, Heber's wife, took a nail of the tent, and took a hammer in her hand, and went softly unto him, and smote the nail into his temples, and fastened it into the ground: for he was fast asleep and weary. So he died.

"And, behold, as Barak pursued Sisera, Jael came out to meet him, and said unto him, Come, and I will shew thee the man whom thou seekest. And when he came into her *tent*, behold, Sisera lay dead, and the nail *was* in his temples.

"So God subdued on that day Jabin, the king of Canaan, before the children of Israel.

"And the hand of the children of Israel prospered, and prevailed against Jabin, the king of Canaan, until they had destroyed Jabin, king of Canaan." (Judges iv. 21–24.)

We are glad to say here that the movement now being made by the women of our churches is accomplishing much for missions abroad and at home. An evangelical power is being felt that will save the churches from the dead calm of a stupid formality. Deborah was compelled to be in the vanguard, taking the place of the man who should have been first. (See Judges iv. 4–9.) Let it be the prayer of the church for the Lord to raise up Deborahs all over the land. Let every man in Zion do something to advance the cause of our common Christianity. We need not wait for the colleges and theological schools to send them out. If the laymen of the churches would only take this thing in hand, under the all-controlling influence of the Spirit of God, our whole land would resound with the voice of singing and victory, from Maine to California, from Florida to the Canadas. We need Sunday school men and women who have vim and religious vivacity. We need more life and spiritual power in our prayer and social meetings of the church. Exhortation that is stirring in its appeals to the impenitent, when do we hear? The world is God's workshop, in which He demands help of every kind to carry on the work of saving sinners, and to bring this conflict to a successful close. We need another Ehud in our camp. (See Judges iii. 14–22.)

> "Soldiers of Christ, arise and gird your armor on,
> Strong in the strength which God supplies
> Through His eternal Son."

Let us call your attention,

III. To the evident Results of this Contest.

1. It will lead each individual disciple of Jesus to examine his motives for enlisting in this campaign against sin. Quite a number have gone into the conflict for the spoils, as their fruits do show—loaves and fish followers of Christ! They have joined the church to be made comfortable and to be pleased with the "brilliant discourses" of some minister who has the reputation of being an eloquent pulpit orator, who was never so vulgar as to pronounce that awful category of words, "hell," "perdition," "damnation," "lost souls," "judgment day," "day of wrath." (See Ezekiel xxxiii. 31, 32.)

"And they come unto Thee as the people cometh, and they sit before Thee *as* my people, and they hear Thy words, but they will not do them: for with their mouth they show much love, *but* their heart goeth after their covetousness.

"And, lo, Thou *art* unto them as a very lovely song of one that hath a pleasant voice, and can play well on an instrument: for they hear Thy words, but they do them not."

This scene is acted over in our day, to all intents. You take away this kind of bread and butter, these sweet meals of human relish, and they will join a club of infidels: from the simple fact that their motives were not pure when they enlisted. But if they joined the cause for the love of Christ, then they will stand by in storm and sunshine, in battle and in peace, in life and in death.

2. Another result will be that error will yield to the truth when wielded in the name of Jehovah. It is irresistible: "For the Word of God *is* quick, and powerful, and sharper than any two-edged sword, piercing even to the dividing asunder of soul and spirit, and of the joints and marrow, and *is* a discerner of the thoughts and intents of the heart."—(Heb. iv. 12.) I do not believe that one instance can be found where a church or a minister commenced under the guiding and controlling influences of the Truth as it is in Jesus, but sooner or later was victorious over error, and made the infidelity and skepticism of the place bite the dust, and many of the strongest opposers come over to the side of Truth, and say, in the deep simplicity of their natures:

> "I yield, I yield;
> I can hold out no longer."

3. It must result in uniting the people of God in a permanent and healthy fellowship for each other.

Old jealousies and heart-burnings will cease and give place to the song:

"From whence doth this union arise,
That hatred is conquered by love?
It fastens our souls in such ties
As distance and time can't remove."

"Behold, how good and how pleasant *it is* for brethren to dwell together in unity:

"*It is* like the precious ointment upon the head, that ran down upon the beard, *even* Aaron's beard; that went down to the skirts of his garments;

"As the dew of Hermon, *and as the dew* that descended upon the mountains of Zion: for there the LORD commanded the blessing, *even* for life evermore." (Psalm cxxxiii. 1–3.)

Pastor and people will not only work in harmony together, but a growing respect for each other will be manifested in their several spheres of labor. It is only in this sense that a church is edified in the Truth in the highest acceptation of that term, "edified in love." Oh, blessed result to be the people enjoying such a state!

REMARKS.—1. Brethren, are we identified in this conflict, and doing good battle for the Master on Zion's side? God has said: "Woe to them *that are* at ease in Zion, and trust in the mountain of Samaria, *which are* named chief of the nations, to whom the house of Israel came!" (Amos vi. 1.)

2. The day of final celebration of all the victories achieved for Christ is soon to come. What honorable mention shall be made of you and of me in that day? Shall it be like that of Deborah and Barak? or like that of Meroz, Jael and Sisera? God forbid the latter!

3. Victory is sure to all those who enlist under the Captain of our Salvation, and the triumph of the saints is the defeat of the sinner. Our God has said that no weapon formed against Zion shall prosper. He is not wanting in means to carry on the conflict. He can save by many or by few:

"And Jonathan said to the young man that bare his armour, Come, and let us go over unto the garrison of these uncircumcised: it may be that the LORD will work for us: for there is no restraint to the LORD to save by many or by few.

"And his armour-bearer said unto him, Do all that is in thy heart: turn thee; behold, I am with thee according to thy heart." (I Sam. xiv. 6.)

God will hasten the victory in His time. See that ye be not found fighting against God and the Truth. Amen.

CHAPTER XXXIII.

A NIGHT WITH THE "RACKENSACKS" AND "PUKES.

All Western people will understand what is meant by the above names. But, for the instruction of our friends in the East, we "rise to explain."

A Rackensack is a dweller in Arkansas, of the loafer order; and a Puke is a rough of Missouri, or a "border ruffian."

I was called to visit the south-eastern portion of Kansas, in connection with a young minister of our denomination. As we proceeded on our journey, towards evening we discovered that a storm was rising in the north, and that it would overtake us before we could cross Sugar Creek to a settlement, where we expected to find entertainment for the night among friends. So we were obliged to stop at a place called the "Three Stone Houses," lying between Fort Scott and Ottawa.

These three houses were rude structures of stone, laid up without mortar or any visible design. One was a barn, and one of the two houses proper was unoccupied. The third was occupied by an old woman and her son, the husband and father having been killed in the border ruffian war of 1855–56.

We asked for entertainment, and the old lady told us we could stay; but as her son was not at home, we would have to take care of our horses ourselves, at least until her son came. He was expected soon, if he was not delayed by the storm. We complied with the conditions, and went in to wait for supper. While she was making ready our coffee and bacon and corn cake, she looked out of the window and exclaimed:

"Good Lord, have mercy; there comes them devils of Missouri and Arkansas. The Lord only knows what I shall do if Davey don't come." I inquired: "Why, what's the matter with them? They won't hurt you, I think."

In they came, and addressed the old matron: "Wall, old woman, have you got any whisky in these diggins? If you have, draw et out quicker than a badger can hunt his hole." The old lady replied by saying: "We don't keep it for anybody. Dave did have a little he got for snake bites; but I don't know where he keeps it, if he has got any." At this one of the Pukes said: "Wall, he haint got any now—we sucked out the last of that air stuff when we were here last week;" and continued by asking, "Where is your Davey?" "He has been gone all day at Mapleton, and will be at home, if he can get here, before the storm comes." "Wall, there'll be a storm if he don't bring some of the critter, for we want to liquidate as bad as ——." At which all set up a coarse and vulgar laugh.

A Rackensack bawled out, "Come, old gal, stir your dancing pegs and get us something to eat, for we are as hungry as five wolves, and can eat all there is in this shanty as quick as lightning can strike a dry cottonwood."

She replied: "I have no more coffee until Dave gets here, as I have just made all I have for these strangers, and a scant mite for them. I reckon it will be mighty weak too, but it's all I had in the house until Dave gets home. There, strangers, set up and take such as it is." Poor coffee, rusty bacon, and corn-cake baked on the stove, as griddle-cakes are baked, only it was about an inch thick, browned on both sides, and looked about as much like a No. 7 griddle to a stove, as a cake.

As we sat down to the table, I said to my young Reverend companion: "Ask a blessing." He shook his head, and said: "I will join with you." So I gave thanks in words something like the following: "Ever blessed Father of all our mercies, sanctify this sweet portion of Thy bounty, to our nourishment and comfort, and may we consider the heart and hand that supply us, for Christ's sake, Amen." And the old woman said: "Amen; bless the Lord."

At that moment, a voice at the door called out: "mam, come and take the things in quick." Dave had come. Soon she returned with a paper of coffee, a dozen of candles, and three boxes of matches. As she laid them on the bed in the corner of the room, one of the Pukes said: "Wall, hain't Dave brought any whisky, old gal?" She answered: "Not as I can see, if he has, it is in his saddle-bags."

Up jumped three of them and they went to the stone shed to find Dave, or what they most desired, the whisky. Soon the storm of wind and rain burst upon the house with great fury and force, and in came Dave and the hunters after whisky, in great haste, but no whisky had come.

The old lady at once set herself to get supper for her son and the roughs.

As we closed our frugal meal, the young Domine said to me in a whisper: "Brother Stimson, I wish we had gone on, I don't feel safe here. These are a bad set of roughs, and there is no knowing what they may do before morning." I replied in a low whisper: "Well, now hold up your head and stop your looking so much like a coward. Be a man. It will only make the matter worse if they see your timidity."

I sat down by the stove and stirred the coffee for the old woman, and then ground it for her and her guests, while she baked the second installment of corn-cake, and fried the second batch of bacon, filling the whole house with an odor similar to what I have enjoyed in a soap-chandler's establishment, only more so. As soon as I had finished my task in the cooking department, I commenced singing a hymn that my young friend could have joined in if he would:

> "Hark, my soul, it is the Lord,
> 'Tis the Savior, hear his Word;
> Jesus speaks, and speaks to thee:
> Say, poor sinner, lovest thou me."

All was as still and quiet as a funeral, the moment the singing commenced. When we came to the third stanza:

> "Can a woman's tender care
> Cease towards the child she bare?
> Yes, she may forgetful be;
> Yet will I remember thee."

One large, brawny fellow took his coat-tail up and wiped his eyes, turning his face away from the light. By this time supper was ready, and they gathered around the table to supply their needs. They sat and ate their meal in quietness, speaking in respectful terms to the old lady.

The storm had now so abated that my companion and myself stepped out of the door, and going a little way from the house, I said: "I shall call on you to read the Bible, and I want you to read the xviiith chapter of Luke, and then we will sing again and have prayers. The old lady is a Christian, I am quite confident, and one of these roughs has a tender spot in his heart. So we went in again. I spoke to the old lady: "Well, madam, shall we spend a little time in devotion, before we lie down to rest? We all need protection, and it is well for us to commit ourselves to God as our Father and Protector."

"Oh yes, I reckon it would be so nice; I have not heard a man pray since my poor husband was shot in 1856. We then had a man here to help bury him out on the prairie, and he prayed."

"Was your husband shot, madam?" we asked. "Yes, he was shot while we were milking our cows. It was in the time of our troubles here on the border. Dave was then a little boy, and we had a pretty little girl, next younger than Dave, and she never got over the fright of that awful time. If we could a got back to Injiana, we should a gone, but we had no money, and all our oxen had been stolen, and here Dave and I have stayed ever since."

I called on the young brother, and we sang again, and then I asked them all to kneel down with us while I made supplication to the Almighty Father for protecting care during the watches of the night. There was no more loud talking or profanity there that night. As we stepped out of the door while the young man covered the floor with blankets for our beds, I heard one of them say to his companion, as they stood around in the dark: "Wall, Buck, I should think that old 'feller was John Brown, if he wan't hung by them Virginians." His friend replied: "It may be him arter all. He was a slippery old cuss, and it may be he gave them the dodge, or got somebody hung in his place."

There was no more said about whisky, no more swearing, no more impertinent talk to the old lady of the house. All was as quiet as a first-class hotel, except the loud snoring. At daylight my young brother and myself started off on our journey again, driving twelve miles before breakfast.

THE IRISHMAN'S MIRACLE OF THE LOAVES AND FISHES.

An Irishman in his travels found a New Testament, and, having a moment's leisure, sat down and read the Miracle of the Loaves and Fishes, after which he went on his journey, and, meeting a countryman, said, "Pat, I have just read a curious book to-day." "An' pfat book have ye read, Mike?" "Well, it's about the Lord Jesus, ye know; it tells all about the twelve Apostles, ye know, Pat. How, wänst upon a time they were all out in the woods together, and the Apostles got farefully hungry, ye know: and the Lord Jesus took five hundred fishes and seven thousand loaves of bread and blessed them—an' the twelve Apostles ate them all up, sure." "But Mike," said Pat, "I don't see any miracle." "Hunch me Honey, isn't it a miracle they didn't all bust afther aitin so many?"

The above story has served Father Stimson so well on such a variety of occasions, it well deserves a place among those in which he has been a personal actor. The story itself, if not the application he made of it, will be remembered a long time by those who laughed over his inimitable telling of it at the General Association, held at Topeka, Kansas, October 1873.

CONCLUSION.

A PERSONAL SKETCH, BY THE EDITOR.

Father Stimson is a character; every man is not. He isn't just like anybody else. When in his presence, you are at once satisfied that he has opinions. When you have heard him talk, either in conversation or public discourse, you are more convinced that his ideas are his own, and that he would sacrifice everything rather than yield them. He is not obstinate. Mere human opinions on which men have a right to differ, he is as ready to change or give up as any man need to be. Religious principles he holds as inviolably sacred. No one who has ever heard him preach, can forget the solemnity with which he speaks of these. Rather than yield one of them, he would suffer the loss of all things. Bred according to the Scotch-Irish Presbyterian rule, and educated in the high school of Baptist faith and practice, it is not to be wondered at that he has the grit of a reformer. He has preached the gospel the Master has bidden him, asking no questions, and neither daring nor wishing to make the least modification. He couldn't have been anything else but a Baptist. His impatience of human authority in matters of conscience, his radical nature, his disregard of what is simply time-honored, his scorn of the double-edged weapons of ridicule and custom, his loyalty to the truth, and his supreme love of his Divine Master, have qualified him for the enjoyment of the fellowship and service of the church for a place in which he made such a struggle in early life. Certainly in these qualities he is a representative Baptist.

If Father STIMSON should find a weak Baptist church in a place, with little or no "social standing," he would go to work at once to make it stronger. He would do the same thing if he were not a minister. If there were no church in the place, he would set himself to the delightful task of preparing a people, by Divine help, for church fellowship.

All must respect the man who, without the advantages of an education, rises superior to the majority—the great majority—of those who are educated. College-bred men often leave school so conscious of their advantages over uneducated men as to make no habitual efforts afterwards to maintain their advantages. Those not so favored in youth, often go through life with the spur of conscious disadvantage. By this they are stimulated to great and constant effort for self improvement, and soon outstrip those who were far in advance to begin with—hare and tortoise. Father STIMSON has accomplished more in the world for God and humanity than is the average work of a College and Seminary educated minister.

Two or three of the natural qualities that have helped him in his otherwise unassisted work deserve special mention. First, his memory. This is remarkable. It's not a memory for one class of subjects alone, but for facts and principles, dates, names and words, and for one as much as for another. Memory is as distinguishing a faculty as man possesses. It gives a man more aid in public life than any other faculty, unless it be the gift of superior speech. It has helped him more than any one knows, except himself, in all his public work. It has given him a great command of Scripture and hymn quotations in the pulpit and prayer-meeting. It has given him the apt story in public addresses and private conversation. It has given him great advantage in argument, supplying him with the needed quotations from authors. It has been absolutely indispensable in the preparation of this auto-biography. With the previously-prepared manuscript all lost in Chicago, he had to begin again, and after two years had passed. The facility with which he remembered dates and facts and names and conversations, and dashed them down with his pencil, is known to at least one other person. I shall always have one proof that I am not lazy in the speed with which my pen followed his pencil.

His tact in reply to grave argument or witty personal assault, is another trait of mind that will be remembered as long as he is remembered. An Irishman by parentage, he is never wanting in quick repartee and apt anecdote most forcibly told. He has an almost exhaustless fund of humor and anecdote. If argument would not serve his purpose when attacked or making a point, some quaint saying of somebody's or some resistless story would always come in at the right moment, and he would carry off the laurels. He is the soul of any company in which he feels at home. As to others, his wit makes them feel at home. No sketch of him would have been complete without a chapter of stories and jokes.

He is a man of large practical common sense. He despises shams. He sees the best way out of a tight place as soon as he is in it. His advice to people similarly situated is of great value. His common sense doesn't desert him when he comes to matters of religion. He reasons upon Christianity as he would on any subject requiring the use of reason, but never without making the broad distinction that exists between it and all other forms of religion.

He has a fair share of originality of thought and expression. His imagination, too, is more than ordinary. The happy combination of these qualities and others, and the conscientious use of them through public life, have made him a power in the denomination.

He belongs to a race of men that is rapidly passing away. The places that now know them will soon know them no more. The need of pioneer men—especially of the angular, eccentric, original, self-made stamp to which he belongs—is fast ceasing to exist. They have nobly done a great work, a work smoother men could not have done. Peace to their ashes. Peaceful years to those who remain among us.

www.ingramcontent.com/pod-product-compliance
Lightning Source LLC
LaVergne TN
LVHW021148110826
845150LV00005B/1156
* 9 7 8 1 4 2 5 5 4 6 7 9 3 *